OLD TESTAMENT MESSAGE

A Biblical-Theological Commentary

Carroll Stuhlmueller, C.P. and Martin McNamara, M.S.C.
EDITORS

Old Testament Message, Volume 23

INTERTESTAMENTAL LITERATURE

Martin McNamara, M.S.C.

 Michael Glazier, Inc.
Wilmington, Delaware

First published in 1983 by MICHAEL GLAZIER, INC., 1723 Delaware Avenue,
Wilmington, Delaware 19806
Distributed outside U.S., Canada & Philippines by: GILL & MACMILLAN,
LTD., Goldenbridge, Inchicore, Dublin 8 Ireland

Library of Congress Catalog Card Number: 83-81652
International Standard Book Number
  Old Testament Message series: 0-89453-235-9
  INTERTESTAMENTAL LITERATURE
    0-89453-256-1 (Michael Glazier, Inc.)
    7171-1187-3 (Gill & MacMillan, Ltd.)

Cover design by Lillian Brulc
Typography by Richard Reinsmith
Printed in the United States of America

TABLE OF CONTENTS

Editors' Preface

Old Testament Message brings into our life and religion today the ancient word of God to Israel. This word, according to the book of the prophet Isaiah, had soaked the earth like "rain and snow coming gently down from heaven" and had returned to God fruitfully in all forms of human life (Isa 55:10). The authors of this series remain true to this ancient Israelite heritage and draw us into the home, the temple and the marketplace of God's chosen people. Although they rely upon the tools of modern scholarship to uncover the distant places and culture of the biblical world, yet they also refocus these insights in a language clear and understandable for any interested reader today. They enable us, even if this be our first acquaintance with the Old Testament, to become sister and brother, or at least good neighbor, to our religious ancestors. In this way we begin to hear God's word ever more forcefully in our own times and across our world, within our prayer and worship, in our secular needs and perplexing problems.

Because life is complex and our world includes, at times in a single large city, vastly different styles of living, we have much to learn from the Israelite Scriptures. The Old Testament spans forty-six biblical books and almost nineteen hundred years of life. It extends through desert, agricultural and urban ways of human existence. The literary style embraces a world of literature and human emotions. Its history began with Moses and the birth-pangs of a new people, it came of age politically and economically under David and Solomon, it reeled under the fiery threats of prophets like Amos and Jeremiah. The people despaired and yet were re-created with new hope during the Babylonian exile. Later reconstruction in the homeland and then the trauma of apocalyptic movements prepared for the revelation of "the mystery hidden for ages in God who created all things" (Eph 3:9).

While the Old Testament telescopes twelve to nineteen hundred years of human existence within the small country of Israel, any single moment of time today witnesses to the reenactment of this entire history across the wide expanse of planet earth. Each verse of the Old Testament is being relived somewhere in our world today. We need, therefore, the *entire* Old Testament and all twenty-three volumes of this new set, in order to be totally a "Bible person" within today's widely diverse society.

The subtitle of this series—"A Biblical-Theological Commentary"—clarifies what these twenty-three volumes intend to do.

Their *purpose* is theological: to feel the pulse of God's word for its *religious* impact and direction.

Their *method* is biblical: to establish the scriptural word firmly within the life and culture of ancient Israel.

Their *style* is commentary: not to explain verse by verse but to follow a presentation of the message that is easily understandable to any serious reader, even if this person is untrained in ancient history and biblical languages.

Old Testament Message—like its predecessor, *New Testament Message*—is aimed at the entire English-speaking world and so is a collaborative effort of an international team. The twenty-one contributors are women and men drawn from North America, Ireland, Britain and Australia. They are scholars who have published in scientific journals, but they have been chosen equally as well for their proven ability to communicate on a popular level. This twenty-three book set comes from Roman Catholic writers, yet, like the Bible itself, it reaches beyond interpretations restricted to an individual church and so enables men and women rooted in biblical faith to unite and so to appreciate their own traditions more fully and more adequately.

Most of all, through the word of God, we seek the blessedness and joy of those

who walk in the law of the Lord!...

who seek God with their whole heart (Ps. 119:1-2).

Carroll Stuhlmueller, C.P.   Martin McNamara, M.S.C.

INTRODUCTION

The term "Intertestamental" found in the title of this book merits a few words of explanation. It is a somewhat rare word, and in fact is not registered in a number of standard English dictionaries. Then again, the very concept "intertestamental" is not a clear one, since from more than one point of view there can be neither time nor literature between the Old Testament and the New — the testaments from which the adjective is derived. The expression "the intertestamental period" or "the period between the testaments" is used to designate the period between 200 B.C. and A.D. 100. This is the age in which the greater part of the books known in Protestant Bibles as "The Apocrypha of the Old Testament" were composed, books that in some Protestant Bibles were, and still are, printed between the Old and New Testaments. These books, and the period over which they were composed, could be described as "intertestamental" in this sense. Jewish scholars would prefer to refer to this same period and the literature composed during it as "between the Bible and the Mishnah".

Whatever of the origins or aptness of the designation, in this work we are considering the non-canonical literature composed during the three centuries between 200 B.C. and A.D. 100. The Old Testament Apocrypha of the Protestant Canon which are regarded as canonical in the Catholic

Church (Sirach, the Wisdom of Solomon, Baruch, Tobit, Judith, 1-2 Maccabees), are treated in special volumes in this present series. The same holds true for other works composed during the period, e.g. the Book of Daniel.

Our main interest will be the works actually written during this period. These are of importance from our point of view mainly for the evidence they contain on how religious men and women of those ages viewed God, the world and the relationships between the two — that is for the thoughts that moved the minds of men and women during the centuries in question. But precisely because we are interested in thoughts and trends of thought, we shall not limit our consideration to works actually consigned to writing during the centuries in question. To do so would oblige us to pass over a good portion of the rabbinic tradition which came to be written down only after A.D. 100, even though we must suppose that a good part of it existed as oral tradition during the first century A.D., and even before the Christian era.

And just as the intertestamental period saw the origins of the rabbinic tradition that would only later be consigned to writing, so also was this period itself heir to an earlier post-exilic tradition, one that in part influenced its manner of thinking. Since history and historical periods must be treated not in isolation but as parts of larger units, we begin this work by a preliminary chapter on the formation of the tradition which the intertestamental period in its own way articulated.

NOTE ON THE TERMS "APOCRYPHA," "PSEUDEPIGRAPHA," "DEUTEROCANONICAL."

Writings composed during the intertestamental period are often referred to as the Apocrypha. Pseudepigrapha, or by Roman-Catholic writers as deuterocanonical. The terminology has originated in denominational settings and can at times be confusing. The Roman-Catholic tendency would be to use only two terms: canonical and apocryphal. A writing not part of the canon, whether it be the canon of the Old or of the New Testament, would be designated apocryphal, the Apocrypha being the non-canonical writings. Those writings not part of the Hebrew Scriptures but recognized by the Roman Catholic Church as canonical are called deuterocanonical, because their canonicity was formally declared only after a period of discussion. The seven books in question have been listed earlier. To these books we may add the deuterocanonical additions in the Book of Esther and in the Book of Daniel (i.e. the Prayer of Azariah and the Song of the Three Young Men, Susanna, Bel and the Dragon). The Letter of Jeremiah is included in the Roman-Catholic canon as chapter six of the Book of Baruch. The

Roman Catholic Church has also traditionally highly respected some writings which she refused to accept as canonical, e.g. 2 (or 4) Esdras, the Prayer of Manasseh which were also printed as Appendices to the Latin Vulgate rendering. The Reformers refused to accept any of these as canonical, and designated them as Apocrypha. The other books relating to the Old Testament period which were neither in the Hebrew Bible nor in the western Canon are given the designation Pseudepigrapha. However, since other Christian Churches, such as the Greek, Slavonic or Armenian, have in their Bibles writings not found in the western Canon (e.g. 3 and 4 Maccabees), these too tended to be regarded as among the Apocrypha and to feature in later translations, as in the newer editions of the *Revised Standard Version*.

Within the Apocrypha there is some confusion in the manner in which the various Books of Ezra are referred to. The first problem concerns the number to be attached to the name. In the Vulgate the canonical books of Ezra and Nehemiah are entitled respectively 1 and 2 Ezra (as already in the Greek Septuagint). Consequent on this the Vulgate designates the two apocryphal books of Ezra as 3 and 4 Ezra. These are now generally referred to as 1 and 2 Ezra — although some prefer to use the form "Esdras," the better to distinguish them from the canonical works.

1. FORMATION OF A TRADITION

The destruction of Jerusalem by the Roman armies in A.D. 70 brought an end to the diversity which had been a feature of Jewish life and religion for the two preceding centuries. For most of this earlier period, Jewish life was characterized by the presence of the three major religious groups, the Sadducees, Pharisees and the Essenes. Apocalyptic writings also were as much part of the picture as legal tradition. With the destruction of the city by the Romans and after the reorganization at Jamnia, Rabbinism reigned supreme and regarded itself as the successor of Pharisaism. Sadducism and Essenism were no more, and the apocalyptic world of ideas, which had helped engender false hopes and the revolt, soon fell into disfavour.

When treating of the characteristics of these three religious groups within Judaism it is customary to stress the points in which they differed one from the other. And yet the matters in which the Sadducees, Pharisees and Essenes were at one were probably more numerous than those in which they were divided. To begin with, all were sufficiently united in the main tradition as to be classed as genuinely Jewish, in contradistinction, say, to the Samaritans — the remnant of the northern kingdom who were ill at ease with the post-exilic community of Judah and broke with Jerusalem some time after the exile to become the alienated and hostile neighbours of both Galilee and Judea as we know from the pages of the New Testament. All three belonged not merely to the central tradition of Hebrew religion, but represented this in its late and post-exilic form, as distinct from pre-exilic or exilic Hebrew religion. All groups, most probably, accepted the same basic canon of the Scriptures and regarded the Pentateuch as in some sense more sacred, more basic and more normative than the other books, although the Sadducees may have done this to a greater extent than the other two groups. It is also highly probable that all three groups had much in common in the matter of liturgical prayers. While all three groups had a not inconsiderate central unity, the relationship of the Pharisaic tradition to that of the monks of Qumran (which we can suppose to have been Essene) appears to have been rather close in many respects, despite evident differences in a number of points.

These agreements and divergences between the various Jewish groups during the intertestamental period can probably be accounted for by the origin of all three in the Judaism of the post-exilic period and the development which this underwent during the earlier period of the second century B.C. These considerations indicate that the intertestamental period proper may profitably be introduced by a summary description of the development of Jewish religion and religious tradition during the post-exilic period prior to 200 B.C.

1. Political Situation of Post-Exilic Judaism

The wars, destruction and deportation which accompanied the Babylonian invasions during the early sixth century must have drastically reduced the population of Judah. It has been estimated that in the eighth century, in the time of Isaiah, Judah had a population of about a quarter of a million. By the time of the first deportation to Babylon in

597 it seems to have been reduced to half this figure. The effects on the population of the next, and the final destruction of 586 and its aftermath were simply disastrous and by the time of the renewed attempt to rebuild the temple in 522, it is reckoned that the population of the little province of Yehud could hardly have been much above 20,000, reckoning those recently returned from Babylon with the Jews who had never gone into exile.

The numbers actually exiled from Judah to Babylon in the deportations of 597, 587-86 and 582 do not appear to have been very large. Jeremiah (Jer 52:28-30) gives the figure of 4,600 in all, a number which many scholars take as exact but most probably as including the males only. This would give a grand total of about 13,800 to 18,400. These deportees, however, represented the cream of Israelite society. They also represented the nucleus from which in exile and adversity the new Israel would be born.

Humanly speaking, during the decades that followed on the destruction of Jerusalem, the situation must have appeared hopeless to both the exiles and those remaining behind in Judah. The changed circumstances that emerged with the rumours of Cyrus' victories about 550 would have begun to relieve the despair. Then came the capture of Babylon by Cyrus and the edict permitting the Jews to return to their homeland and rebuild the temple. The prophecy of Jeremiah, accentuated through the brilliant preaching of Second Isaiah, could be seen as fulfilled in part at least by the rebuilding of the temple in 515. Even though its completion, like the laying of its foundations, could be described as "a day of small things" (cf. Zech 4:10; Ezra 3:12), it did give genuine foundation to the hope that a new age had dawned and that the promise made to David, and renewed through Jeremiah (cf. Jer 23:5-6), was about to be fulfilled (cf. Zech 3:8), and this in the person of Zerubbabel (see Zech 3:8; 6:9-14; both texts re-edited to have Zerubbabel's name changed to that of Joshua). An outburst of messianic fervour seems to have occasioned the end of Zerubbabel's reign as governor of Judah. He was probably withdrawn or replaced by the Persian authorities.

After the completion of the temple, the next major event recorded in the life of the post-exilic community of Judah was the advent of Nehemiah from the Persian court to become governor of the province about 445 B.C. He came to a community still small in numbers and limited in the extent of the territory it controlled — about 25 miles from north to south. Jerusalem itself was still unwalled and mainly in ruins and the Jewish community in danger of extinction through mixed marriages. The reorganization under Nehemiah and Ezra is considered elsewhere in this series (see volumes 13 and 14).

From the biblical and other evidence we can infer that, during the exile and later, the Jewish community in Babylonia continued to grow in strength and in devotion to the reforms that had begun after the fall of Jerusalem. Reflection on the earlier religious tradition and the efforts to have it recast so as to suit later needs also went on apace, as did the interest of the Jewish religious leaders in Babylon in the affairs of the brethren in Judah. The biblical tradition as recast in Babylon would be taken to Palestine to become part of the canon of Jewish scriptures.

There were Jewish colonies in Egypt before the fall of Jerusalem. During the early days of the exile, and also later, the numbers of Jews there most probably increased (cf. Jer 42-43). The band of refugees that forced Jeremiah to go into Egypt with them settled at Tahpanes (Daphne), just within the eastern border (cf. Jer 43:7). Other groups were to be found in cities of Lower Egypt (Jer 44:1; cf. Isa 19:18-19). From papyri discovered at Elephantine, at the first cataract of the Nile, we know that a Jewish military colony existed there by 525 B.C. It was very probably already there in 580 B.C., soon after Jeremiah had been taken to Egypt. These Jews at Elephantine had a temple of their own, and maintained certain contacts with Jerusalem. This we know from the so-called "Passover Papyrus" written in 419 B.C. All the evidence at our disposal suggests that, unlike Babylonian Judaism, the religion of these Jews in Egypt was syncretistic. It had not undergone the reform that had taken place in the eastern exile.

Politically, first under Persia (539-333) and then under the Ptolemies of Egypt (312-200), Judah enjoyed religious autonomy and generally speaking good relations with its overlords. The situation changed when the political control of Palestine passed from the Ptolemies to the Seleucids of Syria in 198 B.C.

2. The Religious Situation of the Jews 500-200 B.C.

Among the many fruits of biblical criticism is the insight it has given us into the workings of the Hebrew mind. It has shown us that the tradition now enshrined in the Bible is due in good part to the formulation and reformulation of an earlier tradition. This is evident from the Yahwist onwards. In the seventh century, if not already in the eighth, the Deuteronomistic School was again reformulating the tradition. The Priestly School was active at the same task already before the destruction of the southern kingdom. Belief in the God of the fathers, the just God who could do no wrong and would be faithful to his promises, imposed it as an obligation on Israel to think and rethink its relationship with him and recast its tradition to have it speak in a meaningful fashion to a new generation. The prevailing preoccupations seemed to have determined the manner of the reformulation.

This activity continued in a more intense manner during the exile in Babylon, especially in the Deuteronomistic and Priestly schools. It was done by pious scholars whose names have been lost to history, if indeed they were ever known outside their own very limited circles. Outstanding prophets such as Ezekiel and Second Isaiah (towards the beginning and the end of the exile respectively) were also active in this work. Much of the earlier prophetic tradition, especially the teaching of Jeremiah, seems to have been edited by the Deuteronomistic School. Ezekiel's preaching appears to have been treasured, developed and added to by a band of disciples whose teaching is so intimately linked with that of their master that scholars often simply despair of distinguishing what is genuinely from one and what from the other. An interesting feature some scholars have noted in the Book of Ezekiel is the presence in it of inner-biblical interpretation. Ezekiel himself depends upon and re-uses earlier biblical tradition. He also seems to have used written texts, regarded no doubt as sacred and authoritative, i.e. as scripture. And the expansion of his oracles by his disciples and followers is a further example of inner-biblical exegesis. The reinterpretation carried out by the Deuteronomistic and Priestly schools very probably continued for some time after the exile, either in Babylon or Palestine. So, too, apparently did the development of the Jeremiah and Ezekiel traditions.

This explicit reference to earlier tradition and to early prophecy was a marked characteristic of the post-exilic era and became all the more clearly expressed with the passage of time. It is something to which we shall return again in this chapter. We have already noted the partial fulfilment of Jeremiah's prophecy (cf. Jer 25:11-12; 29:20) in the return from exile. This fulfilment is explicitly mentioned in the work of the Chronicler (cf. 2 Chr 36:22-23; Ezra 1:1-4). The very presence of Zerubbabel in the events of 522 and later was regarded as a fulfilment of another prophecy of Jeremiah by the prophet Zechariah (cf. Zech 3:8; 6:12 and Jer 23:5-6).

While the reconstruction of the temple was important for the history of the post-exilic community, the major event in the reconstruction of the community, however, was the advent and mission of Ezra, to which we now turn.

3. *The Work of Ezra*

The significance of Ezra's work consists principally in his mission to make known and observed a work referred to as "the law of Moses which the Lord, the God of Israel, had given" (Ezra 7:6). This is the first clear evidence we have of the existence of the Law of Moses as a written document.

Ezra himself is presented more than once in his capacity as priest (Ezra 7:11; 10:10, 16; Neh 8:2,9; 12:26) and scribe — in Hebrew *sopher* (Ezra 7:6, 11; Neh 8:1, 4, 9; 12:13; 12:26,36) — indeed on a number of occasions as priest and scribe. His competence in the Law of Moses is stressed (e.g. Ezra 7:6, 11). Since a predominant meaning of the Hebrew word *sopher* in pre-exilic times is "minister of state, secretary of state affairs", some scholars believe that Ezra was actually a sort of secretary of state for Jewish affairs in the Persian system of administration. This, in fact, he may have been. It is clear from the biblical evidence, however, that his principal concern was with the law of Moses. He had a command of its content and felt commissioned to make it known and applied. He was, thus, a scribe also, if not principally, in the later meaning of this word. He came from the Persian government with a mandate to have this law become the basis and centre of the Jewish community and to bring all Jews within the Persian province of Abar-Nahara to a knowledge of it (cf. Ezra 7:25).

It is somewhat unfortunate that we are unable to determine exactly when Ezra's mission took place. We are told in our present text of Ezra 7:7-8 that it was in the seventh year of king Artaxerxes. This would have been 458 if the king intended is Artaxerxes I. This date, however, is considered unlikely since it would place Ezra's mission thirteen years before the commissioning of Nehemiah which was done in the twentieth year of Artaxerxes, i.e. 445 B.C., whereas Ezra's reform seems to presuppose Nehemiah's work. For this reason, some scholars take it that 398 B.C. and the seventh year of Artaxerxes II is intended. Others still believe that the year of the king's reign which originally stood in the text was "thirty-seventh", not "seventh," and that the king in question was Artaxerxes I, giving us the date 428 B.C. (See further J. Kodell in vol. 14 of this series, pp. 113-117, and C. Mangan, in vol. 13, pp. 165-166) Ezra arrived in Jerusalem on the fifth month, and in the seventh (i.e. Tishri) held a solemn assembly to promulgate the law. This event, of enduring importance for the whole of later Judaism, is thus described in Neh 7:73—8.6:

[73]So the priests, the Levites, the gatekeepers, the singers, some of the people, the temple servants, and all Israel, lived in their towns.

And when the seventh month had come, the children of Israel were in their towns.

8 [1]And all the people gathered as one man into the square before the Water Gate; and they told Ezra the scribe to bring the book of the law of Moses which the Lord had given to Israel. [2]And Ezra the priest brought the law before the assembly, both men and women and all who could hear with understanding, on the first day of the seventh month. [3]And he read from it facing the square before the Water Gate from early morning until midday, in the presence of the men and the women and of those who could understand; and the ears of all the people were attentive to the book of the law. [4]And Ezra the scribe stood on a wooden pulpit which they had made for the purpose; and beside him stood Mattithiah, Shema, Anaiah, Uriah, Hilkiah, and Maaseiah on his right hand; and Pedaiah, Misha-el, Malchijah, Hashum, Hashbaddanah, Zechariah, and Meshullam on his left hand. [5]And Ezra opened the book in the sight of all the people, for he was above all the people; and when he opened it all the people stood. [6]And Ezra blessed the Lord, the great God; and all the people answered, "Amen, Amen," lifting up their hands; and they bowed their heads and worshipped the Lord with their faces to the ground.

The text goes on to say that Ezra read from the law and that both he and the Levites taught the people, helping them to understand it (cf. Neh 8:7-9):

> ... the Levites helped the people to understand the law, while the people remained in their places. And they read from the book, from the Law of God, clearly; and they gave the sense, so that the people understood the reading.

The meaning of this text is probably that given more clearly in the apocryphal work known as I Esdras (9:48):

> "The Levites taught the law of the Lord, at the same time explaining what was read".

What the explanation, or interpretation, given by the Levites consisted in is a matter of scholarly debate. Some believe that a translation from Hebrew (the language of the Pentateuch and of the Law of Moses) into Aramaic is intended. In fact, the Hebrew word in Neh 8:8 rendered "clearly" in the RSV could also be rendered as "with interpretation", and this in turn is understood by some scholars to mean "translation into the vernacular", or an Aramaic targum. Some, in fact, would like to understand 1 Esdras 9:48 as implying an Aramaic rendering as well. However, it seems clear that only an explanation of the contents of the law is intended there, a point made clearer in 1 Esdras 9:49 which says that Esdras was chief priest and reader and that the Levites were teaching the multitudes. This also appears to be the best understanding of Neh 8:8. In any event, an Aramaic rendering would not appear to have been necessary for the Jewish community of Ezra's day, since it now seems clear that their language then was Hebrew, not Aramaic.

On that solemn occasion, on the seventh month (September-October) of 428 or 398 B.C. Judaism, the religion of the book, was officially born, a religion that would have a book as its centre and its basis, the book being "the law of Moses which the Lord God of Israel had given" to his people. There is a strong probability that the book in question on that occasion was the Pentateuch. But even if it was not, all that was said of the law, and done concerning the law, on that occasion held true for the Torah, the Pentateuch, in later Judaism: it was to be at the centre of religion, taught to the people and explained to them so that they could understand its message. We are not told what steps were actually taken at that time to have all Israel come to a knowledge of the law of Moses. It would, however, be fair to say, I believe, that with Ezra the planned programme of bringing all Jews to a knowledge of this law began to take effect. By New Testament times it was recognized that this was already an immemorial custom. As James said at the Council of Jerusalem: "From early generations Moses has had in every city those who preach him, for he is read every sabbath in the synagogues" (Acts 15:21). Or as Flavius Josephus puts it: "He (i.e. Moses) has proclaimed the law to be the best and most necessary instruction of all; but once or twice or many times must one listen to it; for he has ordained that every week, other works being set aside, the people should come together to hear the law and learn it exactly" (*Contra Apionem* II, 17 (18), 175).

4. *Priests, Levites and Scribes*

After the exile until 200 B.C. or so, the restored community had a theocratic constitution and was governed by priests. In the early years of the restoration mention is made of both a civil and a religious leader, Shesbazzar the governor, then Zerubbabel the Governor and Joshua the High Priest. Apart from Shesbazzar, Zerubbabel and Nehemiah, no mention is made of governor (*pehah*) in the post-exilic province of Yehud, and when it had one he was probably Persian rather than Jewish. Either the absence of a governor or the fact that he would have been non-Jewish would have given all the more prestige to the High Priest in the affairs of the restored community.

The life of the community centered around the temple and was governed by the priests and the Levites. It was a community small in numbers — probably not much more than 20,000 in all — set on living after the model of the assembly of the desert as put before them in the Priestly Holiness Code and other parts of the Pentateuch.

Already in the time of the prophets Zechariah and Haggai, the period of classical prophecy seems to have been considered as past. Zechariah (1:4; 7:7, 12) speaks of the "former prophets" as if they already stood out as normative and a class apart (see also Zech 1:6; 7:3). By the time of Ezra prophecy would have receded further into the background.

Coupled with this, the post-exilic theocratic community seemed to have looked on itself as living the reality of which these prophets had spoken — that is, they believed that the prophecy of a return from exile and of a new age had actually come (see the interpretation of Jeremiah's prophecy — Jer 25:11-12; 29:20 — in 2 Chron 36:22-23 and Ezra 1:1-4). With such a faith there was little need to look forward.

In this religious community the Levites played an important role as temple singers and as teachers. Ezra, the scribe of the law of Moses, was a priest, and, in this sense, of the levitical class. We have seen the role of the Levites at the promulgation of the Law of Ezra: they taught the people and helped them understand the message of the law of Moses. We can presume that this is but a reflection of a major role they played during the post-exilic period. In the Books of Chronicles mention is also made of the teaching activity of the Levites in the pre-exilic period. Examples of this can be seen in the texts known as Levitical Sermons which we find in Chronicles (see, e.g. 2 Chron 17:7-9; 35:3; see also 30:6-9). Here we probably are in the presence of the retrojection into pre-exilic times of the situation obtaining in the Chronicler's own day (perhaps ca. 300 B.C.) and in the earlier post-exilic period.

Prophetic activity is also attributed to the Levites in Chronicles. In 2 Chron 20:14 we read of a Levite who took the lead in prophecy in king Jehoshaphat's day and in 2 Chron 20:20 the same king seems to refer to the Levites as prophets. We have an interesting text in the Chronicler's account of Josiah's reform in which he replaces "prophets" of his source (which was 2 Kings 23:2) with "Levites" (2 Chron 34:30). Even in their temple service the Levites are said to prophesy (cf. 1 Chron 25:1-3). This may reflect a belief of the Second Temple period that the spirit of prophecy had passed to the Levites, now that prophecy in the older sense of the word had ceased. The Levites, then — and this probably in their varied activities of teaching as well as liturgical service — may have been regarded as the successors of the prophets. If this is so, the Pharisaic view that the

Scribes were the successors of the Prophets would have very old roots.

This takes us to a consideration of the Scribes during the post-exilic period, especially before 200 B.C. Before this date, it is generally stated, and probably rightly so, that the scribes were from the priestly or the levitical classes. Ezra the priest was also a scribe of the law of Moses. His activity, and the activity of the Levites of his time, would be that of the scribes of succeeding generations: to study the law and teach it to others.

It must be admitted, however, that we are not too well informed about the origins and development of the later scribal system. As their forerunners we may envisage those scholars of the Deutronomistic and Priestly schools and the disciples of Ezekiel who reformulated and transmitted an earlier tradition. And to these we may add the scholars of the wisdom tradition who performed a like task for that other inheritance of Israel. These would have worked during the exile in Babylon and later both in Babylon and Palestine. They would both have reflected on Israel's sacred traditions and where required taught the Law as Ezra and the Levites had done. Within this larger group, some at least would have had a special role of working to produce the definitive text of Israel's varied traditions which was to become accepted as canonical. It would be within this group that the books of the Hebrew scriptures received their final form. In the process of producing the final text they would have reformulated, added, juxtaposed one item of tradition with another, as they believed was indicated by the situation of their day and by the work in which they were involved. We may look on these as inspired scribes.

It would be unwise, however, to look on the scribes of this post-exilic period as all of one sort. Together with those whose chief concern was the sacred traditions of Israel, there were presumably others, especially those of the wisdom tradition, who were open to the international wisdom of the east, just as the sages of pre-exilic times were. These would have maintained contact with the learned schools of Babylon, and possibly of Egypt and Canaan as well. We know from Greek and Roman writers that the ancient Chaldaean learning of Babylonia continued right down to Roman times. Pliny (*Natural History* 6, 30, 123, see also Strabo, *Geography* 16, 1, 6) mentions three cities which were famous at a later date for their "Chaldean learning", namely Babylon, Warka and Hipparene. The ancient texts continued to be copied and studied in Babylon long after the Persian, and indeed the Greek, conquest. They were collected and published in Greek by the Babylonian priest Berossus in a work dedicated to Antiochus I (281—261 B.C.). The ancient traditions of Egypt also continued to be studied. The best-known collection of them is that made by Manetho, an Egyptian priest, of the third century B.C. in his history of Egypt (*Aegyptiaca*) composed in Greek.

The ancient traditions also probably continued to be transmitted in Canaan, but in what formal way, if any, is difficult to say. In the first or second century of our era Philo of Byblos composed an account of Phoenician tradition under the title *Phoenician History*, which is further presented as simply a translation of a native source written by a person called Sanchuniathon. The Neo-Platonist writer Porphyry goes further and asserts that Sanchuniathon was a figure of remote antiquity, prior to the time of the Trojan war. While the real date of Sanchuniathon, if he really existed, is a matter of debate, and even though scholars are still divided as to the amount of genuine and ancient (hence Canaanite) tradition in Philo of Byblos, it seems legitimate to assume that the ancient traditions of Canaan were transmitted into later times and were available to Jewish writers.

That Jewish scribes had access to Chaldean and Babylonian tradition seems indicated by the presence in the Enochic material (*The Book of Giants*) of Qumran of the names of ancient Babylonian heroes such as Gilgamesh, and even of his adversary Humbaba (under the form Hababesh). The use of older material in the book of Daniel, and the references to Daniel's education in the letters and language of the Chaldeans (cf. Dan 1:4) is further proof of this continued contact with Babylonian learning. It is also worth noting in this regard that the name of the Babylonian hero Gilgamos

(Greek form of Gilgamesh) occurs in the Italo-Greek writer Aelian of the 2nd-3rd century A.D. (*On the Nature of Animals* 12, 21) where he is presented as grandson of Euechoios (or Seuechoros) king of the Babylonians. Aelian may have come on this information in Berossus' work. The Greek chronographer Georgios Synkellos, however, also mentions Euechoios, first king of Babylon and in this, as in other matters, he may be dependent on the *Book of Enoch*.

The books of Job and Koheleth can be presumed to have originated within wisdom circles, and circles that must have been regarded as orthodox. Yet they were scarcely representative of the scribes of their day, in their unconventional treatment of the problem of retribution. And despite this, it appears that Koheleth was a school teacher (cf. Ecclesiastes 12:9).

The earlier sections of Enoch belong to the period before 200 B.C. In some of these Enoch is presented as "scribe of righteousness" (in 1 Enoch 12:3; 12:4; 15:1). He is called "the scribe", even though he was not of the tribe of Levi.

The post-exilic period, then, can truly be called "the Age of the Scribes", yet probably of a scribal learning that was rich and varied, faithful to tradition yet open to the larger world, mainly, but not necessarily completely, priestly or levitical.

5. Biblical Interpretation between 500 and 200 B.C.

We now return to a point already treated of in passing, namely the ongoing development of the biblical tradition and the inner-biblical interpretation of scripture.

Before the tradition has been consigned to writing and has attained at least semi-canonical status we can speak of the development of tradition. After this comes interpretation which is here understood as reflection on and explanation of a written text, in a sense exegesis. It is not necessary that the text be formally accepted as authoritative and canonical, although the very fact that it is being accepted as the basis of reflection within the believing community would seem to imply that it is regarded as in some sense "canonical". In so complex a matter as that of the canon, however, it would be unwise to probe further at this stage.

There is general agreement among more recent scholars that in the books composed during the post-exilic age, both proto-canonical and deutero-canonical, there is a fair degree of dependence on earlier books of the canon. The relationship of these later works to the earlier ones can vary in nature. Sometimes it is a question of a recasting of the earlier text to have it bear a message for a later date. At other times there is question of use of the language of the earlier books to convey the later author's message, without there being necessarily any inner connection between the teaching itself. The manner of the use can vary, while the fact of contact with the earlier tradition and writings is clear. While often there seems to be question of dependence on actual written texts, at times there may be more a question of dependence on the tradition itself without it being clear whether the later writers had access to this in its written or oral form.

We have already spoken of the manner in which the tradition found in the Book of Ezekiel seems to have developed: a basic tradition representing the teaching of the prophet, together with the development of this by later disciples and students. The question of biblical exegesis within the Book of Ezekiel can be approached in a number of ways. There is the question of the possible influence of earlier biblical books upon the prophet Ezekiel himself. Then there is the question of Ezekiel's message being linked in the process of interpretation with other biblical books. Some scholars believe that the section of Gog from Magog (chaps 38-39) falls within this category: Ezek 38:17 refers to the earlier prophets who foretold the coming of the enemy from the north, and because of this the language of Isa. 5, Jer 4-6 and Ps 46 is introduced into Ezekiel's composition to make the fulfilment clear. In like manner, the original description of the theophany in Ezek 1 is regarded as embellished by the introduction of the imagery from other epiphanies, e.g. Exod 24:9ff., Isa 6:1ff. and Ps 18:11. A further kind of internal exegesis is the expansion of one text of Ezekiel by another text of his. The clearest example of this in Ezekiel is the introduction of elements from the theophany of chapter 1 into that of chapters 8-11. A similar phenomenon may explain the relationships between chapters 16 and 23.

No one doubts that there is a very definite relationship between the Third Isaiah (Isa 56-66) and the Second Isaiah (Isa 40-55). How explain this relationship is less certain. One view is that Third Isaiah (whether from one or more authors) is a conscious re-interpretation of themes and words in Second Isaiah and this at more than one level. In some cases there would be merely re-adaptation of key-words and phrases, in other cases it looks more like a sermon or commentary on a sacred text. The purpose of this interpretative activity was apparently to draw lessons for the later age of Trito-Isaiah (say about 520-515 B.C.) from the words of an acknowledged religious leader who lived in different circumstances — even though this was but a few decades earlier. To quote John J. Scullion in volume 12 of this series: "He (Trito-Isaiah) resumed, adopted and applied words, phrases and verses from (Isaiah) chaps. 40-55 to the post-exilic situation in Jerusalem and Judah" (p. 147).

The Book of Jeremiah has an interesting and informative history of composition, which is explained in detail by Lawrence Boadt in volumes 9 and 10 of this series. What interests us here is the development that almost certainly went on after the Hebrew text on which the Greek Septuagint text is based was composed. The Septuagint, as is well known to scholars in this field, is about one eighth shorter than the Hebrew — or by about 2700 words. Often the difference is only of a single word, but sometimes it is of a shorter or longer passage. Since fragments of a shorter Hebrew text, corresponding with the Greek translation, have been found in Qumran, the best explanation of the difference seems to be the existence of two Hebrew texts — a first one (composed perhaps in the fifth century at latest) of the shorter type translated in Greek. The Jeremianic tradition, however, would have continued to develop, and this development would have led to the insertions which have given us the present longer Masoretic text. All these insertions, of course, need not have actually come into existence after the Greek translation was made.

An instance of one such expansion in the later history of transmission can be seen in Jer 33:14-26 as compared with Jer. 23:5-6. Jer 23:5-6 is generally taken as a genuine oracle of Jeremiah, in fact the only genuine Jeremianic oracle on the Messiah. It reads:

> [5]"Behold, the days are coming, says the Lord, when I will raise up for David a righteous branch, and he shall reign as king and deal wisely, and shall execute justice and righteousness in the land. [6]In his days Judah will be saved, and Israel will dwell securely. And this is the name by which he will be called: 'The Lord is our righteousness.'

The lengthy section, Jer. 33:14-26, not found in the Greek Septuagint translation, appears to be an expansion of this. It reads:

> [14]"Behold, the days are coming, says the Lord, when I will fulfil the promise I made to the house of Israel and the house of Judah. [15]In those days and at that time I will cause a righteous Branch to spring forth for David; and he shall execute justice and righteousness in the land. [16]In those days Judah will be saved and Jerusalem will dwell securely. And this is the name by which it will be called: 'The Lord is our righteousness.'
>
> [17]"For thus says the Lord: David shall never lack a man to sit on the throne of the house of Israel. [18]and the Levitical priests shall never lack a man in my presence to offer burnt offerings, to burn cereal offerings, and to make sacrifices for ever."
>
> [19]The word of the Lord came to Jeremiah: [20]"Thus says the Lord: If you can break my covenant with the day and my covenant with the night, so that day and night will not come at their appointed time, [21]then also my covenant with David my servant may be broken, so that he shall

not have a son to reign on his throne, and my covenant with the Levitical priests my ministers. 22As the host of heaven cannot be numbered and the sands of the sea cannot be measured, so I will multiply the descendants of David my servant, and the Levitical priests who minister to me."

23The word of the Lord came to Jeremiah: 24"Have you not observed what these people are saying, 'The Lord has rejected the two families which he chose'? Thus they have despised my people so that they are no longer a nation in their sight. 25Thus says the Lord: If I have not established my covenant with day and night and the ordinances of heven and earth, 26then I will reject the descendants of Jacob and David my servant and will not choose one of his descendants to rule over the seed of Abraham, Isaac, and Jacob. For I will restore their fortunes, and will have mercy upon them."

The reader will note that the oracle is modified somewhat in the expanded version. It is Jerusalem, not the son of David, which will be called "The Lord is our righteousness". The expanded version also contains a blessing on the Levitical priests, mention of the union of North and South, of God's covenant with creation, and his promises to the patriarchs.

We agree with Lawrence Boadt's judgment expressed in volume 10 of this series: "...we can scarcely come to any other conclusion than that vv. 14-26 represent a later period's reflection upon the meaning of Jeremiah's words in chaps. 22-23, with their lack of hope, when mixed with his words of promise in chaps. 30-32" (p. 71). It is less easy to assign a date of composition to this prophecy, although L. Boadt, with others, opts for the days of the activity of Zerubbabel the Davidide and governor, and Joshua the high priest —sometime between 520 and 516 B.C. The important fact, from our point of view, is not so much its date: we are concerned with the process by which a later text reflects upon an earlier one and reinterprets it. This instance from Jeremiah is another good example of internal exegesis of the kind we have seen in the Book of Ezekiel.

We have already seen how the prophet Zechariah looks on the earlier prophets ("the former prophets", Zech 1:4; 7:7, 12) as a class apart, in some sense already classical and canonical. We have also seen how he (Zech 3:8-10) seems to make a direct reference to the prophecy of Jeremiah 23:5 (that expanded in the Masoretic text of Jer 33:14-26), just as the words of his contemporary Haggai in Hag. 2:23 which are addressed to Zerubbabel seem to be a recasting of the oracle which Jeremiah (Jer 22:24) had directed against Zerubbabel's grandfather Jehoiachin.

Both the date and the purpose of the Book of Jonah are difficult to determine, but it is most probably post-exilic and possibly from about 475-450 B.C. One view is that it is a midrash on Jeremiah 18:1-10, on Yahweh's readiness to forgive a repentant city despite the apparently absolute threats of punishment he had made against it. Jonah would be a story illustrating the principle enunciated in Jer 18:1-10.

The Book of Malachi appears to have been composed around 400 B.C. Some time later the prophet Joel wrote and seems to have borrowed from Malachi (compare Joel 2:11 with Mal 3:2), but also from Amos (compare Joel 3:18 with Amos 9:13). In 3:18 Joel takes up a prophecy of Ezekiel (Ezek 47:1-8) on the fountain of water flowing from the temple of the Lord, an idea that occurs again in Deutero-Zechariah (Zech 14:18).

The prologue of the Book of Proverbs (Prov 1-9) is most probably post-exilic, possibly from the fifth century B.C., although some would reckon it later still — from the fourth or even the third century. In the mid-thirties the French biblical scholar André Robert made a study of the literary connections of this section of the book and maintained that it contained echoes of Deuteronomy, Jeremiah, Isaiah and in particular Deutero-Isaiah. Its use of the earlier scriptures he described as "the anthological style" and many scholars see this style present in a number of the later works of the Old Testament.

The Books of Chronicles were probably composed in the fourth century, after the law of Moses had been made

central to Judaism by Ezra. 1 Chronicles in particular
makes extensive use of earlier Hebrew literature, which
most probably lay before the Chronicler in written form,
and as sacred text — canonical or authentic Sacred Scripture. It has been ascertained that the author or editor of 1 - 2
Chronicles had before him the law of Moses (the Pentateuch). In fact he was convinced that this work already
existed in writing and was being explained to the people in
the days of the kings of Judah. The Chronicler in 1-2 Chronicles mentions "the Torah of the Lord" (or, "of God", "of the
Lord God") 14 times, whereas the expression is used only
once in the Books of Kings. On 9 occasions the law is
referred to as a book. Both books of Chronicles also hold
the prophets in high regard. We have already noted that 2
Chron 36:22-23 and Ezra 1:1 make the point that Yahweh
inspired Cyrus to issue his proclamation in favour of the
Jews "so that the word of the Lord by the mouth of Jeremiah might be accomplished" (of "fulfilled"). Later history
was seen to relate to earlier prediction. That the Pentateuch
was a specially sacred text may be seen in the manner in
which the Chronicler introduced texts from it. He uses a
formula that will later become sacrosanct, e.g. "as it is
written"; in Hebrew *kᵉkatūb* (2 Chron 30:5; 31:3), "as it is
written in the law of Moses" (2 Chron 23:18); "what is
written in the law, in the book of Moses" (2 Chron 25:4,
citing Deut 24:16). The presence of certain hortatory passages in both books of Chronicles has already been mentioned — the sections to which the title "Levitical Sermons"
has been given. In these passages in particular, but also
elsewhere in the books, we meet a number of biblical quota-
tions and allusions. Among others the following texts cited
or alluded to may be instanced: Zeph 3:5; Jer 17:5; 29:14, 18;
Zech 4:10; Isa 19:2; 7:4; 7:9; 1 Sam 13:13; 17:47; Josh 10:25;
Deut 4:29-30; 10:17; Exod 14:13-14; Ps 132:7. In short, in
the work of the Chronicler the process already begun in
earlier post-exilic writings is taken a step further. Furthermore, together with citation and allusion, the Chronicler's
manner of using earlier scriptural tradition has advanced far

along the road to the form of interpretation which will be later known as midrash. It is a point to which we shall return presently.

The use of earlier biblical tradition is also a feature of the final chapters of Zechariah (Zech 9-14), collectively referred to as Second Zechariah. This section of the book was probably composed in the early Greek period (330-300 B.C.). Some scholars see in Second Zechariah a development of the tradition of Proto-Zechariah (i.e. Zech 1-8). It has also been shown that these final chapters make use of Ezekiel, Trito-Isaiah (Isa 56-66), Job, Malachi, Joel and Chronicles. Many of the borrowings from these books are in the area of apocalyptic teaching, e.g. Joel 4, Ezekiel 38-39 and Isa 60-62. In these chapters we have the continued development of such earlier themes as the temple on a high mountain (Zech 14:10; Ezek 43:12), living waters flowing from Jerusalem (Zech 14:8; Ezek 47:11), the coming of the messianic king to Zion (Zech 9:9; Zeph 3:4). In these chapters such early motifs as the divine warrior and the holy war are used and developed in a novel manner. There is also a distinct possibility that in 9:1-8 a very ancient piece of Israelite prophecy is being used, but if so only to have it understood in the new context of the early Greek empire in Palestine.

The Book of Tobit was probably composed about 200 B.C. In this work we have clear evidence of dependence on the earlier scriptures. In the words of John Craghan in volume 16 of this series (p.132) introducing Tobit: "The most obvious influence on the book is the Old Testament. The author clearly dialogues with his scriptural heritage and adapts it to the needs of his audience". The influence of Gen 2 is clearly visible in Tobit 8, and Gen 24 can be compared with Tobit 6 and 7. There is an especially strong influence from the Book of Deuteronomy. To cite the words of J. Craghan again (p. 132): "Tobit may be called 'Deuteronomy revisited' since the story reflects the living out of the covenant implications of that book."

6. *Fixation of Text and Biblical Interpretation*

We can terminate this survey on the development of tradition and on the interpretation of the Bible between 500 and 200 B.C. with some words on the end of the process, namely the redaction of the biblical books and the formation of the canon.

In the books of the bible as we now have them biblical criticism has identified what appear to be a juxtaposition of texts which seems to be editorial, not original, and the presence of texts which appear to be later than the main body of the tradition. These, and other of the phenomena identified by critics, can be attributed to the scribes responsible for producing the final form of the biblical text that was to become canonical. Thus their activity can also be regarded as interpretation. Their aim can be presumed to have been the presentation of the tradition of the Law, the Prophets, etc. in a manner that would continue to have a message for later generations.

This editorial work of the inspired scribes was manifold: for instance in the prophetical corpus the completion of a prophecy of woe with one of welfare, prophecies of doom against foreign nations occasionally rounded off by a prediction of their conversion to the religion of Yahweh "in the days to come" (e.g. Isa 17:3; 18:7; 19:18-24; Jer 48:47; 49:39).

Other examples of editorial additions can probably be seen in the presence of brief texts on the future life and on angelology in contexts which appear to be older than the time of the emergence of these ideas in Israel. Examples of this kind could be multiplied.

In the abstract one could say that these later elements are mere haphazard intrusions into the corpus of earlier tradition as it was being transmitted. Much more likely, however, they are evidence of an intentional updating of the tradition by the authorized scribes as they set down to give definitive shape to the tradition, a form that would become concrete in a book intended for the believing and worshipping community, one that would have the particular book speak to the contemporary and to a later generation. Writing on this point Père R. Tournay has expressed himself as follows:

> It is interesting to see to what extent the Scriptures continued to live within the community of believers and how the faith of these believers poured itself into the very text of the ancient writings, thus registering the development of revelation for future generations. The forward thrust of this revelation went beyond the material content of the texts, and the latter were not considered as dead documents, fixed once for all; they always remained open to eventual enrichment. The Bible was already read and meditated on within a living tradition, a tradition anxious to answer the spiritual need of the Jewish people at every moment of its existence.

Revelation developed between the time of an original oracle or teaching and the date of the final redaction of the work that contained it, this was registered in the final edition of the work. Sometimes even after the final edition of a biblical book had been made, newer insights could be worked into the now completed composition to become part of the canonical text. Once the text was finally closed, however, development of thought and revelation would have to find expression in some form other than in the canonical writing itself.

In the matter of fixation of the text and of the ensuing interpretation of this within the community, one must keep in mind the prevailing mental climate. We have already noted that an enlarged world view had later generations interpret and formulate earlier tradition in the light of its faith on matters such as messianic teaching, afterlife, angelology and such like. And these later ideas were read into the final form of the text, the one that was to become canonical.

We may have good instances of how the overall view of the covenant relationship affected interpretation of scripture in both First and Second Zechariah, but in quite different ways in each. It appears that the age of Proto-Zechariah believed that fulfilment of the prophecies was to come immediately on the rebuilding of the temple and that this belief has coloured his interpretation of the prophecies of Jeremiah.

It also seems that the theocratic community that followed on the restoration believed that fulfilment had already taken place in the community then gathered around the temple and bonded together by the law of Moses. They had little need to look forward and could interpret the prophecies as already fulfilled. By 300 B.C. or so disillusionment had set in, forcing the community to look towards fulfilment in the future, in a new divine intervention. This is what we find in Second Zechariah. The whole outlook had by then become eschatological.

With the conviction that salvation and fulfilment lay in the future, the scriptures were regarded as prophesying about future salvation rather than as narrating past events or predictions already fulfilled. This shift was facilitated both by the prevailing eschatological outlook and the decline of the prophetic word, or the belief in the cessation of prophecy. The scriptures themselves were now becoming regarded as the word of God and as such prophetic, predictive of future salvation. The prophets were now regarded primarily as foretellers of the end rather than as spokesperson for God in the society of their day. This attitude to prophecy seems implied in the Book of Sirach (about 200 B.C.). In his introduction to the praise of famous persons he says in 44:3 according to the Hebrew text, which probably best represents the original: "There were persons renowned for their power, counsellors of all things in their prudence, seers of all things in (their) prophecy" (cf. *New American Bible*). Writing of the prophet Isaiah Sirach is more explicit: "He revealed what was to occur to the end of time, and the hidden things before they came to pass" (48:25). Thus the RSV, but the Hebrew text has literally: "before their coming", which is better rendered by NAB as: "(hidden things) yet to be fulfilled." "What was to occur in the end of time" and "the hidden things yet to be fulfilled" are not so much individual prophecies of Isaiah which had already occurred in history, as the course of history which in Ben Sirach's day was yet to come. In this understanding of the text, Ben

Sirach would have regarded Isaiah (and possibly other scriptures) as foretellers of the end of time. The Bible was being interpreted eschatologically by 200 B.C., a situation that would obtain right through into the New Testament period. With this change in perspective, the stage was set for apocalyptic.

Excursus on Midrash

We have spoken on a number of occasions in the preceding pages on midrash and the midrashic interpretation of Scripture. Since the term will return again in the course of these pages, and in fact since mention of midrash cannot be avoided in any discussion of the literature and biblical interpretation of the intertestamental period, it merits separate consideration here.

Midrash itself belongs in a special way to rabbinic Judaism and rabbinic literature. In this literature it is a term rich in meaning, but has always to do with the exposition of scripture of an actualizing, contemporizing kind. It can designate the spiritual and mental approach to the study or the reflective reading of the scriptures. It can mean the actual exposition itself, and also the result of this interpretative activity—the writings in which the exposition is found. An attempt was made in recent years to restrict the meaning of the term, and to regard midrash as a literary genre. In his review of a work on this matter, one with the significant title, *The Literary Genre Midrash*, Roger Le Déaut has the following to say on midrash:

> It forms part of a specific "mental constellation" in which it is endowed with a charge which is both affective and religious and which, in our view, obliges us to retain for it its exclusive traditional meaning. Now, this traditional understanding of the term has a very broad range of meaning, that range which has been adopted by the Jewish and Christian authors who have devoted the most important studies to it (Zunz, Bacher, Albeck....). Mid-

rash, in effect, is an entire universe, which one does not discover except by accepting its complexity all at once. Midrash permeates the entire Jewish approach to the Bible, and can even designate this approach in all its variety. One cannot separate the techniques and the methods of midrash, even if these lead to different literary genres. Midrash can be described; it cannot be defined for the reason that it is a way of thinking and of reasoning often disconcerting for us.

That midrash is found within the Hebrew Scriptures has been affirmed by some scholars for many years. It is this point that I would like to consider briefly here.

The term *midrash* itself occurs twice in 2 Chronicles: the *Midrash* of the prophet Iddo (2 Chron 13:22) and the *Midrash* of the Book of Kings (2 Chron 24:27). This latter work may be the same as that referred to elsewhere in Chronicles under other titles: *The Book of the Kings of Israel and Judah* (2 Chron 27:7, 35:27, 36:8, cf. 1 Chronicles 9:1), *The Book of Kings of Judah and Israel* (2 Chron 20:34, cf. 1 Chron 9:1), *The Words (affairs) of the Kings of Israel* (2 Chron 33:18). *The midrash of the Prophet Iddo* may have been part of this Midrash of Kings in so far as it contained narratives concerning the prophet Iddo (cf. 2 Chron 12:15). It appears, however, that besides the *Midrash* of the Kings the Chronicler had a similar source with information concerning prophets.

The meaning of *midrash* as title of the book or books in question is not clear. The *Midrash* of Kings was probably a work based on the books of Samuel and Kings, but with extra information of the supplementary, interpretative kind found in Chronicles themselves. Some take the term as title of a work to mean no more than "book"; others render it as "treatise", "commentary."

The word *midrash* comes from the Hebrew verb *darash* which means "to seek." It is often used of "seeking God", inquiring concerning the will of God from a prophet, etc.; seeking for the word of God. It is also used in the sense of seeking out the meaning of a thing, to inquire, to investigate a matter, to seek with application, to study. The word *midrash* denotes the action of so doing, or its result, i.e. study, interpretation, exposition. The *midrash* of the book of kings, and of Iddo, may have been writings of an exhortatory, didactic nature.

After Chronicles the next attested use of the term *midrash* is found in the text of two of the Rules from Qumran, i.e. the *Community Rule* (1QS) and the *Damascus Rule* (CD) composed respectively about 150 and 100 B.C. In both these texts it is used in relation with the law of Moses and means the *study* or interpretation of the law.

In the *Community Rule* (1QS) 8:15 we read concerning the Community:

> And when these become members of the Community in Israel according to all these rules, they shall separate from the habitation of the ungodly and shall go into the wilderness to prepare the way before him; as it is written, *Prepare in the wilderness . . . make straight in the desert a path for our God* (Isa 40:3). This (path) is the study (*midrash*) of the Law which he commanded by the hand of Moses, that they may do according to all that has been revealed from age to age, and as the Prophets have revealed by his Holy Spirit.

The *Damascus Rule* (CD) 20:6, text B has this statement about a community member who has proved unfaithful to his rule:

> When his deeds are revealed, according to the interpretation (*midrash*) of the Law in which the men of perfect holiness walk, let no man defer to him with regard to money or work, for all the Holy Ones of the Most high have cursed him.

In these two texts *midrash* deals with scripture and its interpretation. The Qumran actualizing interpretation of Scripture, in which the words of the sacred text were usually interpreted as actualized in their own community, is generally called *pesher* in the Qumran texts. A text of scripture is first given and then applied with the words: "its interpretation (*pesher*) concerns . . . . ." One such piece is the text of 4Q174, which is a *Florilegium* in which we have select texts interpreted of the Community and the Messiah, each interpretation introduced by the expected *pesher*. However, the section on Ps 1 is first introduced as a *midrash*: "Explanation (*midrash*) of (the text): *How blessed is the man who does not walk in the counsel of the wicked* (Ps 1:1). The interpretation (*pesher*) of the word concerns . . . . ."

It is thus clear that the term *midrash* and the reality itself existed before the Christian era. The point of departure of midrash was the Scripture text which it took up and applied to a later, generally contemporary, situation. The basis for such an application of the Scriptures was established with the formation of the canon and the religious conviction that the Bible itself was the word of God and prophetic. We have already considered some evidence for the existence of this view in the Book of Sirach. To this we may add the text of 1 Mac 3:48 (cf. also 2 Mac 8:53). This text speaks of Judas Maccabee and his brothers assembled at Mizpah, in preparation for battle. There they fasted and mourned and then (in the most probable translation of a difficult text), "opened the book of the Law to inquire into these matters about which the Gentiles were consulting the images of their gods." Their purpose in opening the book of the law was probably to get direction from it concerning the divine will — an exercise in midrash.

The Books of Chronicles seem to provide a good example of midrash within the Hebrew Scriptures. In the words of B.S. Childs: "Perhaps the crucial discovery of the modern study of Chronicles is the extent to which the Chronicler sought to interpret Israel's history in relation to a body of authoritative scripture. . . . . Indeed, most of the crucial exegetical moves which comprise the chronicler's method derive directly from his concept of authoritative writings through which the will of God is revealed to every generation of Israel." Childs himself instances the following features of the Chronicler's method: exegesis of authoritative scripture, harmonization of accounts, arising from taking the entire Bible as a unit; supplementation of earlier accounts in the light of later and more fully developed teaching; typology or the ordering of biblical material according to patterns, and finally, coherence of action and effect. Such an approach and method, can be aptly described as midrashic.

We may be permitted to go beyond these larger principles into details. I believe that we find a good illustration of the Chronicler's midrashic technique in the manner he treats the tradition of Mount Moriah of Genesis 22 and links it with the later narrative concerning the site of the temple. According to Gen 22 Abraham was about to sacrifice his son Isaac on Mount Moriah. With an obvious play of the presumed root of the place-name, the corresponding or related verb *ra'ah*, "to see" is used four times in the Genesis narrative (Gen 22:4, 8, 13, 14). Abraham called the name of that place "The Lord will provide" (literally, "will see"). The Genesis narrative gives us no exact location for Mount Moriah and the place is not mentioned again in biblical literature before 2 Chron 3:1, where it is identified as the place where Solomon built the temple, and likewise with the threshing floor of Araunah: "Then Solomon began to build the house of the Lord in Jerusalem on Mount Moriah, where the Lord had appeared to David his father, at the place that David had appointed, on the threshing floor of Ornan the Jebusite." But this is not all. The same tradition on the identity of Moriah (and all that the name from the supposed root *ra'ah* evoked) seems to underlie the manner in which the Chronicler rewrites his source 2 Sam 24:15-17 in 1 Chron 21:15. The narrative here concerns the plague in David's day and how it ceased. The text of 2 Samuel simply says that the angel sent to destroy Jerusalem was standing by the threshing floor of Araunah (called Ornan in Chronicles) when Yahweh stayed his hand. As retold by the Chronicler (1 Chron 21:15) this becomes: "the Lord saw (*ra'ah*) and he repented of the evil .... and the angel of the Lord was standing by the threshing floor of Ornan...." The Lord *saw* as the angel stood by the threshing floor of Ornan, identified with Moriah — a name taken to mean "the Lord will see" (Gen 22:14). The link can scarcely be accidental. What the Lord actually saw we are not told. Jewish tradition as later expressed in the Targum of Chronicles will say he saw the blood of Isaac, as if shed on Mount Moriah. This may not have been in the Chronicler's mind. The approach to scripture, however, the midrashic one, which led to this development, appears to have been very much part of the Chronicler's religious outlook.

2. APOCALYPTIC LITERATURE

1. A Matter of Definition

The term "apocalyptic" is one of those words which require definition or explanation before use. It has on occasion been employed rather loosely, in the broad sense of eschatological, relating to the end time. More recently, however, the dangers inherent in the imprecise use of the term have been adverted to and attempts have been made to arrive at a more refined and exact definition.

The very word "apocalyptic" itself is a sophisticated term, coined by scholars to designate a number of late Jewish and early Christian writings. It was so used because these books were seen as having much in common with the last writing in the New Testament Canon, known to us as "The Apocalypse" or "Revelation" — *apokalypsis* being the Greek for revelation. In the opening words of this book John introduces his message as follows: "The revelation (*apokalypsis*) of Jesus Christ, which God gave him to show to his servants what must take place soon; and he made it known by sending his angel to his servant John" (Rev. 1:1). In this description we can find the more important elements of what is regarded as the apocalyptic genre, viz. (1) a divine revelation, (2) communicated through an intermediary, often, as in this case, an angel, (3) regarding future events, (4) to take place soon. From this New Testament writing, as just noted, the term apocalyptic was applied by scholars to the larger body of related works, although the writers of these works did not describe them as apocalyptic nor speak of themselves as apocalypticists.

Further features of the body of apocalyptic writings is that they contain accounts of otherworldly journeys, and often describe the geography of the heavenly realms. The contents of works of this genre also tend to be of a certain kind, having to do generally with salvation, and at least with regard to the greater part of them, salvation in an afterlife at that.

Modern writers distinguish between apocalyptic (or apocalypse), apocalyptic eschatology and apocalypticism. Apocalypse (or apocalyptic) is taken as the literary form of this particular kind of writing. Apocalyptic eschatology is the form of eschatology found in apocalypses (or in apocalyptic literature) — eschatology being the doctrines, beliefs, hopes for the end time, for the future, the unfolding of God's plan for his people and the universe. Apocalypticism is: "a system of thought produced by visionary movements; builds upon a specific eschatological perspective in generating a symbolic universe opposed to that of the dominant society. This symbolic universe serves to establish the identity of the visionary community in relation to rival groups and to the deity..." (P.D. Hanson). Apocalypticism is thus a sociological ideology.

2. The Origins of Apocalyptic

In the not too recent past it was much easier than it is now to have neat and definite ideas as to when and how apocalyptic originated. One school of thought regarded it as the child of prophecy. Another preferred to see the origins of apocalyptic within the wisdom movement. It was, however, generally accepted that the first apocalyptic work (or at least the first great apocalyptic writing) was the canonical Book of Daniel, written during the Maccabean revolt, ca. 164 B.C.

The Qumran finds have obliged us to reassess our views on the priority of Daniel in this regard. Research in the field of apocalyptic has also shown that the origins of the genre are more complex than had once been thought. Much of this research has been done by John J. Collins who has written the commentary on Daniel and 1-2 Maccabees for this series (*Old Testament Message*, 15), including (pp. 130-145) a very fine excursus on the Apocalyptic genre to which I refer the reader.

The Qumran finds are of especial importance for an understanding of the Ethiopic *Book of Enoch* (also known as 1 Enoch). There are five distinct sections in this book, as follows: (1) *The Book of the Watchers* — sometimes called the Journeys of Enoch (chapters 1-36); (2) *The Parables* —or *Similitudes* (37-71); (3) *The Book of the Heavenly Luminaries* — or *The Astronomical Book* (72-82); (4) *The Dream Visions* — or *The Animal Apocalypse* (83-90); (5) *The Admonitions of Enoch* — called by some *The Epistle of Enoch* (91-107). It has been seen for a long time that these are distinct works, and probably once had separate existence. One or other scholar had even surmised that some of them at least may be as old as or even somewhat older than Maccabean times. They are now joined together in a sort of Enochic Pentateuch. In the Qumran caves Aramaic fragments of all sections, except the *Similitudes*, have been found — in all no fewer than eleven manuscripts of the *Books of Enoch*. Seven of these contain material corresponding to parts of the first (1-36), fourth (83-90) and the fifth (91-107) of the Ethiopic book, while four contain material corresponding to parts of the third section (72-82). A further point worthy of note is that a Qumran manuscript with part 1 (4QEn^a) dates from the first half of the second century B.C., arguing for the existence of the book in the late third century at the latest. A Qumran manuscript (4QEnastr^a), with portion of a longer recension of section of

The Astronomical Book of Enoch, is to be dated to the end of the third century, B.C. at the latest. It is clear, then, that these sections of the books of Enoch were current in the third century, B.C. Some scholars believe that they existed earlier still, e.g. the fourth century. The apocalyptic genre was thus well developed before the composition of the Book of Daniel.

The origins of apocalyptic are also to be sought in a much more complex situation than simply in a prophetic or wisdom tradition. The Israelite apocalyptic tradition has apparently within it and behind it a variety of traditions. It had contact not merely with the wisdom of Israel but also with the wisdom circles of the Middle East, for instance the learned schools of Babylon, and also, it appears, with the Canaanite tradition. Reflection on the prophetic tradition of Israel was very much a feature of Jewish apocalyptic. It conveyed to its devotees the outcome of these reflections in its new categories which make use of the imagery of the ancient east and of the biblical books, especially those of the exilic and post-exilic ages.

3. Method and Message of Jewish Apocalyptic

It is generally agreed that the method and message, the form and content, go together to constitute apocalyptic. The message, the apocalyptic vision, concentrates on certain positions which are central to the genre: that (as God told Ezra, *4 Ezra* 7:50) the Lord did not make one world but two, that reality entails the interplay of these two worlds, this visible one and another one, supernatural and invisible to normal vision; that God and his angels are active in human existence; that the affairs of this world are controlled by the other world; that this world, this age, is in the grips of the evil one, but that beyond this life there is another in which matters are set aright, one in which there is judgment, rewards and punishments; that after this present age a better one will come.

This other world, and with it knowledge of the divine will,

hidden from normal mortals, was made known to the apoc-alyptic visionary. He would receive this knowledge through divine revelation, generally given through an intermediary, not directly. Otherworldly journeys also play a prominent part in apocalypses. These may be of different kinds. In some journeys the visionary is taken up to heaven and is shown the heavenly throne and related realities. He may also be taken on a tour of the extra-terrestrial regions, be shown the souls of the dead awaiting judgment, the location of the heavenly bodies, the treasuries of light and such like. These journeys have a function in the genre and in the apocalyptist's role within his religious community. They serve to accredit the visionary for his readers: he had seen what he narrates regarding heavenly rewards. His hidden knowledge of the heavenly spheres, of the sun, moon, stars, etc., help to lend authority to calendar reckonings based on such information.

4. Old Testament Precedents

Certain sections of exilic and post-exilic books can be regarded as earlier stages in the development of the genre, or they are at least worthy of consideration by reason of their influence on apocalyptic writings, whether with regard to the use of imagery or the sequence of events in the descrip-tion of the end-time. Symbolism and allegory are already employed by Ezekiel, e.g. in chap. 16. In the description of invasion of foreign nations, Ezekiel chapters 38 and 39 makes use of language of the kind found in apocalyptic. The sequence found in the final section of the Book of Ezekiel, i.e. 34-48, would also be used in later apocalyptic writings: restoration after exile (chaps. 34-37), foreign invasion and destruction of invading forces (38-39), a new Israel and a new temple (40-48), with water issuing from the new temple (47:1-12), the place of God's throne.

While the Book of Joel (composed probably ca. 400 B.C.) is not itself apocalyptic, it merits attention in that it speaks almost exclusively of the future; of the future visitation by

Yahweh — in part imminent, in part remote — and employs imagery that will become part of the stock in trade of apocalyptic. The "Day of Yahweh" is looked on as imminent, in the form of a plague of locusts. God is called on to intervene; he becomes jealous for his people and pities them (2:18-19), and promises to remove "the northerner" (2:20), a term which in the context signifies the plague of locusts but which by Joel's day had become the designation of any foreign invader. The remainder of the book speaks entirely of the future. The visionary tells of portents in the heavens. He is also concerned with the fortunes of Judah and Jerusalem. These would be restored and the enemies of the Jews punished. The foreign nations are invited to come and wage war in the valley of Jehoshaphat, where the Lord of hosts who dwells in Zion would destroy them. Fertility on the hills of Judah would follow; a fountain would flow from the temple to water the valley of Jericho.

The date of the so-called "Apocalypse of Isaiah" (Isa 24-27) is still in doubt, although there is a tendency to assign it to about 400 B.C. The chapters belong to the prophetic rather than to the apocalyptic genre, inasmuch as the contents are given as prophecies and not as visions with interpretations, which would be typical of an apocalypse. The chapters have, however, certain themes in common with apocalyptic, such as a universal judgment, an eschatological banquet, signs in the heavens, destruction of God's enemies, resurrection of Israel's dead who perished from suffering and persecution (Isa 26:16-19).

The first eight chapters of the Book of Zechariah, representing the preaching of the prophet from 520 to 518 B.C., have certain material in common with apocalyptic, e.g. heavenly visions with divine interpretations (chaps. 1-6). The remainder of the book (chaps. 9-14) comes from a much later date, probably from the late fourth century B.C. In these chapters we have some of the themes that often occur in apocalyptic writings, e.g. the restoration of Israel and the Day of the Lord (9:1-11, 17; 12:1-14:21), Jerusalem purged of idolatry (12:1-13:6), the final warfare and the final victory over all the pagan nations who have come to wage war against Jerusalem. There are prophecies of the perpetual daylight to follow, of the living waters flowing from Jerusalem (14:6-8), the conversions of the survivors of the pagan nations and of their yearly pilgrimage to Jerusalem for the feast of Booths (14:1-21).

The similarity of Second Zechariah with apocalyptic need not surprise us, since it is probable that the latter genre already existed when the final sections of the Book of Zechariah were being composed.

We shall now examine the various apocalyptic writings of Judaism, following in this survey a chronological order.

5. *1 Enoch 1-36.*
The Book of Watchers, or *Enoch's Heavenly Journeys* (3rd cent. B.C.)

This section of 1 Enoch is itself a composite work. It begins with a Parable of Enoch on the lot of the wicked and of the righteous (1-5). Next comes *The Book of the Watchers* (i.e. the Angels) proper. This recounts the sin of the angels through their sexual union with earthly women, on which follows the demoralization of humankind. We are then told of the doom pronounced by God on the angels and of the joys in store for the just (6-11), e.g. "And . . . the Lord said to Raphael: 'Bind Azazel by his hands and his feet, and throw him into the darkness . . . and let him stay there for ever. . . that on the great day of judgment he may be hurled into the fire'" (10:4-6). "Bind them for seventy generations under the hills of the earth until the day of their judgment and of their consummation, until the judgment which is for all eternity is accomplished. And in those days they will lead them to the abyss of fire; in torment and in prison they will be shut up for all eternity" (10:12-13).

The next section of *The Book of the Watchers* (chaps. 12-16) contains Enoch's dream-vision. At their request, Enoch intercedes for the fallen Angels (the Watchers), but has to preach to them what he has seen in vision, which is that their petition has not been granted and that judgment, not peace, has been decreed against them. Enoch was transported into heaven, an experience which he described in these words (1 Enoch 14:8-23):

> And the vision appeared to me as follows: Behold clouds called me in the vision, and a mist called me, and the path of the stars and flashes of lightening hastened me and drove me, and in the vision winds caused me to fly and hastened me and lifted me up into heaven.

> **14** ⁹And I proceeded until I came near to a wall which was built of hailstones, and a tongue of fire surrounded it, and it began to make me afraid. ¹⁰And I went into the tongue of fire and came near to a large house which was built of hailstones, and the wall of that house (was) like a mosaic (made) of hailstones, and its floor (was) snow. ¹¹Its roof (was) like the path of the stars and flashes of lightning, and among them (were) fiery Cherubim, and their heaven (was like) water. ¹²And (there was) a fire burning around its wall, and its door was ablaze with fire. ¹³And I went into that house, and (it was) hot as fire and cold as snow, and there was neither pleasure nor life in it. Fear covered me and trembling took hold of me. ¹⁴And as I was shaking and trembling, I fell on my face. And I saw in the vision, ¹⁵and behold, another (were) open before me, and (it was) built of a tongue of fire. ¹⁶And in everything it so excelled in glory and splendour and size that I am unable to describe to you its glory and its size. ¹⁷And its floor (was) fire, and above (were) lightning and the path of the stars, and its roof also (was) a burning fire. ¹⁸And I looked and I saw in it a high throne, and its appearance (was) like ice and its surrounds like the shining sun and the sound of Cherubim. ¹⁹And from underneath the high throne there flowed out rivers of burning fire so that it was impossible to look at it. ²⁰And He who is great in glory sat on it, and his raiment was brighter than the sun, and whiter than any snow. ²¹And no angel could enter, and at the appearance of the face of him who is

honoured and praised no (creature of) flesh could look.
22A sea of fire burnt around him, and a great fire stood
before him, and none of those around him came near to
him. Ten thousand times ten thousand (stood) before
him, but he needed no holy counsel. 23And the Holy Ones
who were near to him did not leave by night or day, and
did not depart from him.

After this comes the account of Enoch's journeys through
the earth and Sheol (17-36). In his first journey (17-19) he
has a vision of the location of the luminaries, the storehouses of the stars and of the winds, the flaming fire and the
great abyss, the prison of the stars of heaven and of the host
of heaven who transgressed the Lord's command at the
beginning. He also saw the spirits of the angels who had
sinned with women. In his second journey (21-36) Enoch is
granted a vision of the preliminary and final places of
punishment of fallen angels (symbolized by seven stars), and
then of the underworld. In this vision he sees the places of
the spirits of the just and of the wicked (1 Enoch 22:1-13):

22 And from there I went to another place, and he
showed me in the west a large and high mountain, *and a*
hard rock and four beautiful places, 2and inside it was
deep and wide and very smooth. How smooth (is) that
which rolls, and deep and dark to look at! 3Then
Raphael, one of the holy angels who was with me, answered me and said to me: 'These beautiful places (are
intended for this), that the spirits, the souls of the dead,
might be gathered into them; for them they were created,
(that) here they might gather all the souls of the sons of
men.
4And these places they made where they will keep them
until the day of their judgement and until their appointed
time — and that appointed time (will be) long — until the
great judgement (comes) upon them. 5And I saw the
spirits of the sons of men who were dead, and their voice
reached heaven and complained. 6Then I asked Raphael,
the angel who was with me, and said to him: 'Whose is

this spirit whose voice thus reaches *heaven* and com-
plains?' [7]And he answered me and said to me, saying:
'This spirit is the one which came out of Abel whom
Cain, his brother, killed. And he will complain about him
until his offspring is destroyed from the face of the earth,
and from amongst the offspring of men his offspring
perishes.' [8]Then I asked about him and about the judgement on all and I said: 'Why is one separated from
another?' [9]And he answered me and said to me: 'These
three (places) were made in order that they might separate the spirits of the dead. And thus the souls of the
righteous have been separated; this is the spring of water
(and) on it (is) the light. [10]Likewise (a place) has been
created for sinners when they die and are buried in the
earth and judgement has not come upon them during
their life. [11]And here their souls will be separated for this
great torment, until the great day of judgement and punishment and torment for those who curse for ever, and of
vengeance on their souls, and there he will bind them for
ever. Verily he is from the beginning of the world. [12]And
thus (a place) has been separated for the souls of those
who complain and give information about (their) destruction, when they were killed in the days of the sinners.
[13]Thus (a place) has been created for the souls of men who
are not righteous, but sinners, accomplished in wrongdo-
ing, and with the wrongdoers will be their lot. But their
souls will not be killed on the day of judgement, nor will
they rise from there.

Finally the seer is shown the Tree of Life, Jerusalem and the
portals of heaven.

Despite the mention of "three" places in 22:9 four distinct
places are mentioned in the context for the different categories of dead: (1) the righteous; (2) the wicked who have not
been punished in this life; (3) the martyred righteous; (4) the
wicked who have been punished in this life. The clarity of
the nature of the belief in the afterlife found in this text is
noteworthy.

In the words of J.T. Milik, the Qumran evidence indicates

"that from the first half of the second century B.C. onwards the Book of Watchers had essentially the same form as that in which it is known through the Greek and Ethiopic versions." It can be presumed that it circulated in this form already by 200 B.C. Certain sections of it can be presumed to be older still, e.g. the section on the fall of the angels (chs. 6-11, or even 6-19). G.W. Nickelsburg believes that chapters 6-11 date from the fourth century, while J.T. Milik (somewhat improbably) is of the opinion that 6-19 are older than Genesis 6, which he believes is dependent on them.

6. The Astronomical Book of Enoch (1 Enoch 72-82) — before 200 B.C.

From the opening words in an earlier English translation, this work is also known as "The Book of the Heavenly Luminaries." The contents are described in the opening words (72:1):

> The book of the revolutions of the lights of heaven, each as it is, according to their classes, according to their (period of) rule and their times, according to their names and their places of origin, and according to their months, which Uriel, the holy angel who was with me and is their leader, showed me; and he showed me all their regulations exactly as they are, for each year of the world and for ever, until the new creation shall be made which will last for ever.

Enoch is shown the sun, the moon and its phases, the lunar year, the twelve winds and their portals, the four quarters of the world, the seven mountains, seven rivers, etc., the waxing and waning of the moon. He is told to teach this knowledge to the generations that are to come, and also to teach them the names of the stars (that is, the angels) which lead the seasons and the months.

Chapters 80-82 treat of the perversion of the order of nature through human sin. "In the days of the sinners the years will become shorter, and their seed will be late on their land... and many heads of the stars in command will go astray... and the thoughts of those who dwell upon the earth will go astray over them... And many evils will overtake them, and punishment will come upon them to destroy them" (80:2, 6-8).

There is a passing reference to cosmic transformation in 72:1, cited above. Some find mention of a form of after-life in 81:4-10 but the reference is far from clear. The older translation of R.H. Charles read for 80:4: "Blessed is the man who dies in righteousness and goodness... and against whom no day of judgment shall be found." In the new translation of M.A. Knibb, however, the final sentence reads: "and against whom no guilt has been found."

This *Astronomical Book of Enoch*, then, is mainly concerned with calendars and the base for these in knowledge of the heavenly spheres. The amount of moral and doctrinal matter it contains is negligible. The work is important in that it shows another side of apocalyptic lore: heavenly journeys for the sake of obtaining secret information on the heavenly luminaries.

This astronomical work is presupposed by *Jubilees* 4:17, 21 which may have been composed about the mid-second century B.C. This would indicate a date of composition for *The Astronomical Book* in the first quarter of the second century at the latest. J.T. Milik thinks it is alluded to by the Hellenistic Jewish historian Eupolemus in a work completed 158 B.C. The *Book of Jubilees*, however, may have been composed later in the second century B.C., but this need not affect the date to be assigned to Enoch 72-82. Four copies of an Aramaic Astronomical work attributed to Enoch have been found at Qumran, the earliest in Milik's opinion dating from the late third or the beginning of the second century B.C., the latest from the first years of the first century A.D. These Qumran manuscripts have a longer text than the Ethiopic, especially the section on calendrical reckoning. Milik believes that the original Aramaic text is older than Gen 5:23, which presupposes it and that it was connected with the calendrical reckoning of a highly theoretical nature in the Persian period, but was later introduced by the Essenes into their liturgical life. Milik also thinks that archaic features of the literary and scientific content of the *Astronomical Book of Enoch* link it with ancient Babylonian (and indeed Sumerian) literature, and that the description of the terrestrial orb in Enoch 77 leads us, with complete certainty, to the Mesopotamian centres of scholarship.

7. The Apocalyptic Section of Daniel (Daniel 7-12) — about 164 B.C.

Since this book belongs to the Canon of Scripture and has been provided with a full commentary by a leading specialist in apocalyptic in this very series (John J. Collins in vol. 15) it is sufficient to simply list it here. It will help us to understand the work better when we realize that when it originated apocalyptic was already a well-formed and varied literary genre.

8. Enoch's Book of Dream-Visions (1 Enoch 83-90) — about 165 B.C.

In this part of the Book of Enoch there are two distinct sections, both introduced in 83:1-2 as two visions. The first (chapters 83-84) is a vision of cosmic destruction — presumably at the Flood although this is not explicitly stated.

The second dream-vision, also called *The Animal Apocalypse*, is an allegorical history of the world from creation to a time that can be identified with the Maccabean revolt. After this come the accounts of the last assault of the Gentiles on the Jews (90:13-19), the judgment of the fallen angels, shepherds and apostates (90:20-27), the replacement of "the old house" (the old temple? the world?) by the new, the conversion of the Gentiles to Judaism, the resurrection of the righteous, the birth of the Messiah, and the transformation of the righteous to be like him (90:28-42).

In this vision of history mortals are symbolized as animals and birds of various kinds: for example, the patriarchs by bulls, the faithful of later times by sheep, the Gentiles by wild beasts (cf. Ezekiel 39:17). The symbolism, however, is not consistent throughout the book.

Adam is symbolized by a white bull, Eve by a heifer, Cain by a black bullock, Abel by a red one. The Messiah, like Adam, is symbolized by a white bull, and in the end of time all beasts and birds become white bulls like him. The Messiah comes after the judgment and the general idea appears to be the messianic age will amount to paradise regained. This interpretation supposes, however, that the Messiah is intended by the white bull to be born at the end of time.

In the *Book of Jubilees* 4:19 mention is made of Enoch's dream visions of the course of history, by which the second vision of this section may be intended. No fragment of the first vision (83-84) has been found in Qumran. The second vision seems to have been composed in Maccabean times, and possibly before Jonathan's assumption of the high priesthood in 153 B.C. The author seems to have belonged to the Hasidic movement.

I give here some illustrative texts of *The Animal Apocalypse*. The first text is on the creation of Adam (a white bull), and Eve (a heifer), on Cain and Abel and the sin of the angels (stars) (1 Enoch 85-86):

> **85** And after this I saw another dream, and I will show it all to you, my son. ²And Enoch raised (his voice) and said to his son Methuselah: 'To you I speak, my son. Hear my words, and incline your ear to the dream-vision of your father. ³Before I took your mother Edna, I saw in a vision on my bed, and behold, a bull came out of the earth, and that bull was white; and after it a heifer came out and with the heifer *came two bullocks*, and one of them was black, and the other red. ⁴And that black bullock struck the red one, and pursued it over the earth, and from then on I could not see that red bullock. ⁵But that black bullock grew, and a heifer went with it; and I

saw that many bulls come out from it which were like it and followed behind it. [6]And that cow, that firt one, came from the presence of that first bull, seeking that red bullock, but did not find it; and thereupon it moaned bitterly, and continued to seek it. [7]And I looked until that first bull came to it and calmed it, and from that time it did not cry out. [8]And after this she bore another white bull, and after it she bore many black bulls and cows. [9]And I saw in my sleep that white bull, how it likewise grew and became a large white bull, and from it came many white bulls, and they were like it. [10]And they began to beget many white bulls which were like them, one following another.

86 And again I looked with my eyes as I was sleeping, and I saw heaven above, and behold, a star fell from heaven, and it arose and ate and pastured amongst those bulls. [2]And after this I saw the large and the black bulls, and behold, all of them changed their pens and their pastures and their heifers, and they began to moan, *one after another.* [3]And again I saw in the vision and looked at heaven and behold, I saw many stars, how they came down and were thrown down from heaven to that first star, and amongst those heifers and bulls; they were with them, pasturing amongst them. [4]And I looked at them and saw, and behold, all of them let out their private parts like horses and began to mount the cows of the bulls, and they all became pregnant and bore elephants and camels and asses. [5]And all the bulls were afraid of them and were terrified before them, and they began to bite with their teeth, and to devour, and to gore with their horns. [6]And so they began to devour those bulls, and behold, all the sons of the earth began to tremble and shake before them, and to flee.

The account of Maccabean times, given in 90:6-12, is brief. The "white sheep" are the loyal Jews. The "lambs" born to them may be the members of the Hasidic movement. The "horned lambs" are apparently the Maccabees and the "great horn" Judas Maccabee.

90 [6]And small lambs were born from those white sheep, and they began to open their eyes, and to see, and to cry to the sheep. [7]But the sheep did not cry to them and did not listen to what they said to them, but were extremely deaf, and their eyes were extremely and excessively blinded. [8]And I saw in the vision how the ravens flew upon those lambs, and took one of those lambs, and dashed the sheep in pieces and devoured them. [9]And I looked until horns came up on those lambs, but the ravens cast their horns down; and I looked until a big horn grew *on* one of those sheep, and their eyes were opened. [10]And it looked at them, and their eyes were opened, and it cried to the sheep, and the rams saw it, and they all ran to it. [11]And besides all this those eagles and vultures and ravens and kites were still continually tearing the sheep in pieces and flying upon them and devouring them; and the sheep were silent, but the rams lamented and cried out. [12]And those ravens battled and fought with it, and wished to make away with its horn, but they did not prevail against it.

The New Jerusalem(?), the Conversion of the Gentiles surviving after their chastisement by God, the Resurrection of the righteous, and what appears to be the advent of the Messiah, are described as follows in 90:28-42:

[28]And I stood up to look until he folded up that old house, and they removed all the pillars, and all the beams and ornaments of that house were folded up with it; and they removed it and put it in a place in the south of the land. [29]And I looked until the Lord of the sheep brought a new house, larger and higher than that first one, and he set it up on the site of the first one which had been folded up; and all its pillars (were) new, and its ornaments (were) new and larger than (those of) the first one, the old one which he had removed. And the Lord of the sheep (was) in the middle of it [30]And I saw all the sheep which were left, and all the animals on the earth and all the birds of heaven falling down and worshipping those sheep, and

entreating them and obeying them in every command. [31]And after this those three who were dressed in white and had taken hold of me by my hand, the ones who had brought me up at first — they, with the hand of that ram also holding me, took me up and put me down in the middle of those sheep before the judgement was held. [32]And those sheep were all white, and their wool thick and pure. [33]And all those which had been destroyed and scattered and all the wild animals and all the birds of heaven gathered together in that house, and the Lord of the sheep rejoiced very much because they were all good and had returned to his house. [34]And I looked until they laid down that sword which had been given to the sheep, and they brought it back into his house, and it was sealed before the Lord; and all the sheep were enclosed in that house, but it did not hold them. [35]And the eyes of all of them were opened, and they saw well, and there was not one among them that did not see. [36]And I saw that the house was large and broad and exceptionally full. [37]And I saw how a white bull was born, and its horns (were) big, and all the wild animals and all the birds of heaven were afraid of it and entreated it continually. [38]And I looked until all their species were transformed, and they all became white bulls; and the first one among them was a wild-ox, and that wild-ox was a large animal and had big black horns on its head. And the Lord of the sheep rejoiced over them and over all the bulls. [39]And I was asleep in the middle of them; and I woke up and saw everything. [40]And this is the vision which I saw while I was asleep, and I woke up and blessed the Lord of righteousness and ascribed glory to him. [41]But after this I wept bitterly, and my tears did not stop until I could not endure it; when I looked, they ran down on account of that which I saw, for everything will come to pass and be fulfilled; and all the deeds of men in their order were shown to me. [42]That night I remembered my first dream, and because of it I wept and was disturbed, because I had seen that vision.

9. The Admonitions of Enoch (1 Enoch 91-107) — about 100-75 B.C.

This section of the work is also known as *The Epistle of Enoch*. For these chapters we have fragments of two Qumran manuscripts: one (4QEnᶜ), written about 75 B.C. with fragments of chapters 104-107 and the other (4QEnᵍ), written about 50 B.C., with fragments of chapters 91-94. In a Greek papyrus codex of the fourth century (preserved partly in the Chester Beatty Library, Dublin and Michigan University) we have more or less the complete Greek version of 97-107. The present Ethiopic text has a final chapter 108, which is not attested either by the Qumran fragments or by the Greek version and is probably a later addition.

The material in this final section (91-107) is not all of one sort. First of all we have Enoch's admonition to all the children of righteousness (91:1-10; 92). Next comes *The Apocalypse of Weeks* (93 + 91:11-17 — the order of the Qumran text and that required by the sequence) in which Enoch (himself the seventh of the first week, 93:3, cf. Jude 14) narrates the history of the world in a scheme of ten weeks.

Some scholars maintain that this latter part was once an original work and that it is pre-Maccabean, thus antedating even Daniel. If once independent, by the time the Qumran text came to be written it had become part of a larger composition. In *The Apocalypse of Weeks* Enoch recounts the history of creation from his own time to the end. His birth was the first week in which judgment and righteousness still endured. The second week was one of great wickedness in which a man (i.e. Noah) would be saved. Abraham was to come in the third week. The fourth week was that of the exodus, the fifth of the building of the temple, the sixth the ages of the divided kingdom, of Elijah and the burning of the temple, the seventh week, that of the author's time, would be one of apostasy. The eighth week would be one of righteousness, when the sinners would be delivered into the hands of the righteous. *The Apocalypse of Weeks* ends thus (91:13-17):

[13]And at its end they will acquire houses because of their righteousness, and a house will be built for the great king *in glory* for ever. [14]And after this in the ninth week the righteous judgement will be revealed to the whole world, and all the deeds of the impious will vanish from the whole earth; and the world will be written down for destruction, and all men will look to the path of uprightness. [15]And after this in the tenth week, in the seventh part, there will be the eternal judgement which will be executed on the watchers, and the great eternal heaven which will spring from the midst of the angels. [16]And the first heaven will vanish and pass away, and a new heaven will appear, and all the powers of heaven will shine for ever (with) sevenfold (light). [17]And after this there will be many weeks without number for ever in goodness and in righteousness, and from then on sin will never again be mentioned.

No mention is made in this text of a resurrection. Apparently eternal life is conceived of as coming immediately after the judgment.

Material of a variety of kinds follows on *The Apocalypse of Weeks:* Enoch's admonitions to the righteous (94:1-5) and woes on sinners (94:6-11; 95); reasons why the righteous should have hope (96:1-3), and why sinners should fear (96:4-8). There are woes on those who acquire unrighteous gain (97), and once more on sinners in general (98-104). The central motif of this section is the economic differentiation betwen rich and poor, the classes being practically identified with the sinners and righteous respectively. The rich are accused of idolatry in certain texts (99:6-9; cf. 91:9 and 104:9). The rich sinners are presented as oppressing the righteous poor (95:7; 96:5, 8; 103:9-15; 104:3). The statement that sin originated with man ("Sin has not been sent upon the earth, but man himself has created it", 98:4) may be intended to stress human responsibility but may also be directed against other sections of the Enochic corpus which present the Watchers as having introduced it at the Flood (e.g. 1 Enoch 6-11).

Since chapter 105:1 has corresponding material in the Qumran fragments, it may be that this entire chapter formed part of *The Admonitions of Enoch* (or *The Epistle of Enoch*) in the first century B.C. The brief chapter of only three verses, however, seems alien in spirit to the remainder and is probably not original. The apparently messianic reference in 105:3 is particularly doubtful: "For I and my son will join ourselves with them for ever in the paths of uprightness during their lives, and you will have peace."

It is difficult to assign a date to the composition of this section of 1 Enoch. The Qumran fragments show that the sections they cover must have been composed before 75 and 50 B.C. It is also hard to determine the setting of the social condition referred to. J.T. Milik thinks it was a prosperous Greek city where the Jews lived as an economically "under-developed" minority. The author may have been a pious Pharisee, but this is far from certain.

10. The Enochic Book of Giants
— about 125-100 B.C.

J.T. Milik has identified fragments of this work among the Enoch material from Qumran. Among its many interest-ing features is the fact that it contains the name of Gilga-mesh, the hero of the well-known Babylonian epic.

11. The Parables of Enoch (1 Enoch 37-71)
— probably first century A.D.

In this section of *The Book of Enoch* we have three divisions, each of which is called a parable in the text itself, namely chaps. 37-44; 45-57; 58-69; 69:29 being given as the end of the third parable of Enoch. Chapter 70 speaks of the final translation of Enoch and chap. 71 contains two of his earlier visions.

The first parable speaks of the coming judgment of the

wicked, of the abode of the righteous and of the elect one. "And there I saw another vision, the dwelling of the righteous and the resting-places of the holy. There my eyes saw their dwelling with the angels and their resting-places with the holy ones, and they were petitioning and supplicating and praying on behalf of the sons of men. . . " (39:4-5). This parable also speaks of the four archangels and of astronomical secrets.

The second parable (45-57) is the most important for the eschatology of the work. It speaks of the lot of the apostates, of the new heaven and the new earth, the Head of Days and the Son of Man, the prayer of the righteous for vengeance and their joy at its coming; the Son of Man, the stay of the righteous; the judgment of the kings and the mighty, the glorification and victory of the righteous and the repentance of the gentiles; the resurrection of the dead and the separation of the righteous from the wicked; the valley of judgment and final judgment of the fallen angels; the last struggle of the pagan powers against Israel; the ingathering of the exiles.

45 And this (is) the second parable about those who deny the name of the dwelling of the holy ones and of the Lord of Spirits. [2]They will not ascend into heaven, nor will they come upon earth: such will be the lot of the sinners who deny the name of the Lord of Spirits; who will thus be kept for the day of affliction and distress. [3]On that day the Chosen One will sit on the throne of glory, and will choose their works, and their resting-places will be without number; and their spirits within them will grow strong when they see my Chosen One and those who appeal to my holy and glorious name. [4]And on that day I will cause my Chosen One to dwell among them, and I will transform heaven and make it an eternal blessing and light. [5]And I will transform the dry ground and make it a blessing, and I will cause my chosen ones to dwell upon it; but those who commit sin and evil will not tread upon it. [6]For I have seen, and have satisfied with peace, my righteous ones, and have placed them before me; but for the sinners my judgement draws near before me, that I may destroy them from the face of the earth.

46 And there I saw one who had a head of days, and his head (was) white like wool; and with him (there was) another, whose face had the appearance of a man, and his face (was) full of grace, like one of the holy angels. ²And I asked one of the holy angels who went with me, and showed me all the secrets, about that Son of Man, who he was, and whence he was, (and) why he went with the Head of Days. ³And he answered me and said to me: 'This is the Son of Man who has righteousness, and with whom righteousness dwells; he will reveal all the treasures of that which is secret, for the Lord of Spirits has chosen him, and through uprightness his lot has surpassed all before the Lord of Spirits for ever. ⁴And this Son of Man whom you have seen will rouse the kings and the powerful from their resting-places, and the strong from their thrones, and will loose the reins of the strong, and will break the teeth of the sinners. ⁵And he will cast down the kings from their thrones and from their kingdoms, for they do not exalt him, and do not praise him, and do not humbly acknowledge whence (their) kingdom was given to them. ⁶And he will cast down the faces of the strong, and shame will fill them, and darkness will be their dwelling, and worms will be their resting-place, for they will have no hope of rising from their resting-places, for they do not exalt the name of the Lord of Spirits. ⁷And these are they who judge the stars of heaven, and raise their hands against the Most High, and trample upon the dry ground, and dwell upon it; and all their deeds show iniquity...and their power (rests) on their riches, and their faith is in the gods which they have made with their hands, and they deny the name of the Lord of Spirits. ⁸And they will be driven from the houses of his congregation, and of the faithful who depend on the name of the Lord of Spirits.

47 And in those days the prayer of the righteous and the blood of the righteous will have ascended from the earth before the Lord of Spirits. ²In these days the holy ones who dwell in the heavens above will unite with one voice, and supplicate, and pray, and praise, and give thanks, and bless in the name of the Lord of Spirits, because of the blood of the righteous which has been poured out, and (because of) the prayer of the righteous, that it may not cease before the Lord of Spirits, that justice may be done to them, and (that) their patience may not have to last for ever.' [3]And in those days I saw the Head of Days sit down on the throne of his glory, and the books of the living were opened before him, and all his host, which (dwells) in the heavens above, and his council were standing before him. [4]And the hearts of the holy ones were full of joy that the number of righteousness had been reached, and the prayer of the righteous had been heard, and the blood of the righteous had been required before the Lord of Spirits.

The third parable has a number of the same themes as the second: the blessedness of the saints, judgment of the kings and mighty, and their unavailing repentance, the place of punishment of the fallen angels and of the kings, the names and functions of fallen angels.

No fragment of any part of *Parables* has been found in Qumran. For this, and for other reasons besides, some scholars doubt its pre-Christian and Jewish character. J.T. Milik maintains that it was composed in the second or third century of our era. However, contemporary scholarship tends to reckon the parables Jewish, and to assign their composition to the first century of the Christian era.

12. 2 Enoch or The Slavonic Book of Enoch — 1st century A.D.

The work is extant in Slavonic manuscripts and in two recensions, a longer and a shorter one. Its contents are as follows: Enoch informs his sons about his ascension soon to take place (1-2); he ascends through seven heavens (3-21:5; expanded to ten heavens by a later editor in 21:6-22:1a);

Enoch meets the Lord and records the secrets which God reveals to him (22-38). He then returns to earth and admonishes his children (39-66). The angels finally carry Enoch to the highest heaven (67). The longer recension adds to a further chapter (68) on how the people praised God for the sign he had given them through Enoch.

In the third heaven Enoch found Paradise the abode of the just, and is told (2 Enoch 9):

> "This place, Enoch, is prepared for the righteous, who suffer offence in their lives and spite in their souls, and avert their eyes from injustice and make righteous judgment, to give bread to the hungering, to clothe the naked and cover them with a garment, to raise the fallen, and help the wronged, who walk before God's face and serve him alone; now for these is this place prepared for an eternal inheritance."

He is then lifted up from there and taken to the north of the heaven, and shown the place of torture and torment for the wicked.

As early as 1896 R.H. Charles assigned the work to the period before A.D. 70 since it presupposes the existence of the temple. He also maintained that it was composed in Egypt, probably in Alexandria, by a Hellenistic Jew. J.T. Milik in more recent times wished to assign it a date in the ninth century A.D. but has had little following. Scholars still prefer Charles' opinion both as to date and place of origin, although some believe that there are arguments for a Palestinian origin for the short recension. It is generally agreed that the original text was the short one and that the other is an expansion of this.

13. 2 (4) Esdras — about A.D. 100

This work was written in Palestine either in Hebrew or Aramaic. It is preserved, however, only in a Latin translation and in some other versions, the most important of which is the Syriac. The Latin work has 16 chapters. The original, however, is found in chapters 3-14, the remaining chapters being later additions. It is now generally agreed that this original work was composed by a single author and planned as one work.

Ezra (called Salathiel in the book) received seven visions. The first three of these (3:1—5:20; 5:21—6:34; 6:35—8:25) have to do with the problem of God's justice in his dealings with Israel and the world. Ezra is extremely perturbed by this problem. He has dialogue with an angel (Uriel) on the matter and is told by him (4:2-10):

> **4** "Your understanding has utterly failed regarding this world, and do you think you can comprehend the way of the Most High?" ³Then I said, "Yes, my lord." And he replied to me, "I have been sent to show you three ways, and to put before you three problems. ⁴If you can solve one of them for me, I also will show you the way you desire to see, and will teach you why the heart is evil."
>
> ⁵I said, "Speak on, my lord."
>
> And he said to me, "Go, weigh for me the weight of fire, or measure for me a measure of wind, or call back for me the day that is past."
>
> ⁶I answered and said, "Who of those that have been born can do this, that you ask me concerning these things?"
>
> ⁷And he said to me, "If I had asked you, 'How many dwellings are in the heart of the sea, or how many streams are at the source of the deep, or how many streams are above the firmament, or which are the exits of hell, or which are the entrances of paradise?' ⁸perhaps you would have said to me, 'I never went down into the deep, nor as yet into hell, neither did I ever ascend into heaven.' ⁹But now I have asked you only about fire and wind and the day, things through which you have passed and without which you cannot exist, and you have given me no answer about them!" ¹⁰And he said to me, "You cannot understand the things with which you have grown up; ¹¹how then can your mind comprehend the way of the Most

High? And how can one who is already worn out by the corrupt world understand incorruption?"

The dialogue continues (4:12-21);

When I heard this, I fell on my face [12]and said to him, "It would be better for us not to be here than to come here and live in ungodliness, and to suffer and not understand why."

[13]He answered me and said, "I went into a forest of trees of the plain, and they made a plan [14]and said, 'Come, let us go and make war against the sea, that it may recede before us, and that we may make for ourselves more forests.' [15]And in like manner the waves of the sea also made a plan and said, 'Come, let us go up and subdue the forest of the plain so that there also we may gain more territory for ourselves.' [16]But the plan of the forest was in vain, for the fire came and consumed it; [17]likewise also the plan of the waves of the sea, for the sand stood firm and stopped them. [18]If now you were a judge between them, which would you undertake to justify, and which to condemn?"

[19]I answered and said, "Each has made a foolish plan, for the land is assigned to the forest, and to the sea is assigned a place to carry its waves."

[20]He answered me and said, "You have judged rightly, but why have you not judged so in your own case? [21]For as the land is assigned to the forest and the sea to its waves, so also those who dwell upon earth can understand only what is on the earth, and he who is above the heavens can understand what is above the height of the heavens."

The advent of the Messiah, the resurrection and general judgment are described to Ezra as follows: (2 Esdras 7:25-44):

[25]"Therefore, Ezra, empty things are for the empty, and full things are for the full. [26]For behold, the time will come, when the signs which I have foretold to you will

come to pass, that the city which now is not seen shall appear, and the land which now is hidden shall be disclosed. [27]And every one who has been delivered from the evils that I have foretold shall see my wonders. [28]For my son the Messiah shall be revealed with those who are with him, and those who remain shall rejoice four hundred years. [29]And after these years my son the Messiah shall die, and all who draw human breath. [30]And the world shall be turned back to primeval silence for seven days, as it was at the first beginnings; so that no one shall be left. [31]And after seven days the world, which is not yet awake, shall be roused, and that which is corruptible shall perish. [32]And the earth shall give up those who are asleep in it, and the dust those who dwell silently in it; and the chambers shall give up the souls which have been committed to them. [33]And the Most High shall be revealed upon the seat of judgment, and compassion shall pass away, and patience shall be withdrawn, [34]but only judgment shall remain, truth shall stand, and faithfulness shall grow strong. [35]And recompense shall follow, and the reward shall be manifested; righteous deeds shall awake, and unrighteous deeds shall not sleep.

[36]Then the pit of torment shall appear, and opposite it shall be the place of rest; and the furnace of hell shall be disclosed, and opposite it the paradise of delight. [37]Then the Most High will say to the nations that have been raised from the dead, 'Look now, and understand whom you have denied, whom you have not served, whose commandments you have despised! [38]Look on this side and on that; here are delight and rest, and there are fire and torments!' Thus he will speak to them on the day of judgment— [39]a day that has no sun or moon or stars, [40]or cloud or thunder or lightning or wind or water or air, or darkness or evening or morning, [41]or summer or spring or heat or winter or frost or cold or hail or rain or dew, [42]or noon or night, or dawn or shining or brightness or light, but only the splendor of the glory of the Most High, by which all shall see what has been determined for them.

⁴³For it will last for about a week of years. ⁴⁴This is my judgment and its prescribed order; and to you alone have I shown these things."

Ezra is still perturbed and inquires about the number of those who will be saved. His query and the angel's response are as follows: (7:45-61):

⁴⁵I answered and said, "O sovereign Lord, I said then and I say now: Blessed are those who are alive and keep thy commandments! ⁴⁶But what of those for whom I prayed? For who among the living is there that has not sinned, or who among men that has not transgressed thy covenant? ⁴⁷And now I see that the world to come will bring delight to few, but torments to many. ⁴⁸For an evil heart has grown up in us, which has alienated us from God, and has brought us into corruption and the ways of death, and has shown us the paths of perdition and removed us far from life—and that not just a few of us but almost all who have been created!"

⁴⁹He answered me and said, "Listen to me, Ezra, and I will instruct you, and will admonish you yet again. ⁵⁰For this reason the Most High has made not one world but two. ⁵¹For whereas you have said that the righteous are not many but few, while the ungodly abound, hear the explanation for this.

⁵²"If you have just a few precious stones, will you add to them lead and clay?"

⁵³I said, "Lord, how could that be?"

⁵⁴And he said to me, "Not only that, but ask the earth and she will tell you; defer to her, and she will declare it to you. ⁵⁵Say to her, 'You produce gold and silver and brass, and also iron and lead and clay, ⁵⁶but silver is more abundant than gold, and brass than silver, and iron than brass, and lead than iron, and clay than lead.' ⁵⁷Judge therefore which things are precious and desirable, those that are abundant or those that are rare?"

⁵⁸I said, "O sovereign Lord, what is plentiful is of less worth, for what is more rare is more precious."

⁵⁹He answered me and said, "Weigh within yourself

what you have thought, for he who has what is hard to get rejoices more than he who has what is plentiful. ⁶⁰So also will be the judgment which I have promised; for I will rejoice over the few who shall be saved, because it is they who have made my glory to prevail now, and through them my name has now been honored. ⁶¹And I will not grieve over the multitude of those who perish; for it is they who are now like a mist, and are similar to a flame and smoke—they are set on fire and burn hotly, and are extinguished."

Later in this long dialogue comes Ezra's well-known reflection on the tragedy of the human condition, exacerbated if anything by the stipulations of the covenant (7:116-131):

I answered and said, "This is my first and last word, that it would have been better if the earth had not produced Adam, or else, when it had produced him, had restrained him from sinning. ¹¹⁷For what good is it to all that they live in sorrow now and expect punishment after death? ¹¹⁸O Adam, what have you done? For though it was you who sinned, the fall was not yours alone, but ours also who are your descendants. ¹¹⁹For what good is it to us, if an eternal age has been promised to us, but we have done deeds that bring death? ¹²⁰And what good is it that an everlasting hope has been promised us, but we have miserably failed? ¹²¹Or that safe and healthful habitations have been reserved for us, but we have lived wickedly? ¹²²Or that the glory of the Most High will defend those who have led a pure life, but we have walked in the most wicked ways? ¹²³Or that a paradise shall be revealed, whose fruit remains unspoiled and in which are abundance and healing, but we shall not enter it, ¹²⁴because we have lived in unseemly places? ¹²⁵Or that the faces of those who practiced self-control shall shine more than the stars, but our faces shall be blacker than darkness? ¹²⁶For while we lived and committed iniquity we did not consider what we should suffer after death."

¹²⁷He answered and said, "This is the meaning of the

contest which every man who is born on earth shall wage,
[128]that if he is defeated he shall suffer what you have said,
but if he is victorious he shall receive what I have said.
[129]For this is the way of which Moses, while he was alive,
spoke to the people, saying, 'Choose for yourself life, that
you may live!' [130]But they did not believe him, or the
prophets after him, or even myself who have spoken to
them. [131]Therefore there shall not be grief at their destruction, so much as joy over those to whom salvation is
assured. "

The fourth vision of the book (9:26-10:59) speaks of the
abiding glory of the law of Moses. Even though Israel has
sinned and will perish, the law cannot perish because it is
from God. It remains in its glory (9:29-37). The visionary is
given a vision of Jerusalem as a disconsolate woman but is
also permitted to see in vision the heavenly Jerusalem.

The fifth vision (11:1-12:51), the Eagle Vision, is a reinterpretation of the Son of Man vision of Daniel 7, especially of
the fourth beast. In Ezra's vision the corresponding creature
is an eagle (representing Rome). A lion is seen coming out
of the forest and reproving the eagle for its wickedness. The
lion is interpreted as "the anointed one (i.e. the Messiah)
whom the Most High has reserved till the end of days, who
will arise from the seed of David" (12:31-32). The fact that
he has been reserved by the Most High seems to indicate not
only an origin from the seed of David but also pre-existence.

The sixth vision (13:1-58) also has to do with Daniel 7. It
treats of the Danielic Son of Man ("one like a son of man" in
Daniel) who is here interpreted as the Messiah, "the one
whom the Most High has been keeping for many ages, who
will himself deliver his creation, "and he will direct those
who are left" (13:26). Ezra sees him as a Man coming out of
the heart of the sea and flying with the clouds of heaven. An
innumerable multitude (i.e. the Gentiles) gather to make
war on him, but he slays them with fire from his mouth.
Then the Man calls about him another, peaceful host.

The seventh and final vision (14:1-8) speaks of Ezra writing the Hebrew scriptures — both the canonical and the

apocryphal: twenty-four books to be read by the worthy and the unworthy (the canonical books) and seventy others (the apocrypha) to be reserved for the wise among his people (14:44-47; cf. 12:37-38).

It is now generally accepted that *2 (4) Esdras* was composed in Palestine some time between the destruction of the temple (A.D. 70 and 100). A special feature of the work is its relationship in themes, thought and language with rabbinical writings. It was very probably composed by one trained in the schools of the rabbis.

14. 2 Baruch (The Apocalypse of Baruch) — about A.D. 100

This work is very closely related to *2 (4) Esdras* and like it can be presumed to have been written by one trained in the rabbinic schools. It, too, was composed after the fall of Jerusalem and seems to be later than *2 (4) Esdras*. The original language appears to have been Aramaic or Hebrew. It is now preserved, however, only in Syriac.

Baruch announces the destruction of Jerusalem and, in chap. 4 (which some regard as interpolated) is shown the heavenly Jerusalem. Like Ezra, Baruch is made to see that God's ways are incomprehensible. He is told that the holy city of Zion has been taken away so that God might hasten the day of judgment (20). God's final judgment will come in God's own time, that is when all the souls destined to be born have been born. "Because when Adam sinned and death was decreed against those who should be born, then the multitude of those who should be born was numbered, and for that number a place was prepared where the living might dwell and the dead might be guarded. Before therefore the number aforesaid is fulfilled, the creature will not live again..., and Sheol will receive the dead. And again it is given to thee to hear what things are to come after these times. For truly My redemption has drawn nigh, and is not far distant as aforetime"(23:4-7). Signs will precede the end.

Twelve woes will come on the earth and then the Messiah and his kingdom "will begin to be revealed" (27-29). Then, "after these things, when the time of the advent of the Messiah is fulfilled, he shall return in glory" (30:1). His return to heaven may be intended. The resurrection follows (30:2-5). The nature of the resurrection body of both the good and the wicked is described in some detail and likewise the final destinies of the good and the wicked (49-52). Baruch tells us of his query on this matter and of the heavenly response (chaps. 49-52):

49 'Nevertheless, I will again ask from Thee, O Mighty One, yea, I will ask mercy from Him who made all things.

² "In what shape will those live who live in Thy day?
Or how will the splendour of those who (are) after that time continue?

³ Will they then resume this form of the present,
And put on these entrammelling members,
Which are now involved in evils,
And in which evils are consummated,
Or wilt Thou perchance change these things which have been in the world
As also the world?"

50 And He answered and said unto me: 'Hear, Baruch, this word,
And write in the remembrance of thy heart all that thou shalt learn.

² For the earth shall then assuredly restore the dead,
[Which it now receives, in order to preserve them].
It shall make no change in their form,
But as it has received, so shall it restore them,
And as I delivered them unto it, so also shall it raise them.

³ For then it will be necessary to show to the living that the dead have come to life again, and that those who had

⁴ departed have returned (again). And it shall come to pass, when they have severally recognized those whom they now know, then judgement shall grow strong, and those things which before were spoken of shall come.

51 'And it shall come to pass, when that appointed day has gone by, that then shall the aspect of those who are condemned be afterwards changed, and the glory of those

2 who are justified. For the aspect of those who now act wickedly shall become worse than it is, as they shall suffer torment.

3 Also (as for) the glory of those who have now been justified in My law, who have had understanding in their life, and who have planted in their heart the root of wisdom, then their splendour shall be glorified in changes, and the form of their face shall be turned into the light of their beauty, that they may be able to acquire and receive the world which does not die, which is then

4 promised to them. For over this above all shall those who come then lament, that they rejected My law, and stopped their ears that they might not hear wisdom or

5 receive understanding. When therefore they see those, over whom they are now exalted, (but) who shall then be exalted and glorified more than they, they shall respectively be transformed, the latter into the splendour of angels, and the former shall yet more waste away in wonder at the visions and in the beholding of the forms.

6 For they shall first behold and afterwards depart to be

7 tormented. But those who have been saved by their works,

And to whom the law has been now a hope,

And understanding an expectation,

And wisdom a confidence,

Shall wonders appear in their time.

8 For they shall behold the world which is now invisible to them.

And they shall behold the time which is now hidden from them:

9 And time shall no longer age them.

10 For in the heights of that world shall they dwell,

And they shall be made like unto the angels,

And be made equal to the stars,

And they shall be changed into every form they desire,

From beauty into loveliness,

And from light into the splendour of glory.

11 For there shall be spread before them the extents of Paradise, and there shall be shown to them the beauty of the majesty of the living creatures which are beneath the throne, and all the armies of the angels, who [are now held fast by My word, lest they should appear, and] are held fast by a command, that they may stand in their places till their advent comes.

12 Moreover, there shall then be excellency in the righteous surpassing that in the angels.

13 For the first shall receive the last, those whom they were expecting, and the last those of whom they used to hear that they had passed away.

14 For they have been delivered from this world of tribulation,
And laid down the burthen of anguish.

15 For what then have men lost their life,
And for what have those who were on the earth exchanged their soul?

16 For then they chose (not) for themselves this time,
Which, beyond the reach of anguish, could not pass away:
But they chose for themselves that time,
Whose issues are full of lamentations and evils,

52 And I answered and said:
'How can we forget those for whom woe is then reserved?

2 And why therefore do we again mourn for those who die?
Or why do we weep for those who depart to Sheol?

3 Let lamentations be reserved for the beginning of that coming torment,
And let tears be laid up for the advent of the destruction of that time.

4 [But even in the face of these things will I speak.

5 And as for the righteous, what will they do now?

6 Rejoice ye in the suffering which ye now suffer:
For why do ye look for the decline of your enemies?

7 Make ready your soul for that which is reserved for you,
And prepare your souls for the reward which is laid up for you.]

Following on this section we are given a panorama of Israelite history from Adam to the fall of Jerusalem and the final consummation (53-70). The symbols used in the vision are black and white waters. The seer is interested in the sin of Adam and on its disastrous effects. The consequences are most clearly expressed in 56:6:

> For (since) when he transgressed
> Untimely death came into being,
> Grief was named
> And anguish was prepared,
> and pain was created,
> And trouble was consummated,
> And disease began to be established,
> And Sheol kept demanding that it should be renewed in
>   blood,
> And the begetting of children was brought about,
> And the passion of parents produced,
> And the greatness of humanity was humiliated,
> And goodness languished.

Notwithstanding all this, even after Adam's sin man's freedom and responsibility remain intact. This is put as follows in 54:15, 19:

> For though Adam first sinned
> And brought untimely death upon all,
> Yet of those who were born from him
> Each one has prepared for his own soul torment to come,
> and again each one of them has chosen for himself glories
> to come
> . . . .
> Adam is therefore not the cause, save only of his own soul,
> And each of us has been the Adam of his own soul.

15. The Apocalypse of Abraham
— about A.D. 80-100

This work is extant only in a Slavonic version which appears to have been translated from the Greek. It has 32 chapters in all. Of these, chapters 1-8 is a haggadic midrash on Genesis 15:9-17.

The apocalypse is found in chapters 9-32. In it God narrates to Abraham the fall of man and the idolatry of Abraham's own descendants. This their infidelity will bring about the judgment. The end is said to be near. The pagan nations are soon to be punished or destroyed. The trumpet will sound and God's elect one (the Messiah) will come to gather together his own people and burn his enemies with fire.

16. The Life of Adam and Eve (The Apocalypse of Moses) — probably 1st cent. A.D.

The Apocalypse of Moses, the title found in Greek manuscripts of the work, is really a misnomer. The work is not an apocalypse. The other title is that given it in Latin manuscripts. The original of the work, now lost, was probably Hebrew or Aramaic.

In 51 chapters this work recounts the lives of Adam and Eve after their expulsion from Paradise (1-11). It also tells of the fall of the devil (12-17) and gives us the lives of Cain, Abel and Seth (18-24). In chapters 25-29 Adam tells Seth of his visit to Paradise, in words somewhat reminiscent of the literature of Jewish Merkabah mysticism:

> And Adam said to Seth, 'Hear, my son Seth, that I may relate to thee what I heard and say after your mother and I had been driven out of paradise. When we were at prayer, there came to me Michael the archangel, a messenger of God. And I saw a chariot like the wind and its wheels were fiery and I was caught up into the Paradise of righteousness, and I saw the Lord sitting and his face was flaming fire that could not be endured. And many thousands of angels were on the right and the left of that chariot' (25:1-3).

Adam goes on to tell Seth the remainder of the secrets revealed to him when he had eaten of the Tree of Knowledge, also giving a brief history of the Jewish people, laying stress on the temple. We are told that in the end God will dwell on earth with men and that righteousness will then begin to shine (29:7). He will drive away the wicked from his presence, but the just shall shine in his sight (29:9).

The apocalyptic-like section in the work merits it inclusion in this present survey. The writing is also of interest for Jewish eschatology but its value is diminished by the fact that we cannot always be sure what is genuinely Jewish and what Christian interpolation. The work is generally assigned to the first century A.D.

17. 3 Baruch or the Greek Apocalypse of Baruch — early second century A.D.

This work is extant in two Greek manuscripts and in Slavonic versions. It tells of Baruch's journeys through five heavens and what he saw in each: in the first heaven (chapter 2) he saw a plain, and the builders of the Tower of Babel; in the second (chap. 3) — a plain, and the designers of the Tower of Babel; in the third (chaps. 4-9) — a great serpent; Hades; the sun, moon and attendant angels; the Phoenix; in the fourth (chap. 10) — a monotonous plain; birds (i.e. the souls of the righteous) singing praise to God; in the fifth (chap. 11ff.) —Michael, commander of the angels, who receives men's prayers from the angels. It is nowhere stated in the work that the number of heavens was restricted to five.

3 Baruch was probably composed at the beginning of the second century A.D. Its original language is uncertain. It may have been Greek, Aramaic or Hebrew.

18. The Apocalypse of Zephaniah and Others

We know of *The Apocalypse of Zephaniah* chiefly from a citation in Clement of Alexandria. A few Coptic fragments known to us are also probably from this work. It will suffice to mention the existence of the work here. The same holds true of other works such as *The Apocalypse of Elijah*, *The Apocalypse of Sedrach* and *The Ascension of Isaiah*. These may have originally been Jewish apocalypses reworked by Christians.

3. TESTAMENT LITERATURE

1. Definitions

Testament Literature or the Farewell Discourse literature as it is also called, is a body of Jewish literature closely related to Apocalyptic, yet sufficiently different from it to merit separate treatment.

The similarity lies in the fact that in both there generally is prediction of the future. They differ in that, whereas in Apocalyptic this prediction is through a heavenly being to a visionary (often an angel), in Testament Literature it is made by some noted person in Israel (e.g. a patriarch) to his children and their descendants. The setting of the Testament or Farewell Discourse generally is that the patriarch or notable figure about to die calls his children to him in order to reveal to them what their future fortunes are to be. Very often he also warns them of dangers to come their way when he has gone, and gives them instructions on how they are to conduct themselves.

Farewell Discourses occur already in the Old Testament, the earliest clear example being the Blessing or the Farewell Discourse of Jacob (Gen 49). Passages or entire works belonging to this genre have also been isolated in the New Testament. In the Old Testament examples the Farewell Discourses occur within a larger setting, and this is also the case in some Jewish writings. In the case of a number of the later writings, however, the entire work, not merely a section within it, constitutes the genre of Testament.

It is natural that given this long history of the genre and the variety of contexts in which Testaments are found, there will be significant differences between the genre in one book and another. All this notwithstanding, scholars who have studied the genre, especially in the New Testament, have isolated certain common features in these biblical and post-biblical farewell speeches. In his study of the farewell discourse in the Fourth Gospel Raymond Brown lists the features of the biblical and farewell speeches that are found also in John's Last Discourse. His list coincides basically with that drawn up by Ethelbert Stauffer in his *New Testament Theology*. Brown's list is as follows:

i.   The speaker announces the imminence of his departure.

ii.   Occasionally this announcement produces sorrow, and some form of reassurance is necessary.

iii.   In the older Old Testament farewells the speaker tends to support his instructions by recalling what God has done for Israel, but in the later Jewish examples it became more customary for the speaker to recall his own past life.

iv.   The directive to keep God's commandments is often part of the advice passed on by the speaker.

v.   In particular, the speaker often commands his children to love one another.

vi.   Unity is another frequent theme in the later forms of the farewell speeches.

vii.   The speaker tends to look into the future and see the fate that will befall his children.

viii.   In looking to the future the speaker curses those who persecute the just and rejoice over their tribulation.

ix.   The speaker may call down peace upon his children.

x.   The speaker may promise to his children that God will be close to them if they are faithful.

xi.   The dying man may worry about the endurance of his name.

xii.   As part of Moses' farewell to Israel, he picks as a successor Joshua, who in many ways will be another Moses.

xiii.   Finally the speaker often closes his farewell address with a prayer for his children or for the people he is leaving behind.

2. Some Old Testament Farewell Discourses

i. Isaac's Blessing — Genesis 27:27-29; 38-40

This blessing of Isaac on Jacob merits consideration with the Farewell Discourse since it contains the words of one who is soon to die, and concerns the fate of his descendants through the one to be blessed. The same holds in its own way for the "curse" on Esau in verses 38-40.

ii. Jacob's Blessing (or Farewell Discourse) — Genesis 49.

This is generally classed as belonging to the literary form of Blessing (cf. 49:28). It is a good example of a Farewell Speech. Jacob, about to die and conscious of this, calls his children together to tell them beforehand what is in store for them.

iii. Moses' Farewell Discourse — Deut 33.

In one sense the entire Book of Deuteronomy is a series of Farewell Discourses of Moses. He is assumed to have delivered all the discourses on the same day, and even to have died on that same day; see Deut 1:3 and 32:48 together with the comments on these verses by Richard Clifford in volume 4 of this series. In a very special way, however, Moses' "Blessing", his Farewell Discourse, is found in Deut 33, given immediately after Yahweh had told him he was about to die. The "Blessing" or Farewell Discourse closely parallels Jacob's Blessing in Gen 49.

iv.   Joshua's Farewell Discourses — Joshua 23 and 24.

In the Book of Joshua we have two Farewell Speeches of the leader, the one (24) earlier, the other (23) later and Deuteronomistic. The speech in 23 is modelled on 24, which it may have intended to replace. It is exilic in perspective (cf. v.15) and was probably intended for the exiles in Babylon. In this speech, Joshua represented as far advanced in years and about to die (cf. vv. 1-2, 14), reminds the people of God's mighty deeds towards them, exhorts them to fidelity and warns them of the consequences of infidelity.

In its present context in the book, Joshua 24 is also a Farewell Speech, although this is mainly due to the editorial work of the Deuteronomistic writer. With regard to content, in the speech Joshua asks Israel to remember God's intervention on its behalf. All Israel declare for Yahweh and renounce false gods. Finally, the covenant is ratified and its statutes committed to writing.

v.   Samuel's Parting Discourse — 1 Sam 12.

Samuel presents himself to the people as one old and grey. His day, and the period of the Judges, has ended. The age of the monarchy is about to begin with Saul, their new king. In the discourse Samuel protests his honesty in his dealings with the people. (Paul's parting discourse to the Elders at Ephesus is in part inspired by these words; cf. Acts 20:18-35.) Samuel also recalls Yahweh's mighty deeds for their ancestors and urges them to reverence and serve Yahweh in the new age that lies ahead. In its present context in the Deuteronomistic history the main concern of the passage is to subordinate the institution of the monarchy to the obligation of total obedience to God's word in the covenant relationship. See further, Charles Conroy's comment on the passage in volume 6 of this series.

vi.   Tobit's Farewell Discourse — Tobit 14:1-11.

Tobit's Farewell Discourse is presented as having been delivered just before he died in his bed. In this discourse he speaks to his son about the exile, destruction of the temple and the return from exile, and the conversion of the Gentiles to the fear of the Lord — all represented as future events. He also exhorts him to act uprightly, in fidelity to the law and the commandments. See further, John Craghan in volume 16 of this series.

vii.   *Farewell Discourse of Mattathias the Maccabee — 1 Mac 2:49-70.*

The discourse is represented as having been delivered as "the days drew near for Mattathias to die." In it he exhorts his children to show zeal for the law and to give their lives for the covenant of their ancestors, and recalls the mighty deeds which the Lord had done for them throughout history. The lesson from history is that "from generation to generation, none who put their trust in him will lack strength" (v. 61). They are exhorted again to be courageous and to fight. See John J. Collins' comments on the passage in vol. 16 of this series.

After this brief consideration of the biblical testaments we now pass on to consider those in non-canonical literature.

3. The Aramaic Testament of Levi — 3rd or 4th century B.C.

There is a "Testament of Levi" in *The Testaments of the Twelve Patriarchs* (no. 9 below). Fragments of an Aramaic *Testament of Levi* have been discovered in Caves 1 and 4 of Qumran (1 QTLevi ar, possibly with TestLevi 8:11; 4QTLevi ar.^{a}, earlier with siglum 4QTLevi ar.^{b}) and part of the text from Cave 4 has been published in 1955 (text 8 iii 2-8). These fragments differ from the traditional Greek *Testaments of the Twelve Patriarchs* traditionally known, but agree with the Aramaic fragments of this Testament found in the Cairo Geniza and in Greek in the Mount Athos manuscript (Koutloumenos MS 39) of the *Testaments* which has a text different from the traditional one. The Cairo Geniza manuscript was written in the 10th century A.D., but is apparently a copy of a manuscript taken earlier from the Qumran caves. The Qumran MS, 4QTLevi^{a}8 iii 6-7

dates according to J.T. Milik from the second century B.C.
Milik believes that the original text itself was composed in
the course of the third century, if not towards the end of the
fourth. He also believes that it is of Samaritan origin.

I reproduce here an English translation of portion of a
Cairo Geniza fragment of the Testament of Levi, now in
Cambridge, in which among other things Levi speaks of his
son and grandson, Amram and Kohath:

73 In the sixte(enth) year we entered the land of Egypt, and
to my sons (were given) the daughters of my brothers at

74 the time...to them sons. The names of the sons of *Ger-
shon (Libnai and) Shimei: and the names of the sons of
Ko(hath, Amra)m and Izhar and Hebron and Uzziel;
(and the names of) the sons of Merari, Mahli and*

75 *Mushai. (And) Amram (took) to him as wife
Jochebed my daughter*, while I was yet living in the 9(4)th

76 year of my life. And I called the name of Amram, when he
was born, Amram, for I said when he was born, this
(child) shall br)ing out the people from the (land of Eg)ypt.

77 Therefore his name was
called the exalted people. *On one day*

78 *(were they born he) and* Jochebed *my daughter. Eighteen
years old was I when I went in(to the l)and of Canaan,
and (nine)teen years old when I slew She(chem)* and destroyed the workers of violence.

79 *And I was nineteen years old when I became priest, and
twenty-eight years old when I took to me*

80 *a wife. And eight and forty years old was I when we went
into the land of Egypt*, and eighty and nine years I lived in
Egypt.

81 [Col. *e*] And all the days of my life were 1(3)7 *years,* and I
saw my *sons of the th(ird generation)*

82 before I died. And *in the (hundred and eigh)teenth (year)
of my life*, that is, the y(ear) in which *Joseph my brother
died,* I called (my) so(ns) and their sons, and began to
charge them with all that was in my heart.

83 And I answered and said to (my) sons:
(Hear) the word of Levi your father,
And hearken to the commands of God's beloved;

84 *I give you a charge, my sons,*
    And I show you the truth, my beloved,
85 Let the sum of your works be truth,
    And (let) righteousness abide with you for ever.
86 And the tr(uth)...
    And to them the harvest is blessed.
87 *He that soweth good,* reapeth good;
    And he that soweth evil, his seed returneth upon him.
88 And now, my sons, a book of instruction in wisdom *teach
    your sons,*
    And let wisdom be with you an everlasting honour.
89 *He that learneth* wisdom, *she is an honour to him,*
    And whoso despiseth wisdom is given over to contempt.
90 My sons, behold *Joseph my brother,*
    Who gave instruction in the writings and discipline of
    wisdom.

4. The Hebrew Testament of Naphtali

Fragments of a *Testament of Naphtali* in Hebrew have
been found in Qumran Cave 4 (4QTTestNapht I ii 4-5). One
fragment contains the genealogy of Bilhah (mother of
Naphtali) and is longer than that found in the traditional
Greek *Testament of the Twelve Patriarchs* (Test. Naphtali
1:6-11). Other sections of this Qumran Testament of Naphtali are said to contain reflections on the end time which are
scarcely mentioned in the traditional *Testament of
Naphtali.*

5. The Testament of Amram
— probably 3rd century B.C.

Five fragmentary copies of this work have been found in
Qumran cave 4. One of these manuscripts is very old, from
the second century B.C., and possibly even from the first
part of it. The original composition can consequently be
presumed to be from the third century B.C. The text con-

tains the admonition of Amram, son of Kohath, son of Levi, to his children. Amram, in his dream vision, saw the chief Angel of Darkness (Melkiresha), and also addresses the leader of the Army of Light. The name of this leader is lost in the present badly-mutilated text, but it probably was Melchisedek.

J.T. Milik has shown that this *Testament of Amram* was available in Greek translation in the early Christian centuries and was used by the Christian scholar Origen. He likewise believes that three related Testaments circulated in Greek translation, all from Aramaic originals and having to do with patriarchs of the Jewish priesthood, i.e. the Testaments of Levi, of Amram and of Kohath. I here reproduce some passages from the *Testament of Amram* which unfortunately is very imperfectly preserved:

> Copy of the book of the words of the vision of Amram, son of Kohath, son of Levi, a(ll that) he explained to his sons and enjoined on them on the day of (his) death, in his one-hundred-and-thirty-seventh year, which was the year of his death, (in) the one-hundred-and-fifty-second year of Israel's exile in Egypt.
>
> (I saw Watchers) in my vision, a dream vision, and behold two (of them) argued about me and said ... and they were engaged in a great quarrel concerning me ......
>
> I an(nou)nce (this) to you (and al)so I will indeed inform y(ou... for all the Sons of Light) will shine, (and all the Sons) of Darkness will be dark. (For all the Sons of Light) .... and by all their knowledge they will ... and the Sons of Darkness will be burnt .... For all folly and wicked(ness are dar)k, and all (pea)ce and truth are bright(t. For all the Sons of Light g)o towards the light, towards (eternal) jo(y and rej)oicin(g), and all the Sons of Dar(kness go towards death) and perdition ... the people shall have brightness ... and they will cause them to live....

A further text from this Testament of Amram has been noted by J. Fitzmyer, who uses it to illustrate the expression "men of good will. . ." in Luke 2:14. The text in question occurs in fragment 9 of the *Testament* and seems to refer to Aaron, although he is not named. It reads:

> "he will be the seventh among men of (his) good will (and ho)nour and it (he?) will be said . . . he will be chosen as a priest forever."

6. The Aramaic Testament of Kohath — probably 3rd century B.C.

J.T. Milik, as we have seen, postulated the existence of an Aramaic *Testament of Kohath*, son of Levi and father of Amram. He found confirmation of his view in the following text of Cave 4 of Qumran, assigned for publication to l'Abbé Jean Starcky:

> And now to you, Amram, my son, I recommend to you, (I Kohath your father. . .) and to your sons and to their sons, I recommend. . . (. . . .) and they gave (them) to Levi my father, and Levi my father (has given them) to me . . . . all the books as witness, so that by them you may be put on your guard (translation by author).

7. Farewell Discourse of Moses

This Farewell Discourse of Moses has been found among the Qumran manuscripts. In Hebrew it bears the title *Dibre Moshe*: "The Words of Moses." The main inspiration of the piece is drawn from the Book of Deuteronomy and it lays special stress on the appointment of teachers or interpreters of the Law. I give a few passages from it here.

> (God spoke) to Moses in the (fortieth) year after (the children of) Israel had come (out of the land of) Egypt, in the eleventh month, on the first day of the month, saying:
> '(Gather together) all the congregation and go up to (Mount Nebo) and stand (there), you and Eleazar son of

Aaron. Inter(pret to the heads) of family of the Levites and to all the (Priests), and proclaim to the children of Israel the words of the Law which I proclaimed (to you) on Mount Sinai . . . .'.

Then Moses called Eleazar son of (Aaron) and Joshua (son of Nun and said to them,) 'Speak (all these words to the people). . . .'.

And Moses (spoke to the children) of Israel (and said to them): '(Behold) forty (years have passed since) the day we came out of the land (of Egypt, and today has God), our God, (uttered these words) from out of His mouth: all His . . . precepts . . .'.

'When I have (established) the Covenant and commanded (the way) in which you shall walk, (appoint wise men whose) work it shall be to expound (to you and your children) all these words of the law . . .'.

8. The Assumption of Moses (The Testament of Moses) — about 165 B.C.

The original form of this work probably originated about the same time as the Book of Daniel. It was once thought that the date to be assigned to the composition was A.D. 7-30 since chapter 6 clearly speaks of Herod and his sons. It is highly probable, however, that this section is interpolated and was inserted when a second edition, so to speak, of *The Testament of Moses* was brought out in the first half of the first century A.D. *The Testament of Moses* is based on Deut 31-34 and contains Moses' parting words to Israel together with an account of his death.

The work opens imperfectly with the words: ". . . which is the year 2500 from the creation of the world." The event being referred to is probably Moses' commission to Joshua.

The *Testament* tells us that the world was created for the sake of Israel (1:12), that God was pleased to manifest this, the purpose of creation from the foundation of the world and also that he had designed and prepared Moses before the creation of the world so that he should be the mediator

of the covenant (1:14-15). Joshua is commanded to put away
the books which Moses is to give him "in the place that
God has made from the beginning of the world," that his
name might be invoked until the day of repentance in the
visitation at the consummation of the days. From chapter 2
onwards we are given the history of Israel from the conquest
under Joshua to the exile. On this there follows repentance,
return from exile, renewed sin and punishment (cf. 5). The
sequence is broken by chapter 6 which speaks of the
Maccabean-Hasmonean King-priests: "Then shall there be
raised up to them kings bearing rule, and they shall call
themselves priests of the Most High God; and they shall
assuredly work iniquities in the Holy of Holies" (6:1). After
this we have an account of Herod, an insolent king reigning
for 34 years, of his sons, of the advent of the Roman Varus
as governor of Syria (4 B.C.), and the devastation of Jerusalem by him. This section, as already said, is now recognized
as a later interpolation into the original composition.

Chapter 7 speaks of the end time, when impious men shall
rule, claiming to be just. These may be the Hellenizers of Antiochus' day, although some believe that the Sadduccees or
Pharisees are intended. There is also a description of the persecution of Antiochus (chap. 8) and of a man "whose name shall be
Taxo" from the tribe of Levi. Who exactly is intended by the
mysterious figure Taxo is unknown. In a manner reminiscent of the mother of the martyrs in 2 Maccabees 7 and 4
Maccabees, Taxo exhorts his seven sons to die without
fighting, since, he maintains, their pious death will have
God avenge them. On this there follows a description of the
advent of God's kingdom. No mention is made in the work
of a resurrection. God will exalt Israel and cause her to
approach the heavens of the stars, from where she will look
down on her enemies in Gehenna, recognize them and give
thanks to God (10:9-10). The work ends with an address of
Joshua to Moses (cf. 11) and another by Moses to Joshua,
telling him that God knows what is to happen and that he is
in command of his creation.

I reproduce here the texts on Taxo and the advent of the
kingdom (chaps. 9 and 10):

9 ¹ Then in that day there shall be a man of the tribe of Levi, whose name shall be Taxo, who having seven sons shall ² speak to them exhorting (them): 'Observe, my sons, behold a second ruthless (and) unclean visitation has come upon the people, and a punishment merciless and ³ far exceeding the first. For what nation or what region or what people of those who are impious towards the Lord, who have done many abominations, have suffered as ⁴ great calamities as have befallen us? Now, therefore, my sons, hear me: for observe and know that neither did the fathers nor their forefathers tempt God, so as to trans- ⁵ gress His commands. And ye know that this is our ⁶ strength, and thus we will do. Let us fast for the space of three days and on the fourth let us go into a cave which is in the field, and let us die rather than transgress the commands of the Lord of Lords, the God of our fathers. ⁷ For if we do this and die, our blood shall be avenged before the Lord.

10 ¹   And then His kingdom shall appear throughout all His creation,
　　　　And then Satan shall be no more,
　　　　And sorrow shall depart with him.
　² 　Then the hands of the angel shall be filled
　　　　Who has been appointed chief,
　　　　And he shall forthwith avenge them of their enemies.
　³ 　For the Heavenly One will arise from His royal throne,
　　　　And He will go forth from His holy habitation
　　　　With indignation and wrath on account of His sons.
　⁴ And the earth shall tremble: to its confines shall it be shaken:
　　　　And the high mountains shall be made low
　　　　And the hills shall be shaken and fall.

　⁵ 　And the horns of the sun shall be broken and he shall
　　　　　be turned into darkness;
　　　　And the moon shall not give her light, and be turned
　　　　　wholly into blood.
　　　　And the circle of the stars shall be disturbed.
　⁶ 　And the sea shall retire into the abyss,
　　　　And the fountains of waters shall fail,

And the rivers shall dry up.

7 For the Most High will arise, the Eternal God alone,
And He will appear to punish the Gentiles,
And He will destroy all their idols.

8 Then thou, O Israel, shalt be happy,
And thou shalt mount upon the necks and wings of
the eagle,
And they shall be ended.

9 And God will exalt thee,
And He will cause thee to approach to the heaven of
the stars.
In the place of their habitation.

10 And thou shalt look from on high and shalt see thy
enemies in Ge(henna).
And thou shalt recognize them and rejoice,
And thou shalt give thanks and confess thy Creator.

11
12 And do thou, Joshua (the son of) Nun, keep these
words and this book; For from my death
[assumption] until His advent there shall be CCL

13 times. And this is the course of the times which they shall
pursue till they are consummated. And I shall go to sleep
with my fathers. Wherefore, Joshua, thou (son of) Nun,
(be strong and) be of good courage; (for) God hath
chosen (thee) to be minister in the same covenant.

9. The Testaments of the Twelve Patriarchs
— possibly 1st century A.D.

This work is a collection of twelve independent Testaments, one for each of Jacob's twelve sons. In the Testaments the patriarch in question may (a) recall some episode of his own life, (b) admonish his descendants to beware of certain forms of immoral behaviour, and (c) reveal to them the future events of their history.

Reuben looks back with shame on his action against Bilhah (Gen 35:22, 49:4) and warns his sons against immorality and of the dangers that come from women. "For evil are women, my children . . . . Flee, therefore fornication, my children, and command your wives and your children, that they adorn not their heads and faces to deceive the mind; because every woman who useth these wiles hath been reserved for eternal punishment. For thus they allured the Watchers who were before the flood . . ." (*Test. Reuben* 5:1, 5-6). Simeon recalls his sin against Joseph (Gen 42:24) and exhorts his children to beware of the spirit of deceit and envy. Recalling Joseph's beauty and chastity he tells his children: "Make your hearts good before the Lord . . . Beware, therefore, of fornication, for fornication is the mother of all evils, separating from God and bringing near to Beliar" (*Test. Simeon* 5:2-3). They are exhorted to obey Levi and Judah, "for from them shall arise unto you the salvation of God. For the Lord shall raise up from Levi as it were a High-priest, and from Judah as it were a King (God and Man). He shall save all (the Gentiles and) the race of Israel" (*Test. Simeon* 7:1-2). Levi tells how he was transported by an angel of God through the separate heavens (first three, expanded to seven) to the uppermost where he was informed by the Most High that he had been given the blessings and the priesthood until God should come and sojourn in the midst of Israel. He also tells how he took vengeance on Shechem because of Dinah (Gen 34). In a second vision he is clothed with priestly robes by seven men in white garments. He exhorts his children to have reverence for the Law and wisdom. He has learnt, he says, that in the end his sons will transgress against the Lord through wickedness. Finally, a Messianic redeemer will come. The event is described thus (*Test. Levi*, 18):

> **18** And after their punishment shall have come from the Lord, the priesthood shall fail.
> 2 Then shall the Lord raise up a new priest.
> ╷ And to him all the words of the Lord shall be revealed;
> And he shall execute a righteous judgement upon the earth for a multitude of days.
> 3 And his star shall arise in heaven as of a king.

Lighting up the light of knowledge as the sun the day.
And he shall be magnified in the world.

4 He shall shine forth as the sun on the earth,
And shall remove all darkness from under heaven,
And there shall be peace in all the earth.

5 The heavens shall exult in his days.
And the earth shall be glad,
And the clouds shall rejoice;
[And the knowledge of the Lord shall be poured forth
upon the earth, as the water of the seas;]
And the angels of the glory of the presence of the Lord
shall be glad in him.

6 The heavens shall be opened,
And from the temple of glory shall come upon him sanc-
tification,
With the Father's voice as from Abraham to Isaac.

7 And the glory of the Most High shall be uttered over him,
And the spirit of understanding and sanctification shall
rest upon him [in the water].

8 For he shall give the majesty of the Lord to His sons in
truth for evermore,
And there shall none succeed him for all generations for
ever,

9 And in his priesthood the Gentiles shall be multiplied in
knowledge upon the earth,
And enlightened through the grace of the Lord:
In his priesthood shall sin come to an end,
And the lawless shall cease to do evil.
[And the just shall rest in him.]

10 And he shall open the gates of paradise,
And shall remove the threatening sword against Adam.

11 And he shall give to the saints to eat from the tree of life,
And the spirit of holiness shall be on them.

12 And Beliar shall be bound by him,
And he shall give power to His childen to tread upon the
evil spirits.

13 And the Lord shall rejoice in His children,
And be well pleased in His beloved ones for ever.

14 Then shall Abraham and Isaac and Jacob exult,

> And I will be glad,
> And all the saints shall clothe themselves with joy.

Judah in his *Testament* refers to material in the Genesis narrative; especially the affair with Tamar (Gen 38) but also to non-biblical legends. He warns his sons against wine, women and avarice, and exhorts them to be obedient to Levi. Certain events in the history of tribe and kingdom are predicted, culminating with the prediction of a Messiah from Judah, who will be subject to Levi. The text reads (*Test. Judah* 23:5—24:6).

23   ⁵Until the Lord visit you, when with perfect heart ye repent and walk in all His commandments, and He bring you up from captivity among the Gentiles.

24   And after these things shall a star arise to you from Jacob in peace,
   And a man shall arise [from my seed], like the sun of righteousness,
   Walking, with the sons of men in meekness and righteousness;
   And no sin shall be found in him.

   ²And the heavens shall be opened unto him,
      To pour out the spirit, (even) the blessing of the Holy Father;
      ³And he shall pour out the spirit of grace upon you;
      And ye shall be unto Him sons in truth,
      And ye shall walk in His commandments first and last.
      ⁴[This Branch of God Most High,
      And this Fountain giving life unto all.]
      ⁵Then shall the sceptre of my kingdom shine forth;
      And from your root shall arise a stem;
      ⁶And from it shall grow a rod of righteousness to the Gentiles,
      To judge and to save all that call upon the Lord.

The work proceeds in a somewhat similar vein through the other sons of Jacob.

The *Testaments* are extant in Greek, Armenian and Sla-

vonic — this last-mentioned version being the least significant of the three. Two forms of the Greek text are known to
exist: that traditionally known and another recension found
particularly in a manuscript from the Library of Mount
Athos (MS. Koutloumenos mon. 39). The text of this manuscript, as has already been noted, agrees with the Aramaic
Testament of Levi from Qumran against the traditional
text.

Certain sections of the *Testaments* seem closely related to
the New Testament and some texts, at least, in them are of
Christian origin. But there are also resemblances with the
literature of Qumran. For over a century it has been a
matter of discussion among scholars whether the *Testaments* is basically a Jewish work with Christian interpola-
tions or a Christian composition which uses Jewish sources.
The debate has become more acute after the evidence from
Qumran has been brought to bear on the problem. Fragments of only two *Testaments* have been found there, as
already noted — those of Levi and Naphtali, the former in
Aramaic, the latter in Hebrew and these cannot be reckoned
as originals of the corresponding sections of *The Testaments of the Twelve Patriarchs*. Opinion is still divided on
the origins of the present *Testaments*. Some believe that the
work was composed by a Jew or Jewish Christian in the first
or second century A.D. Others maintain that they are of
pre-Christian and Jewish, possibly Essene origin. The original language of the present work, whether Aramaic or
Greek, is also debated.

10. The Testament of Job
— 1st century B.C. or A.D.

This work is found in four Greek manuscripts, in a fragmentary fifth-century Coptic manuscript and in a Slavonic
version, which is reconstructed from three manuscripts. The
original language and place of composition are uncertain. It
could have been composed either in Palestine or Egypt.

Some assign the original composition to the first century B.C., others to the first century A.D.

The work gets its title from the fact that it contains Job's farewell discourse to his children. It is, however, a retelling of the story of Job's life rather than a prediction of the future. The retelling is a midrashic one in which the biblical account is radically changed.

11. The Testament of Abraham
— possibly 1st century A.D.

This work is extant in two Greek recensions, a long one (A) and a shorter one (B). It is also found in a number of other languages. It is given the title *Testament* although no mention is made in the work of Abraham having made one. This, however, seems implied since Abraham is told to "set his affairs in order" (no. 1). The Archangel Michael is sent to Abraham to ask him to render up his soul. This Abraham refuses to do. He agrees only after he has been promised that he will be allowed to survey the entire universe before death. He is taken in a chariot and is shown the inhabited world, but grows very angry on seeing the sins that are committed. He is also shown a vision of God's judgment, with many passing through the broad gate to perdition and only a few through the narrow gate to salvation. Abraham repents of his harsh attitude towards sinners. Michael is again sent to fetch Abraham's soul. God the Father tells him: "Take my friend Abraham to the garden (of Paradise), where the tabernacles of my righteous ones and the abodes of my holy ones Isaac and Jacob are in his bosom, where there is no toil, no sadness, no sighing, but peace and joy and endless life" (no. 20).

Abraham's vision of the judgment scene is thus described (no. 8):

> Going forth, therefore, Michael took up Abraham in the body on a cloud and brought him to the river Oceanus, and Abraham looked and saw two gates, one small

and the other large, and in the midst between the two gates there sat a man upon a throne of great glory, and a multitude of angels was around him and he would weep and then laugh, and the weeping exceeded his laughter seven times. And Abraham said to Michael, "Who is this one who is sitting in the midst between the two gates with great glory, who sometimes laughs and sometimes weeps, and the weeping exceeds the laughter seven times?

Michael said to Abraham, "Do you not know who he is?"

And he said, "No, my Lord."

Then Michael said to Abraham, "Do you see these two gates, the small one and the large one? These are those which lead to life and destruction. This man who sits between them is Adam, the first man whom the Lord created, and He placed him in this place to look upon each soul coming out of its body, since all men are from him. Whenever, therefore, you see him weeping, know that he has looked upon many souls being led away to destruction. Whenever you see him laughing, he has looked upon a few souls being led away to life. Do you see how the weeping exceeds the laughter? Since he looks upon the major part of the world being led away through the wide one to destruction, the weeping exceeds the laughter sevenfold." (no. 8, short recension).

4. THE LITERATURE OF THE QUMRAN COMMUNITY

I. Discoveries in the Dead Sea Area, 1947 — 1967.

The story of the discovery, decipherment and the analysis of the content of the Dead Sea Scrolls has been told so often and so well that the barest essentials of these points are all that is required in a volume such as this. The saga began in the spring of 1947 when Muhammed ed-Dbib, a young goatherd of the Ta'amireh tribe of the Judean desert, went in search of a lost animal and came on a cave with jars containing ancient manuscripts. The area was in the neighbourhood of the ruins known as Khirbet Qumran and the Wadi Qumran, which empties itself into the Dead Sea about ten miles south of Jericho. The ruin itself is about a mile from the sea.

The cave Muhammed lighted on would later be known as Qumran cave 1. The antiquity and importance of the manuscripts found in the jars were soon recognized. In 1949 the cave in which they were found was identified and explored by archeologists and a search was made for other caves in the same area. Between 1952 and 1956 ten more caves were identified, two of them (known as caves 3 and 5) by professional archeologists, four (7, 8, 9, 10) by workmen and four (2, 4, 6, 11) by Ta'amireh tribesmen. Two caves of this last group (4 and 11 discovered respectively in 1962 and 1956) contained very important manuscripts. After 1956 no further manuscript finds have been made in caves of the Qumran area. Even though the largest of the Qumran manuscripts, the Temple Scroll 28 feet in length, only came into the hands of scholars after the Six Days War in 1967, it was known to exist already in 1960 and was probably taken from one of the Qumran caves (presumably Cave 11) some years earlier. All these manuscripts from the Qumran Caves are of especial importance, since they must have been deposited in the caves before the Qumran monastery which used them was destroyed in A.D. 68-69 by the Roman armies during the Jewish War.

In 1949 archeology was brought to bear on the question of the authenticity and origin of the manuscripts. In that year G.L. Harding, Director of the Jordanian Department of Antiquities, and Roland de Vaux, O.P., Director of the Ecole Biblique et Archéologique Française scientifically explored the first cave, discovered in 1947. Initial explorations were also carried out on the ruins at Khirbet Qumran that same year and a full exploration of the ruins began towards the end of 1951. These excavations showed that the ruins were the remains of a monastery of Jewish monks who had written and used the scrolls and finally deposited them in the surrounding caves. The excavations also helped to trace the history of occupation of the site. The oldest building was an Judahite fortress of the eighth or seventh century B.C. (in the days of Isaiah or Jeremiah). Next came the foundation of the Jewish monastery (probably Essene) about 135 B.C. This was enlarged about 100 B.C. and destroyed about 37 or 31 B.C. It was reconstructed about the end of Herod's reign (4 B.C.) and was finally destroyed by the Roman armies during the Jewish War (ca. A.D. 68). This archeological information is highly important for the reconstruction of the history of the Qumran monastic community.

The finds and excavations we have been speaking of occurred in the region of Qumran, at the northwestern end of the Dead Sea. In 1951 the Ta'amireh bedouin discovered further caves in the Wadi Murabba'at, fifteen miles southeast of Jerusalem and about 11 miles south of Qumran. In four caves from this area manuscripts were found, dating in the main from the second century A.D., particularly from the time of the Second Jewish Revolt (A.D. 132-135). These documents comprised a private archive of the Nathapa family, Aramaic, including Nabatean, and Greek deeds, IOUs and such like. One text is the acknowledgment of a debt, dated A.D. 55-56 (the second year of Nero), which contains a clause stipulating that the debt incurred had to be repaid even in the sabbatical year. It is imperfectly preserved and reads as follows:

> The ... of the ... month, in the second year of Caesar Nero, at Siwaya, Abshalom son of Hanin from Siwaya, has declared in my presence to have borrowed from me Zechariah son of Yoqanan, son of H . . . . . resident at Keslon, the sum of 20 zuzim (i.e. denarii), money which I (Abshalom) will repay on ... (and i)f I do not repay it by that date, it (the money) will be restored to you together with one-fifth (as interest), and it will be repaid in full, even if it is a sabbatical year. And should I not do so, recompense shall be made from my possessions and you shall (have the right) to take possession of all that I shall acquire.

(The signatures of Zechariah and of three witnesses follow.)

The text is interesting for the light it throws on the development of Jewish law concerning the sabbatical year. According to biblical law (Deut. 15:2) all debts were to be cancelled in that year. Since such a law made it difficult to get a loan shortly before the sabbatical year began, the noted jurist Hillel who died about 4 B.C. introduced the rule known as *prozbul*, according to which a debtor would formally renounce this privilege of the sabbatical year (see Mishnah, *Shebi'it* 10:4). The text just cited shows us this law of Hillel being put into practice.

In 1960 and 1961 Israeli archeologists systematically investigated the caves within their territory along the Dead

Sea between Ain Geddi and Masada. In one cave at Naḥal Hever they came on letters in Hebrew, Aramaic and Greek from the Bar Cochba period, some of them written by Bar Cochba (or, Bar Cosiba, to use the correct form of his name and that employed by himself).

The rock fortress of Masada at the southern tip of the Dead Sea was built by the Hasmonean ruler Alexander Jannaeus (103 — 76 B.C.) and was enlarged by Herod the Great. It has become renowned especially for the final stand the Jewish garrison took against the Roman army after the fall of Jerusalem in A.D. 70, when 960 Jews preferred self-inflicted death rather than surrender to the enemy. The site was excavated in campaigns during 1963 to 1965, and yielded some important manuscripts, including texts of the Hebrew scriptures, of apocrypha such as the Book of Sirach and Qumran sectarian literature, e.g. part of the text known as *The Angelic Liturgy.*

For the record, we may here note that some manuscripts were also found during this same period at Khirbet Mird, half way between Bethlehem and Qumran. These came, however, from a Christian monastery and are thus beyond the period to which this volume is dedicated.

II. The People of the Scrolls

With regard to the origins of these documents from the Dead Sea area, we must distinguish the manuscripts from the Qumran area proper (caves 1-11, including the Temple Scroll) from those found in the Wadi Murabba'at and at Naḥal Hever. The manuscripts from Qumran proper form a class apart, in that they can be shown to have been transcribed, used, and in good part composed by a definite group which we can identify as Jewish monks from the Qumran monastery. They can, furthermore, be all dated to the era before A.D. 70, since the monastery to which they belonged was destroyed in the Jewish War against Rome. From the excavations at Qumran and from the literature of the sect we can, to a certain extent, trace the history of the community at Qumran from its foundation down to its destruction. By the aid of the same documents we can also reconstruct the central beliefs and expectations of the community.

Many scholars believe that the Qumran monks were Essenes, although some prefer to explain the evidence of the Qumran texts without reference to what ancient authors have to say on this Jewish sect. A major argument in favour of the identification is a text of Pliny the Elder (in *Natural History* 5, 17, 73). He wrote soon after A.D. 70. He speaks of a monastery of the Essenes by the Dead Sea, below Engada (Ain Geddi), a site not far from Qumran. The Essenes are described by the Jewish writers Philo of Alexandria (*That Every Good Man is Free*, chapters 12 and 13), and Josephus (e.g. *Antiquities* 13, 5, 9, §§171-172; 15, 10, 4-5, §§371-378; 18, 1, 5, §18; *Jewish War* 2, 8, 2-13 §§119-160). Philo wrote about A.D. 1. Josephus seems to have had first-hand information on the Essenes of his own day and Bannus, the ascetic with whom he lived for three years (*Life* 2, §§7-12) may have been one of them. His first written account of them is that in the *Jewish War*, written about A.D. 78. The *Antiquities* were written some sixteen years later. Both these writers say that in their day the Essenes in Palestine numbered more than 4000. Josephus first makes mention of them, in conjunction with the other two Jewish "sects" — the Sadducees and the Pharisees — in connection with the reign of Jonathan the Maccabee, 160-142 B.C., as if they originated about that time. He mentions them again as active during the reign of Herod and his son Archelaus. Since our chief concern here is the literature of Qumran we need not enter further into the problems relating to Essene history and beliefs.

Among the various literary genres of the Qumran texts we find neither chronicle nor history. It is chiefly from passing references in works of another nature that scholars are able to piece together the evidence on the origins and history of the community. A very important text in this regard is found in the Rule known as *The Damascus Document*, to which we shall return later. The text in question reads (CD col. 1: 5-12):

For when they were unfaithful and forsook him, he hid his face from Israel and his sanctuary and delivered them up to the sword. But remembering the Covenant of the forefathers, he left a remnant to Israel and did not deliver it up to be destroyed. And in the age of wrath, three hundred and ninety years after he had given them into the hand of king Nebuchadnezzar of Babylon, he visited them, and he caused a plant root to spring up from Israel and Aaron to inherit his land and to prosper on the good things of his earth. And they perceived their iniquity and recognized that they were guilty men, yet for twenty years they were like men groping for the way.

And God observed their deeds, that they sought him with a whole heart, and he raised for them a Teacher of Righteousness to guide them in the way of his heart. And he made known to the latter generations that which God had done to the latter generation, the congregation of traitors, to those who had departed from the way.

The period of 390 years from the destruction of Jerusalem in 587/6 would, in our reckoning, take us to 196 B.C. The further twenty years would take us almost to Maccabean times. While we must admit that a certain error is possible and even likely in any Jewish chronology for the post-exilic period, this particular tradition assigns a date in Maccabean times for the Teacher of Righteousness, who appears to have been the founder of the Qumran community. Scholars are not at one in assigning an exact date for his floruit or for that of his enemy, called "The Wicked Priest" in the Scrolls. The sect, however, appears to have originated within priestly circles and to have broken with the Temple and the Jerusalem priesthood because they believed this latter had fallen into error, possibly because of the introduction of a new calendar into the Temple liturgy. The break may have been occasioned when the high priesthood was assumed by the Maccabean ruler Jonathan (160-142 B.C.) or by his brother Simon (143-134 B.C.). It is possible, however, that it may have come as early as 172 B.C. when Onias of the house of Zadok, ousted from the high priesthood, was murdered and the high priesthood purchased by the non-Zadokite Menalaus.

It is customary to identify or at least connect the Essenes with the Hasideans of early Maccabean times mentioned in 1 Mac 2:42 (see also and 1:62-63; 2:37), and to assign an origin in Maccabean times to both the Essenes and the Qumran community. Another way of reading the evidence, however, has been put forward by Jerome Murphy-O'Connor. In his view the Essene movement originated in Babylonia rather than in Palestine, and from inspired reflection on the causes of the divine punishment on Israel that was the exile rather than as a reaction to Hellenism. In this view the Essenes would have existed for over 300 years in Babylon before some of their members returned to Palestine in the first half of the second century B.C., possibly about 165 B.C. This earlier Babylonian origin of the Essene movement is believed to explain better certain aspects of its legislation, such as rules on contact with pagans. It might also help us understand the relationships that exist between the Epistle to the Colossians and Essene-type teaching. It may have come through the presence in the area of Colossae of Jews from Babylon settled there by Antiochus III some time after 213 B.C. (see Josephus *Ant.* 12, 3, 4, §§ 147-153.

Whatever of this particular point, through archeological and other evidence we can trace the history of the Qumran community from the foundation of the monastery about 135 B.C. down to about A.D. 70. The number of monks during the early period (135 to about 100 B.C.) seems to have been small — no more than fifty or so. The monastery had to be enlarged about 100 B.C., due to a sharp increase in vocations. It has been surmised that this influx came from Pharisees who were then being persecuted by the rulers John Hyrcanus and Alexander Jannaeus. Some time in the thirties of the first century B.C. the monastery was destroyed, either by the invading Parthians (40-37 B.C.) or the earthquake of 31 B.C. It remained in ruins through most of the reign of Herod. This monarch was friendly towards the Essenes and the monks may have lived peacefully outside their monastery. Towards the end of Herod's reign the monastery was rebuilt and was occupied until destroyed by the Romans during the Jewish War A.D. 66-70. Some of the manuscripts may have been deposited in the caves when the monastery was first destroyed in 40-37 or 31 B.C. The remainder would be taken to safekeeping before the final destruction.

As mentioned already, we are here interested in this information for the light it can shed on our principal purpose, which is Jewish literature and the development of doctrine during the intertestamental period. With the Essenes and the Dead Sea Covenanters we may be in the presence of a group which originated well before the Maccabean crisis. This is a possibility which is viewed sympathetically by an increasing number of modern scholars. Indeed this may hold true not merely for the Essenes but also for the other two religious groupings, the Sadducees and the Pharisees. Their roots, if not their actual foundations as organized sects, may go back into earlier post-exilic, if not exilic, times.

The Qumran monastic community originated within levitical and priestly circles. They are, thus, bearers of a priestly tradition which they formulated and reformulated in their own way. Their priestly origins, however, continued to influence their spirituality, with its qualified respect for the temple and its vision of a better and holier temple and Holy City. Their religion would continue to hold much in common with that of the priesthood with which they had broken. It also appears that they had no small amount in common with the Pharisees and were probably influenced in their development by Pharisaic tradition. They seem to have had their immediate, if not their ultimate origins, within or in association with the Hasidim of Maccabean times. The Pharisees may have had a similar origin within this Hasidic movement. And the supposed influx of Pharisees into the community of Qumran about 100 B.C. would not have left unaffected the doctrine of the Covenanters. J.T. Milik calls this second stage of the community's history (which would have lasted to about 65 B.C.) "Essenism with

Pharisaic nuances." Finally, as with so many other Jews and Jewish groups, the final stage of the community's history probably came under Zealot influence, and that its Zealot and anti-Roman stance explains its destruction by the Roman armies during the First Jewish War.

With this information on the history of the group we may now approach the literature they produced or by which their devotion and spirituality was nurtured.

III. The Literature of the Qumran Library

The literature presented to us in the manuscripts found in the Qumran caves 1-11 (including the Temple Scroll) can be divided into four main categories of manuscripts: the Hebrew-Aramaic text of the Bible; (2) the Apocrypha of the Old Testament, which are the Deuterocanonical books of the Catholic Canon; (3) non-sectarian pseudepigrapha; (4) sectarian literature, i.e. works containing the tradition, biblical interpretation and peculiar theological concepts of the Qumran community. Manuscripts, or fragments of manuscripts, of all books of the Hebrew Bible have been found, with the exception of the Book of Esther. These texts are of great importance for the understanding of the origin and transmission of the Hebrew Text of the Bible, as well as for the early history of the Greek versions. It is well known that in some books the Greek translation differs noticeably from the traditional Hebrew text (known as the Masoretic text). Manuscripts with the Hebrew text underlying some books of the Greek Septuagint translation have been found, as well as other manuscripts of these same books with the accepted Masoretic form of the text. There is some evidence also that manuscripts of the Samaritan recension of the Pentateuch were being used in Palestine before the Christian era. Of the Apocrypha, fragments of manuscripts of Sirach, Tobit and the Epistle of Jeremy have come to light. The manuscripts of Sirach are in Hebrew, which must have been the language of the original. Fragments of manuscripts of Tobit have been found both in Hebrew and Aramaic. A Greek fragment of the Epistle (verses 43-44) of Jeremy has been found in Cave 7, a cave discovered during the explorations of the spring of 1955. The few texts published from this cave are all in Greek. The text of the Epistle of Jeremy (7Q2) was copied about 100 B.C.

Our interest in this present volume is with the non-biblical material, which we shall here examine under four headings: (1) Early and nonsectarian literature; (2) the Community's Rules and Regulations; (3) texts on the interpretation of the Bible; (4) Hymns, Prayers and Liturgical Texts; (5) Miscellaneous compositions.

1. EARLY AND NON-SECTARIAN TEXTS

These are texts used by the community and copied in the Qumran scriptorium which are neither part of the Hebrew Bible nor of the Apocrypha as explained above. From the community's point of view the difference between apocryphal (deuterocanonical) and early non-sectarian — or for that matter Community compositions — could have been negligible, if not non-existent. We make the distinction here in this work in the interests of the series of which this volume is part. The importance of the works listed under the present heading lies to a good extent in the information which they might well provide on the origins of the Qumran sect and the earlier non-biblical sources from which it drew its inspiration and which influenced its spirituality.

i. The Books of Enoch.

In the chapter dealing with Apocalyptic Literature we have considered the different books associated with Enoch, of which portions have been found among the Dead Sea Scrolls, viz. *The Book of the Watchers* (1 Enoch 1-36), *The Astronomical Book of Enoch* (1 Enoch 72-82), Enoch's *Book of Dream-Visions* (1 Enoch 83-90), *The Admonitions of Enoch* (1 Enoch 91-107) and the *Book of the Giants*. The first two of these were composed before 200 B.C. and the third apparently before 153 B.C. All three, then, appear to have been composed before the Qumran community was founded. The two remaining sections may also have originated outside the Qumran community, but this point need not detain us here.

ii. The Testaments of Levi, Naphtali, Amram and Kohath.

We have already considered these under Testament Literature. The *Testaments of Levi, Kohath* and *Amram* are apparently from the third century B.C., if not from the fourth. The presence of these texts in Qumran may be due to the priestly and levitical origins of the Dead Sea monastic community.

iii. The Targum of Job.

An Aramaic translation of the entire Book of Job must have existed in Qumran since large portions of the translation of Job 17:14 to 42:11 have been found in Cave 11 and small fragments of the translation of Job 3:5-9 and 4:16 to 5:4 in Cave 4 (4Q157). The editors of the text from Cave 11 have suggested a date of about 100 B.C. for the original composition and believe that its language represents Palestinian Aramaic. Another scholar, however, T. Muraoka, believes it was composed in Babylon between 250 and 150 B.C. It contains no specifically sectarian ideas and was scarcely composed within the community itself, even if a date of about 100 B.C. for the original composition is accepted. It apparently came to the community from outside. It is not easy to see why a community such as that of Qumran, competent in Hebrew, should need an Aramaic translation at all. It may have been due to the extreme difficulty of understanding the original Hebrew text of Job. The rendering itself is fairly straightforward, with relatively little embellishment. In this, and in many other ways, it differs very much from the Targum of Job that has been transmitted to us by rabbinic tradition. Rabbinic sources mention a targum of Job that was known to Rabban Gamaliel the Elder (ca. A.D. 25-50), the teacher of Paul the Apostle (cf. Acts 22:3; see also 5:34). It was used again by Gamaliel II (A.D. 90-110), grandson of the Elder Gamaliel (cf. Tosefta, *Shabbath* 13:2; Bab. *Shabbath* 115a; Pal. *Shabbath* 16, 1, 15c; *Sopherim* 5 and 15).

iv. Fragments of Aramaic Translation of Leviticus chap. 16 (4Q156).
    J.T. Milik has published two fragments of a manuscript with sections of an Aramaic rendering of Leviticus, chapter 16 — the first with the translation of Lev. 16:12-15, the second with a rendering of Lev 16:18-21. The writing, he says, is old — from the second rather than the first century B.C. The orthography, he further notes, resembles that of the book of Daniel, hence of the eastern type. The same writer observes that it is not certain that the two fragments belonged to a targum in the strict sense, i.e. an Aramaic version of a whole book of the Bible. They might have come from a liturgical work or a ritual, certain parts of which could be literal translations of portions of the Pentateuch. The rendering in both fragments is literal, but so, too, we may note is the rendering of the other targums of Onkelos and Neofiti as far as these particular verses of Leviticus are concerned. Linguistically the Aramaic of these fragments belongs to Qumran and literary Aramaic, and to that of Targum Onkelos, rather than to the Aramaic of the Palestinian Targums. However, in certain elements of its rendering such as the choice of specific Aramaic words to translate the Hebrew, the translation is nearer to the Palestinian Targum as found in Codex Neofiti than to Onkelos. After a comparison of the translation of the Qumran fragments with the corresponding texts of the other Targums of the verses, the Jewish rabbinic scholar Menahem M. Kasher expressed the opinion that the two fragments reinforce his conviction that more than the three extant Aramaic translations existed, and that in each of them elements of the Oral Law (which might be written down but had to be transmitted orally) were blended or merged in the course of the translation.

v. The Book of Jubilees
    About ten manuscripts of this Old Testament apocryphon have been found in Qumran (caves 1, 2 and 4). In view

of the insistence of this work on a special form of solar calendar and on fixed dates for the main festivals — both points of capital importance for the Qumran sectaries — some scholars (e.g. J.T. Milik) believe that the *Book of Jubilees* was composed by a member of the sect, and most probably before 100 B.C. Other authorities in the field, however, think that the work was composed before the establishment of the Qumran community and shortly after the Maccabean revolt. The work can be taken as representing the kind of Judaism out of which the Qumran community, and possibly Essenism, emerged.

The *Book of Jubilees* tells the story of origins from the creation of the world to the exodus, from Gen 1:1 to Exod 12:50. It contains the "history of the divisions of the days of the law and of the testimony, of the events of the years, of their (year) weeks, of their Jubilees throughout all the years of the world, as the Lord spoke to Moses on Mount Sinai when he went up to receive the tables of the Law and of the commandment." It gets its title from the fact that it arranges its account in forty-nine periods, each of which is forty-nine years long. The work is, thus, a Jubilee of Jubilees. The account it gives is presented as a revelation to Moses by the angel of the Presence (1:29—2:1) and is a free retelling of the biblical narrative from Gen 1:1 to Exod 12:50. Names are supplied for persons and places of the biblical text and problems arising from the inspired narrative are explained. The less savoury deeds of the ancestors of the nation are whitewashed. The patriarchs are presented as innovators of culture. Writing, medicine and ploughing are said to have originated respectively with Enoch, Noah and Abraham. There is a very clear polemic against the solar calendar.

In connection with the account of the death of Abraham, narrated in chapter 23, a description of the future course of Hebrew and human history is given. The life expectancy of humans would decrease and corruption increase. Woes would descend on the human race. There would be universal strife. The faithful would resort to the use of arms to bring back the faithless (23:11-22). Israel would be invaded by sinners of the Gentiles (23-25). Then, we are told, there would be renewed study of the Law; mankind would be renewed, thus introducing a form of messianic age. The spirits of the dead would enjoy much peace. The description reads (23:26-31):

> 26 And in those days the children shall begin to study the laws,
> And to seek the commandments,
> And to return to the path of righteousness.
> 27 And the days shall begin to grow many and increase amongst those children of men
> Till their days draw nigh to one thousand years,
> And to a greater number of years than (before) was the number of the days.
> 28 And there shall be no old man
> Nor one who is (not) satisfied with his days,
> For all shall be (as) children and youths.
> 29 And all their days they shall complete and live in peace and in joy,
> And there shall be no Satan nor any evil destroyer;
> For all their days shall be days of blessing and healing.
> 30 And at that time the Lord will heal His servants,
> And they shall rise up and see great peace,
> And drive out their adversaries.
>
> And the righteous shall see and be thankful,
> And rejoice with joy for ever and ever,
> And shall see all their judgments and all their curses on their enemies.
> 31 And their bones shall rest in the earth,
> And their spirits shall have much joy,
> And they shall know that it is the Lord who executes judgment,
> And shows mercy to hundreds and thousands and to all that love Him

The work ends (chapter 50) with regulations regarding the jubilees and with strict laws on Sabbath observance:

> And after this law I made known to thee the days of the Sabbaths in the desert of Sin[ai], which is between Elim and Sinai. And I told thee of the Sabbaths of the land on

Mount Sinai, and I told thee of the jubilee years in the
sabbaths of years: but the year thereof have I not told thee
till ye enter the land which ye are to possess. And the land
also shall keep its sabbaths while they dwell upon it, and
they shall know the jubilee year. Wherefore I have
ordained for thee the year-weeks and the years and the
jubilees: there are forty-nine jubilees from the days of
Adam until this day, and one week and two years: and
there are yet forty years to come (lit. 'distant') for learning
the commandments of the Lord, until they pass over into
the land of Canaan, crossing the Jordan to the west. And
the jubilees shall pass by, until Israel is cleansed from all
guilt of fornication, and uncleanness, and pollution, and
sin, and error, and dwells with confidence in all the land,
and there shall be no more a Satan or any evil one, and
the land shall be clean from that time for evermore.

And behold the commandment regarding the
Sabbaths—I have written (them) down for thee—and all
the judgments of its laws. Six days shalt thou labour, but
on the seventh day is the Sabbath of the Lord your God.
In it ye shall do no manner of work, ye and your sons, and
your men-servants and your maid-servants, and all your
cattle and the sojourner also who is with you. And the
man that does any work on it shall die: whoever dese-
crates that day, whoever lies with (his) wife, or whoever
says he will do something on it, that he will set out on a
journey thereon in regard to any buying or selling: and
whoever draws water thereon which he had not prepared
for himself on the sixth day, and whoever takes up any
burden to carry it out of his tent or out of his house [9]shall
die. Ye shall do no work whatever on the Sabbath day
save what ye have prepared for yourselves on the sixth
day, so as to eat, and drink, and rest, and keep Sabbath
from all work on that day, and to bless the Lord your
God, who has given you a day of festival and a holy day:
and [10]a day of the holy kingdom for all Israel is this day
among their days for ever. For great is the honour which
the Lord has given to Israel that they should eat and drink
and be satisfied on this festival day, and rest thereon from

all labour which belongs to the labour of the children of men, save burning frankincense and bringing oblations and sacrifices before the Lord for days and for [11]Sabbaths. This work alone shall be done on the Sabbath-days in the sanctuary of the Lord your God; that they may atone for Israel with sacrifice continually from day to day for a memorial well-pleasing before the Lord, and that He may receive them always from day to day according as thou [12]hast been commanded. And every man who does any work thereon, or goes a journey, or tills (his) farm, whether in his house or any other place, and whoever lights a fire, or rides on any beast, or travels by ship on the sea, and whoever strikes or kills anything, or slaughters a beast or a bird, or [13]whoever catches an animal or a bird or a fish, or whoever fasts or makes war on the Sabbaths: The man who does any of these things on the Sabbath shall die, so that the children of Israel shall observe the Sabbaths according to the commandments regarding the Sabbaths of the land, as it is written in the tablets, which He gave into my hands that I should write out for thee the laws of the seasons, and the seasons according to the division of their days.

Herewith is completed the account of the division of the days.

The mentality expressed in this text reminds us of that of the pious Jews of Maccabean times; cf. 1 Mac 2:29-38. It is the kind of spirituality we find in the Rules of the Qumran community.

Since all the Qumran manuscripts of *Jubilees* are in Hebrew, this, presumably, was the original language of the work. It is extant in its entirety in an Ethiopic translation and partially in a Latin version.

2. COMMUNITY RULES AND REGULATIONS

Among the Qumran documents there are rules concerning the life and administration of the community. These contain a certain amount of the legal tradition (halakah) of the monastic settlement, which in all probability is that of the Essenes. Together with the Community Rules we also have the Temple Scroll which has a special halakic re-reading of Old Testament texts. Finally, we have a text with a commentary on biblical laws, which could be included either here or in the section on biblical commentaries.

We are fortunate in having these texts which give us an insight into the community's rules, regulations and halakah from a very early period down to the final half-century or so of its existence. For lack of historical evidence we can say but little on the origins and development of the Qumran community or the Essenes, but must be grateful for the good fortune that has preserved the major texts we are now to examine.

i. The Community Rule (1QS).

This in Hebrew is known as *Serek ha-Yahad, serek* being the Hebrew for "Rule" — whence the siglum that has been assigned to it. It was first called "The Manual of Discipline." The oldest manuscript of this Rule found in Qumran (4QS^e) was written before 100 B.C., a fact which renders probable a date between 150 and 125 B.C. for the original composition. The author of the work, in fact, may have been the very founder of the Qumran community, the Teacher of Righteousness himself. The Rule seems to have been very much used. We have other manuscripts of it from the period 100-75 B.C. In a later text appendices are found with references to the two messiahs and to the messianic meal. We shall treat of this appendix below as a separate work (no. iii).

This Rule seems to have been composed for the use of the community's teachers, masters and guardians. It was probably a handbook to be used by these for the instruction of others. It begins with an outline of the purpose of the community's being (1:1-18) and then gives an account of the ceremony for entry into the community (1:18-4:26).

The section of the Rule we now cite (1:21-2:10) was to be

recited by the priests and the levites. Authority in the Community, we may recall, was held by these two groups.

> Then the Priests shall recite the favours of God manifested in His mighty deeds and shall declare all His merciful grace to Israel, and the Levites shall recite the iniquities of the children of Israel, all their guilty rebellions and sins during the dominion of Satan. And after them, all those entering the Covenant shall confess and say: 'We have strayed! We have [disobeyed!] We and our fathers before us have sinned and done wickedly in walking [counter to the precepts] of truth and righteousness. [And God has] judged us and our fathers also; 2 but He has bestowed His bountiful mercy on us from everlasting to everlasting. And the Priests shall bless all the men of the lot of God who walk perfectly in all His ways, saying: 'May He bless you with all good and preserve you from all evil! May he lighten your heart with life-giving wisdom and grant you eternal knowledge! May He raise His merciful face towards you for everlasting bliss!'
>
> And the Levites shall curse all the men of the lot of Satan, saying: 'Be cursed because of all your guilty wickedness! May He deliver you up for torture at the hands of the vengeful Avengers! May He visit you with destruction by the hand of all the Wreakers of Revenge! Be cursed without mercy because of the darkness of your deeds! Be damned in the shadowy place of everlasting fire! May God not heed when you call on Him, nor pardon you by blotting out your sin! May He raise His angry face towards you for vengeance! May there be no "Peace" for you in the mouth of those who hold fast to the Fathers!' And after the blessing and the cursing, all those entering the Covenant shall say, 'Amen, Amen!'

Within this long text (1:18—4:26) with the ceremony for entry we find a discussion of one of the central doctrines of the community, that of the Two Spirits within man. The members of the community, the "children of light" were to be instructed on this matter, as we can see from the following text (3:13 — 4:8):

The Master shall instruct all the sons of light and shall teach them the nature of all the chidren of men according to the kind of spirit which they possess, the signs identifying their works during their lifetime, their visitation for chastisement, and all the time of their reward.

From the God of Knowledge comes all that is and shall be. Before ever they existed He established their whole design, and when, as ordained for them, they come into being, it is in accord with His glorious design that they accomplish their task without change. The laws of all things are in His hand and He provides them with all their needs.

He has created man to govern the world, and has appointed for him two spirits in which to walk until the time of His visitation: the spirits of truth and falsehood. Those born of truth spring from a fountain of light, but those born of falsehood spring from a source of darkness. All the children of righteousness are ruled by the Prince of Light and walk in the ways of light, but all the children of falsehood are ruled by the Angel of Darkness and walk in the ways of darkness.

The Angel of Darkness leads all the children of righteousness astray, and until his end, all their sin, iniquities, wickedness, and all their unlawful deeds are caused by his dominion in accordance with the mysteries of God. Every one of their chastisements, and every one of the seasons of their distress, shall be brought about by the rule of his persecution; for all his allotted spirits seek the overthrow of the sons of light.

But the God of Israel and His Angel of Truth will succour all the sons of light. For it is He who created the spirits of Light and Darkness and founded every action upon them and established every deed [upon] their [ways]. And He loves the one **4** everlastingly and delights in its works for ever; but the counsel of the other He loathes and for ever hates its ways.

These are their ways in the world for the enlightenment of the heart of man, and that all the paths of true righteousness may be made straight before him, and that fear

of the laws of God may be instilled in his heart: a spirit of
humility, patience, abundant charity, unending goodness, understanding, and intelligence; (a spirit of) mighty
wisdom which trusts in all the deeds of God and leans on
His great loving kindness; a spirit of discernment in every
purpose, of zeal for just laws, of holy intent with steadfastness of heart, of great charity towards all the sons of
truth, of admirable purity which detests all unclean idols,
of humble conduct sprung from an understanding of all
things, and of faithful concealment of the mysteries of
truth. These are the counsels of the spirit to the sons of
truth in this world.

And as for the visitation of all who walk in this spirit, it
shall be healing, great peace in a long life, and fruitful-
ness, together with every everlasting blessing and eternal
joy in life without end, a crown of glory and a garment of
majesty in unending light.

The greatest part of the Rule (5:1—9:11), however, is
given over to an expression of the Community's legislation.
This covers a variety of topics: the common life, and the
penal code that covered transgressions (6:24—7:25). But
even within the section on the regulations we find clear
expression of the exalted view the community held of itself,
as for instance in the following text (8:1-11):

8 In the Council of the Community there shall be twelve
men and three Priests, perfectly versed in all that is
revealed of the Law, whose works shall be truth, righteousness, justice, lovingkindness, and humility. They
shall preserve the faith in the Land with steadfastness and
meekness and shall atone for sin by the practice of justice
and by suffering the sorrows of affliction. They shall walk
with all men according to the standard of truth and the
rule of the time.

When these are in Israel, the Council of the Community shall be established in truth. It shall be an Everlasting
Plantation, a House of Holiness for Israel, an Assembly
of Supreme Holiness for Aaron. They shall be witnesses

to the truth at the Judgement, and shall be the elect of
Goodwill who shall atone for the Land and pay to the
wicked their reward. It shall be that tried wall, that
precious corner-stone, whose foundations shall neither
rock nor sway in their place (Isa 28:16). It shall be a Most
Holy Dwelling for Aaron, with everlasting knowledge of
the Covenant of justice, and shall offer up sweet fra-
grance. It shall be a House of Perfection and Truth in
Israel that they may establish a Covenant according to
the everlasting precepts. And they shall be an agreeable
offering, atoning for the Land and determining the judgement of wickedness, and there shall be no more iniquity.
When they have been confirmed for two years in perfection of way by the authority of the Community, they shall
be set apart as holy within the Council of the men of the
Community. And the Interpreter shall not conceal from
them, out of fear of the spirit of apostasy, any of those
things hidden from Israel which have been discovered by
him.

At the end of the regulations the text tells us that the men
of the community are to walk in the primitive precepts "until
there shall come the Prophet and the Messiahs of Aaron and
Israel" (9:11).

After this text come directives addressed to the Master on
how he should act in different circumstances, and with this
is tied in the community's teaching on times for worship
(9:12—10:8). The *Community Rule* ends with a beautiful
hymn of Thanksgiving and blessing to be said by the Master
of the Community. A few excerpts from it are given here.

As for me,
  my justification is with God.
In His hand are the perfection of my way
  and the uprightness of my heart.
He will wipe out my transgression
  through His righteousness.

For my light has sprung
  from the source of His knowledge;

my eyes have beheld His marvellous deeds,
   and the light of my heart, the mystery to come.
He that is everlasting
   is the support of my right hand;
the way of my steps is over stout rock
   which nothing shall shake;
for the rock of my steps is the truth of God
   and his might is the support of my right hand.

From the source of His righteousness
   is my justification,
and from His marvellous mysteries
   is the light in my heart.
My eyes have gazed
   on that which is eternal,
on wisdom concealed from men,
   on knowledge and wise design
     (hidden) from the sons of men;

on a fountain of righteousness
   and on a storehouse of power,
on a spring of glory
   (hidden) from the assembly of flesh.
God has given them to His chosen ones
   as an everlasting possession,
and has caused them to inherit
   the lot of the Holy Ones.
He has joined their assembly
   to the Sons of Heaven
to be a Council of the Community,
a foundation of the Building of Holiness,
an eternal Plantation throughout all ages to come.

       . . . .

Blessed art Thou, my God,
   who openest the heart of Thy servant to knowledge!
Establish all his deeds in righteousness,
and as it pleases Thee to do for the elect of mankind,
   grant that the son of Thy handmaid
   may stand before Thee for ever.

For without Thee no way is perfect,
   and without Thy will nothing is done.
It is Thou who has taught all knowledge
   and all things come to pass by Thy will.
There is none beside Thee to dispute Thy counsel
   or to understand all Thy holy design,
or to contemplate the depth of Thy mysteries
   and the power of Thy might.

ii. *The Damascus Rule (CD).*

This text has been known for a long time, thanks to the discovery by Solomon Schechter of two incomplete manuscripts of it in the Geniza of Cairo at the end of the last century. Schechter published them in 1910. The first manuscript (MS A) is from the tenth century A.D., the other (MS B) from the twelfth. These represent two different recensions of the composition. Manuscripts of eight copies of the work have been found in Qumran (caves 4, 5 and 6), the oldest of which was written between 75 and 70 B.C. The date at which the original was composed is less certain. It may have been about 100 B.C. There are two parts in the work. One (chaps 1-8, 19-20) is in the form of an exhortation to those who forsook Judah and went into exile in the land of Damascus. It recounts and comments on God's saving plan in history. The second (9-18) gives detailed rules for the members of the New Covenant (as the members of the group refer to themselves) in their camps in the land of Damascus.

The work draws its title from this reference to the land of Damascus. In general "Damascus" in this work is taken as a designation for Qumran. We have seen already that Jerome Murphy-O'Connor understands it as designating Babylon.

The exhortation recounts the earlier rebellions of humanity and Israel against God's commandments, from the day the Watchers (i.e. the Angels at the flood) sinned until the (New) Covenant was made, apparently during the exile (3:12-4:2):

> But with the remnant which held fast to the commandments of God, He made His Covenant with Israel forever,

revealing to them the hidden things in which all Israel had gone astray. He unfolded before them His holy Sabbaths and His glorious feasts, the testimonies of His righteousness and the ways of His truth, and the desires of His will which a man must do in order to live. And they dug a well rich in water; and he who despises it shall not live. Yet they wallowed in the sin of man and in ways of uncleanness, and they said, 'This is our (way).' But God, in His wonderful mysteries, forgave them their sin and pardoned their wickedness; and He built them a sure house in Israel whose like has never existed from former times till now. Those who hold fast to it are destined to live for ever and all the glory of Adam shall be theirs. As God ordained for them by the hand of the Prophet Ezekiel, saying, *The Priests, the Levites, and the sons* 4 *of Zadok who kept the charge of my sanctuary when the children of Israel strayed from me, they shall offer me fat and blood* (Ezek, 44:15).

Three nets of Satan have been set before Israel to lead them astray: fornication, riches and profanation of the temple. The Rule thus illustrates the snare of fornication (4:19 — 5:6):

> The builders of the wall (Ezek, 13:10) who have followed after 'Precept' — 'Precept' was a spouter of whom it is written, *They shall surely spout* (Mic. 2:6) —shall be caught in fornication twice by taking a second wife while the first is alive, whereas the principle of creation is, *Male and female created He them* (Gen. 1:27) 5 Also, those who entered the Ark went in two by two. And concerning the prince it is written, *He shall not multiply wives to himself* (Deut. 17:17); but David had not read the sealed book of the Law which was in the ark (of the Covenant), for it was not opened in Israel from the death of Eleazar and Joshua, and the elders who worshipped Ashtoreth. It was hidden and (was not) revealed until the coming of Zadok. And the deeds of David rose up, except for the murder of Uriah, and God left them to him.

The second section, the Statutes, contains laws grouped according to subject matter. These are presented as Statutes in which the members of the community were to walk "until the coming of the Messiah of Aaron and Israel who will pardon their iniquity." These Statutes concern oaths and vows, the tribunal, witnesses, judges, purification by water, Sabbath observance, cleanness and uncleanness.

> *Concerning purification by water*
>
> No man shall bathe in dirty water or in an amount too shallow to cover a man. He shall not purify himself with water contained in a vessel. And as for the water of every rock-pool too shallow to cover a man, if an unclean man touches it he renders its water as unclean as water contained in a vessel. (10:10-13).

The longest section of the Statutes concerns Sabbath observance (10:14 — 11:18):

> *Concerning the Sabbath to observe it according to its law*
>
> No man shall work on the sixth day from the moment when the sun's orb is distant by its own fulness from the gate (wherein it sinks); for this is what He said, *Observe the Sabbath day to keep it holy* (Deut. 5:12). No man shall speak any vain or idle word on the Sabbath day. He shall make no loan to his companion. He shall make no decision in matters of money and gain. He shall say nothing about work or labour to be done on the morrow.
>
> No man shall walk abroad to do business on the Sabbath. He shall not walk more than one thousand cubits beyond his town.
>
> No man shall eat on the Sabbath day except that which is already prepared. He shall eat nothing lying in the fields. He shall not drink except in the camp. 11 If he is on a journey and goes down to bathe, he shall drink where he stands, but he shall not draw water into a vessel. He shall send out no stranger on his business on the Sabbath day.
>
> No man shall wear soiled garments, or garments brought to the store, unless they have been washed with

water or rubbed with incense.

No man shall willingly mingle (with others) on the Sabbath.

No man shall walk more than two thousand cubits after a beast to pasture it outside his town. He shall not raise his hand to strike it with his fist. If it is stubborn he shall not take it out of his house.

No man shall take anything out of the house or bring anything in. And if he is in a booth, let him neither take anything out nor bring anything in. He shall not open a sealed vessel on the Sabbath.

No man shall carry perfumes on himself whilst going and coming on the Sabbath. He shall lift neither sand nor dust in his dwelling. No foster-father shall carry a child whilst going and coming on the Sabbath.

No man shall chide his manservant or maidservant or labourer on the Sabbath.

No man shall assist a beast to give birth on the Sabbath day. And if it should fall into a cistern or pit, he shall not lift it out on the Sabbath.

No man shall spend the Sabbath in a place near to Gentiles on the Sabbath.

No man shall profane the Sabbath for the sake of riches or gain on the Sabbath day. But should any man fall into water or fire, let him be pulled out with the aid of a ladder or rope or (some such) tool.

iii. The Messianic Rule (1QSa).

This Rule was originally published in 1955 under the title "The Rule of the Congregation," and is sometimes still so called. It is found as an appendix in a manuscript of the *Community Rule* (1QS), studied earlier. It is designed, however, for the end time when the community would be ruled by the Messiah of Aaron (Priest Messiah) and the Messiah of Israel (the political or Davidic Messiah). This Rule contains a programme for the members of the Community, from childhood until they participate in the community affairs or in its wars. The community, we may recall, was

governed by the sons of Zadok, the priests. This particular
Rule seems to have been composed about the same time as
the *War Rule* which we consider next, i.e. in the final
decades of the first century B.C. or in the early decades of
the first century A.D. The text ends with a description of the
Messianic Meal as follows:

> [*This shall be the ass*]*embly of the men of renown* [*called*]
> *to the meeting of the Council of the Community when*
> [*the Priest-*] *Messiah shall summon them.*
>
> He shall come [at] the head of the whole congregation
> of Israel with all [his brethren, the sons] of Aaron the
> Priests, [those called] to the assembly, the men of
> renown; and they shall sit [before him, each man] in the
> order of his dignity. And then [the Mess]iah of Israel shall
> [come], and the chiefs of the [clans of Israel] shall sit
> before him, [each] in the order of his dignity, according to
> [his place] in their camps and marches. And before them
> shall sit all the heads of [family of the congreg]ation, and
> the wise men of [the holy congregation,] each in the order
> of his dignity.
>
> It is according to this statute that they shall proceed at
> every me[al at which] at least ten men are gathered
> together.

iv. *The War Rule (1QM).*

The contents of scroll with the *War Rule* are as follows:
Proclamation of war against the Kittim (col. 1); reorganization of the temple worship (2); programme of the forty
years' war (2); the trumpets (2); the standards (3-4), disposi-
tion and weapons of the front formations (5), movement of
the infantry and cavalry (5), age of the soldiers (6-7), the
camp duties of the priests and levites (7-9), addresses and
prayers of the battle liturgy (10-12), prayer recited at the
moment of victory (13), thanksgiving ceremony (14), battle
against the Kittim (15-19).

It is possible that cols 1 + 15-19 once formed a separate
work on the final battle against the Kittim, a work drawing
inspiration from Dan 11:40—12:3, and that the remainder

of the Rule concerns a final battle against the entire Gentile world.

The work is a theological treatise on this final battle against the forces of evil and draws inspiration from the Bible. It is not a handbook for the waging of an actual war. However, the weapons mentioned and the tactics of the war seem to correspond to Roman war practice. The fact that it depends on the book of Daniel, written about 164 B.C., and this probable relationship to Roman war practice suggest a date of about 20 B.C. to A.D. 20 for the composition of the original.

From its introduction it is clear that the *War Rule* is intended for those involved in the general battle against the army of Satan. It opens as follows:

> 1 *For the M[aster. The Rule of] War on the unleashing of the attack of the sons of light against the company of the sons of darkness, the army of Satan: against the band of Edom, Moab, and the sons of Ammon, and [against the army of the sons of the East and] the Philistines, and against the bands of the Kittim of Assyria and their allies the ungodly of the Covenant*
>
> The sons of Levi, Judah, and Benjamin, the exiles in the desert, shall battle against them in...all their bands when the exiled sons of light return from the Desert of the Peoples to camp in the Desert of Jerusalem; and after the battle they shall go up from there (to Jerusalem?).
>
> [The king] of the Kittim [shall enter] into Egypt, and in his time he shall set out in great wrath to wage war against the kings of the north, that his fury may destroy and cut off the horn of [the nations].
>
> This shall be a time of salvation for the people of God, an age of dominion for all the members of His company, and of everlasting destruction for all the company of Satan. The confusion of the sons of Japheth shall be [great] and Assyria shall fall unsuccoured. The dominion of the Kittim shall come to an end and iniquity shall be vanquished, leaving no remnant; [for the sons] of darkness there shall be no escape. [The seasons of righteous-]

ness shall shine over all the ends of the earth; they shall go on shining until all the seasons of darkness are consumed and, at the season appointed by God, His exalted greatness shall shine eternally to the peace, blessing, glory, joy, and long life of all the sons of light.

On the day when the Kittim fall, there shall be battle and terrible carnage before the God of Israel, for that shall be the day appointed from ancient times for the battle of destruction of the sons of darkness. At that time, the assembly of gods and the hosts of men shall battle, causing great carnage... And it shall be a time of [great] tribulation for the people which God shall redeem;....

There is a very strong biblical inspiration, and not merely from Daniel. In its concept of the sanctity proper to the war camp it has deep inspiration from the Book of Deuteronomy (cf. Deut 20:1-20; 23:11-14). Since God is present among them, fighting the battle of his people, the camp must be holy. Thus, for instance, col. 7:3-8:

No boy or woman shall enter their camps, from the time they leave Jerusalem and march out to war until they return. No man who is lame, or blind, or crippled, or afflicted with a lasting bodily blemish, or smitten with a bodily impurity, none of these shall march out to war with them. They shall all be freely enlisted for war, perfect in spirit and body and prepared for the Day of Vengeance. And no man shall go down with them on the day of battle who is impure because of his 'fount', for the holy angels shall be with their hosts. And there shall be a space of about two thousand cubits between all their camps and the place serving as a latrine, so that no indecent nakedness may be seen in the surroundings of their camps.

Since victory is of the Lord (citing Deut 20:2-4 and Num 10:9), this is recalled in the battle liturgy (11:17 — 12:10):

For Thou wilt fight with them from heaven ... **12** For the multitude of the Holy Ones [is with Thee] in heaven, and the host of the Angels is in Thy holy abode, praising

Thy Name. And Thou hast established in [a community] for Thyself the elect of Thy holy people. [The list] of the names of all their host is with Thee in the abode of Thy holiness; [the reckoning of the saints] is in Thy glorious dwelling-place. Thou hast recorded for them, with the graving-tool of life, the favours of [Thy] blessings and the Covenant of Thy peace, that Thou mayest reign [over them] for ever and ever and throughout all the eternal ages. Thou wilt muster the [hosts of] Thine [el]ect, in their Thousands and Myriads, with Thy Holy Ones [and with all] Thine Angels, that they may be mighty in battle, [and may smite] the rebels of the earth by Thy great judgements, and that [they may triumph] together with the elect of heaven.

For thou art [terrible], O God, in the glory of Thy kingdom, and the congregation of Thy Holy Ones is among us for everlasting succour. We will despise kings, we will mock and scorn the mighty; for our Lord is holy, and the King of Glory is with us together with the Holy Ones. Valiant [warriors] of the angelic host are among our numbered men, and the Hero of war is with our congregation; the host of His spirits is with our foot-soldiers and horsemen. [They are as] clouds, as clouds of dew (covering) the earth, as a shower of rain shedding righteousness on all that grows on the earth.

This is followed by a prayer of jubilation:

Rise up, O Hero!
Lead off Thy captives, O Glorious one!
Gather up Thy spoils, O Author of mighty deeds!
Lay Thy hand on the neck of Thine enemies
   and Thy feet on the pile of the slain!

Smite the nations, Thine adversaries,
   and devour the flesh of the sinner with Thy sword!
Fill Thy land with glory
   and Thine inheritance with blessing!
Let there be a multitude of cattle in Thy fields,
   and in Thy palaces silver and gold and precious stones!

O Zion, rejoice greatly!
O Jerusalem, show thyself amidst jubilation!
Rejoice, all you cities of Judah;
keep your gates ever open
    that the hosts of the nations
    may be brought in!

Their kings shall serve you
    and all your oppressors shall bow down before you;
    [they shall lick] the dust [of your feet].
Shout for joy , [O daughters of] my people!
Deck yourselves with glorious jewels
    and rule over [the kingdoms of the nations!
Sovereignty shall be to the Lord]
    and everlasting dominion to Israel.

v. *The Temple Scroll (11Q Temple).*

The *Temple Scroll*, presumably from cave 11, was known to have existed in 1960. Only in 1967, however, did it come into the hands of scholars when Yigael Yadin acquired it from an Arab dealer after the Six Days' War. It is the longest and largest of all the Qumran Scrolls, being approximately 28 feet in length when unrolled, with 67 columns of text. This present section on the Scroll is heavily indebted to a study of it made by Jacob Milgrom in 1978.

The Scroll is in what is known as a Herodian hand, indicating that it was written between 30 B.C. and A.D. 70. However, a Rockefeller fragment (43.366) of the same work is in middle Hasmonean script, and thus from the last quarter of the second century B.C. The existence of the Rockefeller fragments indicates that at least two or three copies of the work must have circulated.

The first column of the Scroll is lost. In the second we are given a paraphrase of Exod 34:10-16 and Deut 7:1ff. on the obligation not to succumb to Canaanite religion. After this (cols 3-51) comes a description of the Temple area and the citation of the relevant laws, as key sections of the Temple are described, e.g. the description of the outer court (40-46) presents the occasion to discuss the second tithe (col. 43) which was eaten in that court. The second part of the Scroll, from col. 51 to the end, follows the Deuteronomic Code (Deut 12-26), but neither in sequence nor in its entirety since the author takes occasion of the discussion of a given topic in one section to pass to related topics in other parts of Deuteronomy or of the Bible. Thus, for instance, the legislation on vows in Deut 23:22-24 and Num. 3:3-16 is introduced at the discussion of Deut 12:26. The author also avails of the biblical text to discuss his own sect's special laws or their special interpretation of biblical laws. The Scroll ends with the discussion of Deut 23:1 (col. 66).

In the biblical book of Deuteronomy it is Moses who speaks, mediating God's law to Israel. In the Scroll, however, all these Deuteronomic laws are presented as spoken directly by God, and the laws given in the biblical text as spoken directly by God (e.g. citations from Leviticus) are left unchanged. It seems clear, then, that the contents of the entire Scroll were presented, and intended to be accepted, as the revealed word of God. In many instances the Scroll merely repeats biblical laws. In a number of cases, however, we have innovations in which the sect's own peculiar emphases and points of view are given. There is even a polemical thrust in some of the laws. It is not clear why, but since some of the positions taken in Scroll's halakic understanding of Scripture differ from the rabbinic, the opponents intended may well be early rabbinic and Pharisaic scribes. On other occasions, the temple authorities seem to be the ones intended. The polemical laws in question concern the festivals, sacrifices, the perquisites for priests and levites, impurities, the seducer of Exod 22:15-16 and Deut 22:28-29; on hanging as a mode of execution (Deut 21:22-23); the torah of the king (possibly directed against John Hyrcanus, 134-104 B.C.); a higher status for the levites. Thus, for instance, the rabbis and the Scroll interpret Deut 14:22-27 as referring to the second tithe and the Scroll (with Jubilees 32:10-12; cf. Josephus, *Antiquities* 4, 8, 8.22, §§ 205, 240) maintains that the tithe must be taken to Jerusalem each year, in opposition to the rabbis who claimed that the tithe of the third and sixth years (cf. Deut 14:28-29;

26:12-26) was to be left at home for the levites, sojourners, orphans and widows. The Scroll also maintained that the tithe might be eaten only in the outer courts and only on sabbaths and festivals whereas rabbinic halakah permitted the tithe to be eaten at any time and anywhere in Jerusalem.

The Scroll gives the levites special status, even according them certain priestly functions, thus distinguishing them further from the laity. It even assures them new rights and cultic duties, including some which hitherto were the prerogative of priests.

The torah of the king, which is found in cols 56-59 (on Deut 17:14-20), is also in part polemic, as already noted. Multiple marriages are forbidden lest wives cause "his heart to go astray" (col. 56, 18-19). The king's wife must come from his father's house and he cannot remarry as long as she is alive. He is also to have an advisory council of 36-12 chieftains, 12 priests and 12 levites (cf. Deut 17:20; 19:17). The relevant section of the Scroll reads:

> He shall have twelve princes of his people with him, and twelve priests, and twelve Levites, who shall be seated near him for judgment and for torah. And he shall not exalt his heart above them and shall do nothing in all his counsels without them.
>
> He shall not take a wife from all the daughters of the nations but shall take for himself a wife from the house of his father, of the family of his father. And he shall take no other (wife) together with her but she alone shall be with him all the days of her life. Should she die he shall take for himself another wife from the house of his father, from his family (col. 57, 11-19). (Translation by author).

In stipulating that the king's wife must be from the king's own family, the halakah of the Scroll differs from rabbinic tradition which holds that every Israelite woman was eligible. The rule saying the king can have only one wife, effectively rules out both polygamy and divorce for the king. The rule is in keeping with the sect's interpretation of Genesis 1:27 found in CD 4:20-25 (cited above p. 129). In col. 64, 6-13 we have a reinterpretation of Deut 21:22-23 and Lev 19:16 in which the text from Deuteronomy is understood to refer to death "by hanging on a tree," apparently by crucifixion:

> If a man slanders his people, and delivers his people to a foreign nation, and does evil to his people, you shall hang him on a tree and he shall die. On the testimony of two witnesses, and on the testimony of three witnesses he shall be put to death, and they shall hang him (on) the tree.
>
> If a man is guilty of a capital crime and he flees (abroad) to the Gentiles, and curses his people, and the sons of Israel, you shall hang him also on the tree, and he shall die. But their bodies shall not stay overnight on the tree. Indeed, you shall bury him on the same day, for he who is hanged on the tree is accursed of God and men, and you shall not pollute the ground which I give you to possess.

As one would expect in a work connected with the Qumran community, the Scroll is interested in cleanness and purifications. The Temple City (i.e. Jerusalem) was reckoned as being particularly holy, with the holiness proper to Mount Sinai itself. Only those ritually clean could enter it. Three columns of the Scroll (45-47) are devoted to a consideration of those who are prohibited from entering the Temple City and of the purifications necessary. Those having nocturnal emissions and sexual intercourse (cf. Deut 23:11-12; Lev 15:18) required a three-day purification before entering, together with bathing and laundering on the first and third days. The blind may never enter (cf. Lev 21:17-18; 2 Sam 8:5; Num 5:2); those contaminated by corpses and the lepers as long as they remain impure (cf. Num 5:2-3; Lev 13:46; 14:10-20). An area was to be set aside 3,000 cubits (about a mile; not visible from the city) north-west of the city for toilets for the reception of human excrements. These toilets were not to be visible from the city. They were beyond the 2,000 cubits permitted as the sabbath journey, and consequently not to be used on the Sabbath (cf. Deut 23:13-15). East of the city stood dwellings for lepers, gonnorheics, and those with nocturnal emissions (cf. Num 5:2). All food entering the city must be pure and brought in the skins of animals slaughtered at the temple. Any other skin, even if of a pure animal, was forbidden (cf. Isa 52:1; Joel 4:17). The reason given for these laws is that God dwells among his people. The contention that excrement defiled the Temple city was sectarian, and denied by the rabbis (see Pal. Talmud, *Peshach* 7:11; cf. also Mishnah, *Tamid* 1:1; *Middoth* 1:9. Josephus, too, speaks on the Essene's fear of defilement through defecation and their abstention from it on the Sabbath (*War* 2, 8, 9 §§ 147-149).

vi. *A Commentary on Biblical Laws, (4Q159).*

This text is also known under the title "Ordinances." It contains a reinterpretation of a variety of biblical laws: Deut 23:25-26 (on plucking ears of corn when crossing another's field); Exod 30:11-16 (cf.38:25-26) (on the half-shekel to be contributed to the temple); Lev 25:39-46 (prohibition on selling an Israelite as a slave); a case to be judged by twelve judges (without biblical text); Deut 22:5 (unlawfulness of wearing clothes of the opposite sex); Deut 22:13-21 (charge of non-virginity by a husband against his wife). With regard to the half-shekel to be paid to the temple, the Qumran text stresses that it shall be paid only once in a lifetime. In rabbinic tradition this tax was to be paid annually by every male Israelite (cf. Neh 10:32; Mat 17:24-27). The Qumran understanding abided by the letter of the biblical law without giving undue support to the temple with which it had broken on many matters.

3. WORKS OF BIBLICAL INTERPRETATION

In Qumran the Bible was approached in a variety of ways. First and foremost it was taken as the inspired word of God, full of mysteries concerning the Qumran community itself. The meaning of these mysteries, the members of the sect believed, was revealed to their founder the Teacher of Righteousness and other authorized interpreters within the community. As well as being interpreted in this manner, the biblical narrative could also be rewritten in an imaginative fashion, and new texts composed on the end times taking their inspiration from the sacred page. We shall deal with these different forms of approach to the Bible among the covenanters.

i. The Pesharim.

The most typical form of biblical interpretation among the Qumran monks is that found in the compositions known as *pesharim*. This title is given them because of the fact that in the texts themselves the biblical lemma is given and then we are told that its interpretation (in Hebrew *pesher*) concerns some particular event in the history of the community.

In all we have 18 such texts from Qumran; 4 from cave 1, 1 from cave 3 and the remainder from cave 4. With one obscure exception (4QUnid) the works in question are commentaries on different books of the Bible, the books being indicated by the final element of the abbreviations assigned to them. They are as follows: 1QpHab, 1QpMic, 1QpZeph, 1QpPs, 3QpIsa, 4QpIsa^{a-e}, 4QpHos^{a-b}, 4QpMic, 4QpNah, 4QpZeph, 4QpPs^{a,b}, 4QpUnid (unidentified fragments presumed to be *pesharim*). Fifteen of these texts (the exceptions are 3 QpIsa, 4QpMic and 4 QpUnid) may be regarded as *pesharim* in the strict sense, i.e. a continuous *pesher*-type comment on a biblical book. We also find *pesher*-type comments on certain isolated biblical texts, or on texts grouped thematically together in florilegia. We shall consider these texts later in this chapter.

In the *pesher* commentaries especially we see the central role of the Bible in the life of the community. From the following text of the *Community Rule* (1QS 6:6-8) we get a glimpse of how central it really was:

> Wherever there are ten men of the Council of the Community there shall not lack a Priest among them ....
> And where the ten men are, there shall never lack a man among them who shall study the Law continually, day and night, concerning the right conduct of a man with his companion. And the Congregation shall watch in com-

munity for a third of every night of the year, to read the Book and to study the Law and to pray together.

We see some of the outcome of their meditation in the *Damascus Rule*, which in practice is *pesher* and is sometimes explicitly introduced as *pesher*. Thus in col. 4:13-18:

> During all those years Satan shall be unleashed against Israel, as He spoke by the hand of Isaiah, son of Amoz, saying, *Terror and pit and snare upon you, O inhabitant of the land* (Isa 24:17). Interpreted (literally: "its *pesher*"), these are the three nets of Satan with which Levi son of Jacob said that he catches Israel by setting them up as three kinds of righteousness. The first is fornication, the second is riches, and the third is profanation of the Temple ......(part of this text has already been cited above).

Another text from the same document on the origins of the community combines ancient Jewish lore and biblical interpretation (5:15 —6:10):

> For (already) in ancient times God visited their deeds and His anger was kindled against their works; *for it is a people of no discernment (Isa 27:11), it is a nation void of counsel inasmuch as there is no discernment in them* (Deut 32:28). For in ancient times, Moses and Aaron arose by the hand of the Prince of Lights and Satan in his cunning raised up Jannes and his brother when Israel was first delivered.
>
> And at the time of the desolation of the land there were removers of the bound who led Israel astray .... But God remembered the Covenant with the forefathers, and He raised up from Aaron men of discernment and from Israel men of wisdom, and he caused them to hear. And they dug the Well; *the well which the princes dug, which the nobles of the people delved with the stave* (Num 21:18).
>
> The *Well* is the Law, and those who dug it were the converts of Israel who went out of the land of Judah to sojourn in the land of Damascus ..... The *Stave* is the Interpreter of the Law .... ; and the *nobles of the people*

are those who come to dig the *Well* with the staves with which the *Stave* ordained that they should walk in all the age of wickedness . . . . . .

From the evidence of the *pesharim* themselves we can gather that the commentators worked on three basic assumptions, namely (1) that the words of the sacred books they were commenting on were full of mysteries revealed by God; (2) that these same mysteries referred to the history of their community; (3) that the interpretation of these mysteries was revealed to the Teacher of Righteousness and to other authorized interpreters who came after him. These points will become clear from the citations given here.

> *And the Lord answered and said to me, "Write down the vision and make it plain upon tablets, that he who reads may read it speedily* (Hab 2:2). . . . And God told Habakkuk to write down that which would happen to the final generation, but he did not make known to him when time would come to an end. And as for that which He said, *That he who read may read it speedily* , interpreted this concerns the Teacher of Righteousness, to whom God made known all the mysteries of the words of His servants the Prophets. *For there shall be yet another vision concerning the appointed time. It shall tell of the end and shall not lie* (Hab 2:3a). Interpreted, this means that the final age shall be prolonged, and shall exceed all that the Prophets have said: for the mysteries of God are astounding. *If it tarries, wait for it, for it shall surely come and shall not be late* (Hab 2:3b). Interpreted, this concerns the men of truth who keep the Law, whose hands shall not be slackened in the service of truth when the final age is prolonged. For all the ages of God reach their appointed end as He determines for them in the mysteries of His wisdom.
> . . . . *But the righteous shall live by his faith* (Hab 2:4b). Interpreted, this concerns all those who observe the Law in the House of Judah, whom God will deliver from the House of Judgment because of their suffering and

because of their faith in the Teacher of Righteousness. (1QpHab 7:1-8:1).

Behold the nations and see, marvel and be astonished; for I accomplish a deed in your days but you will not believe it when told (Hab 1:5). [Interpreted, this concerns] those who were unfaithful together with the Liar, in that they [did] not [listen to the word received by] the Teacher of Righteousness from the mouth of the Lord. And it concerns the unfaithful of the New [Covenant] in that they have not believed in the Covenant of God [and have profaned] His holy Name. And likewise this saying is to be interpreted [as concerning those who] will be unfaithful at the end of the days. They will not believe when they hear all that [is to happen to] the final generation from the Priest [in whose heart] God set [understanding] that he might interpret all the words of His servants the Prophets, through whom He foretold all that would happen to His people and [His land]. (1QpHab2:1-10).

The *pesher* on Nahum mentions Demetrius king of Greece (probably Demetrius III, about 88 B.C.) and "the furious young lion" (probably Alexander Jannaeus, 103-76 B.C.) who introduced the abominable practice of crucifixion into Judaea:

And chokes prey for its lionesses; and it fills its caves with prey and its dens with victims (Nahum 2:12-2-b). Interpreted, this concerns the furious young lion (who executes revenge) on those who seek smooth things and hangs men alive, (a thing never done) formerly in Israel. Because of a man hanged alive on (the) tree, he proclaims, *"Behold I am against you, says the Lord of Hosts"* (Nahum 2:13) (4QpNah 1:1-9).

The *pesher* on Ps 37 (4QpPs[a] also known as 4Q171) interprets the psalm as speaking of the sect and its enemies, of the Teacher of Righteousness and of the future:

But those who wait for the Lord shall possess the land (Ps 37:9b). Interpreted, this is the congregation of His elect who do His will. *A little while and the wicked shall be no more* .... (v. 10). Interpreted, this concerns all the wicked. At the end of the forty years they shall be blotted out and not an (evil) man shall be found on the earth. *But the humble shall possess the land....* (v. 11). Interpreted, this concerns (the congregation of the Poor who shall accept the season of penance and shall be delivered from all the snares (of Satan ....).

"The congregation of the poor" is a title given to itself by the community. It recurs in the exposition of v. 22: "... *Truly, those whom He blesses shall possess the land* ...". Interpreted, this concerns the congregation of the Poor, who (shall possess the portion of all ... They shall possess the High Mountain of Israel (for ever), and shall enjoy everlasting delights in his Sanctuary ... ". The word "man" of v. 23 is taken to refer to the Teacher of Righteousness: "*The (steps of man* — or: "*of the Man*") *are confirmed by the Lord* ......" Interpreted, this concerns the Priest, the Teacher of (Righteousness ... whom) He established to build for Himself the congregation of ....." (text broken).

In 4QpIsa^a^ (=4Q161) Isa 11:1 is interpreted messianically:

> "*And there shall go forth a rod from the stem of Jesse* ... (Interpreted, this concerns the Branch) of David who shall arise at the end (of days)... God will uphold him with (the spirit of might, and will give him) a throne of glory and a crown of (holiness) and many-coloured garments .... (He will put a sceptre) in his hand and he shall rule over all the (nations) .....".

In a *pesher* on Isa 54:11 (4QpIsa^d^ = 4Q164) the text is understood of the founders of the sect and the community itself:

> "*Behold, I will set your stones in antimony.* (Interpreted, this saying concerns).... all Israel sought thee according to Thy command. *And I will lay your foundations with sapphires.* Interpreted, this concerns the Priests and the people who laid the foundations of the Council of the

> Community ... the congregation of His elect (shall spar-
> kle) like a sapphire among stones."

These examples should give the reader an idea of the form and content of these *pesharim*. With regard to its approach to the sacred text, the *pesher* method could be compared with rabbinic midrash. The two have much in common, and the term *midrash* itself occurs, as we have seen already (above pp. 44-46) in the sense of "study" and "interpretation." While admitting the strong resemblances between the Qumran *pesher* method and rabbinic midrash, it is best not to press the point. What they have in common can be explained by the view of the sacred text inherited by both from an earlier generation. Each of the two groups, the Qumran community and the Pharisaic-Rabbinic tradition, articulated this in different, even if in similar manners, the former in their *pesharim*, the latter in rabbinic midrash.

The basic meaning of the common Semitic word *pesher* is "to loose," "to untie" — *solvere* in Latin. From this comes a derived meaning of "solution," "interpretation," e.g. the interpretation of dreams, of omens, and such like. The term is used in the Book of Daniel in the sense of the interpretation of dreams, of the mysteries revealed by God to Daniel. The interpretation of the sacred text given in the *pesharim* is somewhat in the tradition of the Book of Daniel. The mysteries are implanted by God in the Scriptures; the interpretation of these mysteries was revealed to the Teacher of Righteousness and his rightful successors.

As to date to be assigned to the Qumran *pesharim*, there are two schools of thought. Since most, if not all, of the manuscripts containing *pesher*-type material are extant in a single copy, and this of a later period of the community's history, J.T. Milik believes that they might be ephemeral compositions preserved in the author's own copy and are to be connected with the exposition of the Bible given in the sect's meeting for worship. There is, however, the other view that the works are basically very old and may take us back to an approach to Scripture found already in the Book of Daniel.

ii. The Genesis Apocryphon (1 QapGen).

This text from cave 1 contains an imaginative rewriting of part of the biblical account of Genesis. The text, which is imperfectly preserved, begins with the account of the miraculous birth of Noah to Bathenosh. Her husband Lamech suspects that the child is not his but is rather the result of Bathenosh's intercourse with an angel. To verify the true situation, Lamech sends his father, Methusaleh, to visit Enoch, Lamech's grandfather, "to learn surely all things from him. For he (i.e. Enoch) was beloved, and he shared the lot (of the Holy ones = angels), who taught him all things" (col. 2, 20). Methusaleh ran to Enoch, his father, going through the length of the Land of Parvain — some mythical, far-distant country (cf. 2 Chron 3:6), probably believed to be the site of Paradise to which Enoch was transported. The main part of the text (col. 19-22) is a paraphrase of Gen 12-15. Sometimes it is almost a direct translation of the Hebrew into Aramaic, at other times it has extensive embellishment.

The work does not fit neatly into any known literary genre. It is best not to classify it either as targum or midrash of the rabbinic type. It is a form of a re-written Bible, and in this is similar to the *Book of Jubilees*. The date of the original composition and its relationship to the Qumran community are matters of debate. Our present text was written about 50 B.C. — A.D. 50. One view is that the original is not much older than 50 B.C., although some scholars consider it was composed in the second century B.C. Since it has no specifically sectarian teaching or language, some believe it was not composed by a member of the Qumran community. Such a conclusion is not necessary: the Qumran monks may well have been capable of more than one approach to the scriptures.

iii. The Ages of Creation (4Q180).

From the fragment of this work preserved in Qumran we can deduce that it is related to the concepts we find in *Jubilees* and in sections of *1 Enoch*. It is presented in the fragment as concerning "the ages made by God," and "the order of the creation of man from Noah to Abraham, until he begot Isaac: ten (weeks of years)". The whole work may have been divided into 70 weeks of years. The only clearly intelligible part of the text deals with the sin of the angels (Gen 6:1-4): ".... the interpretation concerns Azazel and the angels who (came to the daughters of men; and) they bore to them giants."

iv. The Blessings of Jacob (4QpatBless).

The published fragment contains a messianic, *pesher*-like interpretation of the blessing of Judah of Gen 49:10:

> *The sceptre shall not depart from the tribe of Judah* ....
> Whenever Israel rules there shall (not) fail to be a descendant of David upon the throne. For the *ruler's staff* is the Covenant of kingship, (and the clans) of Israel are the *feet*, until the Messiah of *Righteousness comes*, the Branch of David. For to him and to his seed was granted the Covenant of kingship over his people for everlasting generations ......

v. The Testament of Amram (4QAmram).

This has already been considered above under "Testament Literature" (above pp. 153). It merits listing here also by reason of its subject matter and the mention made in it of the chief Angel of Darkness, Melchiresha (Hebrew for "The Angel of Evil") seen by Amram in his vision. This same demon is mentioned in another Qumran text in which he is cursed (see below, p. 153) and has as a heavenly counterpart Melchizedek, mentioned in a text we shall examine later in this section.

vi. The Words of Moses (1Q22).

This text has been studied above under "Testament Literature."

vii. The Vision of Samuel (4Q160).

Only a small section of this badly mutilated text conveys sense. It concerns a vision Samuel is said to have had as a boy serving in the temple with Eli. He is asked by Eli to reveal it to him. It seems connected with 1 Sam 3:14-17.

viii. *The New Jerusalem.*

This is an Aramaic work with a description of the Jerusalem of the eschatological age, based on, or inspired by, Ezekiel chaps. 40-48 (cf. Revelation, chap. 21). The work must have been extremely popular as fragments of manuscripts of it have been found in five caves: 1Q32, 2Q24, cave 4, 5Q15 and 11QJN ar. The texts of caves 4 and 11 have not yet been published. In this text the visionary tells how an angel took him through the Holy City and made detailed measurements of it — the avenues, streets, houses, doors, rooms, etc. J.T. Milik notes that the Aramaic of the text is old, but somewhat more recent than that of Daniel. He also thinks that the author of the Greek New Testament Apocalypse may have known this Aramaic description of the New Jerusalem.

ix. *The Prayer of Nabonidus (4QPsDan ar^{ac}).*

This text is very closely related to Daniel chapter 4. The text of Daniel recounts the healing of Nebuchadnezzar king of Babylon from madness. In the Qumran text, however, the account is of the healing of Nabunai (=Nabonidus, last king of Babylon) from a grievous illness through the prayers of a Jewish exorcist. The text opens as follows:

> The words of the prayer uttered by Nabunai king of Babylon ... (when he was afflicted) with an evil ulcer in Teiman by decree of the (Most High God). I was afflicted (with an evil ulcer) for seven years ... and an exorcist pardoned my sins. He was a Jew from among the (children of the exile of Judah...).

This piece is strictly speaking not a *pesher*, nor an interpretation of Daniel 4. Rather does it belong to the body of literature concerning the Jews in exile which has also provided material for the first part of the Book of Daniel (chaps. 1-6).

x. Pseudo-Daniel (4QPsDan A^a or 4Q243; or 4Q246).
The contents of this Aramaic fragment were revealed by
J.T. Milik at a lecture at Harvard in 1972, and a tentative
English translation supplied by him. It was later studied by
J. Fitzmyer and a new English translation of part of it
published together with the original Aramaic text. The text
is of an apocalyptic nature. It speaks of distress to come
upon the earth, of the rule of enemies, which however is to
be shortlived and which is to last only "until there arises the
people of God." There are also references to the "king of
Assyria" and to "Egypt." There is a divergence of opinion as
to whether the text should be interpreted historically or
eschatologically . The fragment is sometimes referred to as
the "Son of God" text since one of the chief characters is
designated as "Son of God." J.T. Milik believes that by this
title the Seleucid King Alexander Balas (150-145 B.C.) is
intended. J. Fitzmyer prefers to see reference to a Jewish
king. The birth of this personage is thus described (in G.
Vermes' translation):

> . . . he shall be great on earth . . . will make . . . and will
> serve (him). . . great. . . he shall be called and by his
> name shall he be designated. He shall be proclaimed son
> of God and they shall call him son of the Most High. Like
> a shooting star of a vision, so shall be their kingdom.
> They shall reign for some years on the earth and trample
> everything. One nation shall trample on another nation
> and one province on another province until the people of
> God shall rise and all will cease from the sword.

The date of the original composition was probably the last
third of the first century B.C.

xi. Midrash on the Last Days (4QFlor, or 4Q174).
This is a collection of texts from 2 Samuel and the Psalter,
to which citations from a few other books of the Bible are
added. They are interpreted in *pesher* fashion. In this exposition the Community of Qumran is identified with the
temple, and the coming of the two Messiahs (the Branch of

David and the Interpreter of the Law) seen as foretold in prophecy.

> [*I will appoint a place for my people Israel* ...] (2 Sam 7:10). This is the House which [He will build for them in the] last days, as it is written in the book of Moses, *In the sanctuary which Thy hands have established, O Lord, the Lord shall reign for ever and ever (Exod. 15:17-18).* This is the House into which [the unclean shall] never [enter, nor the uncircumcised,] nor the Ammonite, nor the Moabite, nor the half-breed, nor the foreigner, nor the stranger; for there shall my Holy Ones be. ... He has commanded that a Sanctuary of men be built for Himself, that there they may send up, like the smoke of incense, the works of the Law.
>
> And concerning His words to David ....., *I [will be] his father and he shall be my son* (2 Sam 7:14). He is the Branch of David who shall arise with the Interpreter of the Law [to rule] in Zion [at the end] of time. As it is written, *I will raise up the tent of David that is fallen* (Amos 9:11). That is to say, the fallen *tent of David* is he who shall arise to save Israel. Explanation [in Hebrew: *midrash*] of *How blessed is the man who does not walk in the counsel of the wicked* (Ps 1:1). Interpreted, this saying [concerns] those who turn aside from the way [of the people]....
>
> [*Why*] *do the nations* [*rage*] ... *against the Lord and against* [*His Messiah*]? (Ps 2:1). Interpreted, this saying concerns [the kings of the nations] who shall [rage against] the elect of Israel in the last days. This shall be the time of the trial to come...

xii. A Messianic Anthology (4QTestim or 4Q175).

This is a collection of biblical texts which appear to contain the messianic expectations of the Qumran community. First we have two texts from Deuteronomy (5:28-29; 18:18-19) on the need to fear God always and on the advent of the Prophet like Moses. The second is an extract from the prophecy of Balaam (Num 24:15-17) on the Royal

Messiah. The third is a blessing of the levites (from Deut 32:9-11), and probably taken as an implicit promise of the Priestly Messiah. The document ends with a text from the Book of Joshua (Jos 6:26) which is interpreted by a citation from the *Psalms of Joshua*, a non-canonical work originating in the Qumran sect.

xiii. Words of Consolation (Tanḥumim: 4QTanḥumim or 4Q176).

This text contains a citation from Ps 79 (vv. 2-3), ten separate excerpts from Second Isaiah, and Zech 13:19. Some of the excerpts are followed by *pesher*-type comments which are too fragmentary to yield sense.

xiv. Catenae (4QCatena^(a,b) or 4Q177, 182, 183).

In these documents we have chains of texts from the Bible, some of them followed by pesher-type commentary. The comments are again too fragmentary to yield much sense, but some make reference to the community and events in its history. The presence of the following biblical texts has been identified in these catenae: Deut 7:15; Ezek 20:32; Hos 5:8; Isa 37:30, 32:7; Ps 11:1, 12:1; Isa 22:13; Ps 12:7; 13:2-3, 5; Ezek 25:8; Jer 4:4; 18:18, Ps 6:2-3; Joel 2:30; Ps 16:3; Nahum 2:11; Ps 17:1. We cannot say what purpose these catenae served.

xv. The Heavenly Prince Melchizedek (11QMelch).

This document is put together from thirteen fragments from cave 11. It takes the form of an eschatological midrash on certain key-texts, principally Isa 61:1 on the proclamation of freedom to the captives. The eschatological liberation is taken as being part of the general restoration of property in the Jubilee year as found in Lev 25:13, cited at the beginning of the present incomplete text. The heavenly Deliverer is called Melchizedek. He is presented as identical with the archangel Michael and is called the head of the "sons of Heaven" or the "gods of Justice." He is even called in the Hebrew text *elohim* and *el*, words ordinarily meaning "God" but in this context, as sometimes elsewhere, used in the sense of "judge." In this text Melchizedek presides over the final judgment condemning the Prince of Demons, here called Belial, Satan and the Prince of Darkness. In other Qumran texts he is called Melchiresha (see no. v, p. 149 above). Melchiresha in Hebrew means "The King of Wickedness," of which Melchizedek, "The King of Justice" is the exact counterpart. Since neither Genesis 14 nor Ps 110 is quoted or referred to in this text, it i, possible that the name Melchizedek has been chosen simply as contrast to Melchiresha, and without any intended reference to the mysterious personality of Genesis 14 and Ps 110.

> . . . And concerning that which He said, in [*this*] *year of Jubilee* [*each of you shall return to his property* (Lev. 25:13); and likewise, *And this is the manner of release:*] *every creditor shall release that which he has lent* [*to his neighbor. He shall not exact it of his neighbour and his brother*], *for God's release* [*has been proclaimed*] (Deut. 15:2). [And it will be proclaimed at] the end of days concerning the captives as [He said, *To proclaim liberty to the captives* (Isa. 61:1). Its interpretation is that He] will assign them to the Sons of Heaven and to the inheritance of Melkizedek; f[or He will cast] their [lot] amid the po[rtions of Melkize]dek, who will return them there and will proclaim to them liberty, forgiving them [the wrongdoings] of all their iniquities.
>
> EL (*god*) *will judge the peoples* (Psalm 7:7-8). As for that which he s[aid, *How long will you*] *judge unjustly and show partiality to the wicked? Selah* (Psalm 82:2), its interpretation concerns Satan and the spirits of his lot [who] rebelled by turning away from the precepts of God to... And Melkizedek will avenge the vengeance of the judgements of God...and he will drag [them from the hand of] Satan and from the hand of all the sp[irits of] his [lot]. And all the 'gods [of Justice'] will come to his aid [to] attend to the de[struction] of Satan. And *the height is...all the sons of God...this...* This is the day of [Peace/Salvation] concerning which [God] spoke [through Isa]iah the prophet, who said, [*How*] *beautiful*

upon the mountains are the feet of the messenger who proclaims peace, who brings good news, who proclaims salvation, who says to Zion: Your ELOHIM [reigns] (Isa, 52.7). Its interpretation: *the mountains* are the prophets ...and *the messenger* is the Anointed one of the spirit, concerning whom Dan[iel] said, [*Until an anointed one, a prince* (Dan. 9:25)] ... [And he *who*] *brings* [*news*], *who proclaims* [*salvation*]: it is concerning him that it is written ... [*To comfort all who mourn, to grant to those who mourn in Zion*] (Isa. 61:2-3). *To comfort* [*those who mourn*: its interpretation], to make them understand all the ages of t[ime]... In truth...will turn away from Satan...

xvi. *An Essene Edition of the Book of Sirach.*

The Book of Sirach is commented on by R.A.F. MacKenzie in volume 19 of this series. One curious feature of the text history of the book is that while we know fairly precisely when the original Hebrew text was composed (about 180 B.C.) and when and by whom it was translated into Greek (in or soon after 132 B.C. by Sirach's own grandson), we do not know precisely the genesis of the present Greek, Syriac and Latin versions of this work. To begin with, we have two Greek versions, the one presenting an expanded text. And one, or probably both these Greek versions, were made from Hebrew originals. The Syriac version, made from a Hebrew original, also presents an expanded text. So too does the Old Latin (*Vetus Latina*) version taken over as part of the Vulgate since Jerome did not translate this work into Latin (not reckoning it canonical) even though the Hebrew text was still in circulation in his day. The expanded Latin text, we may add, is not a direct rendering of any single known Greek manuscript. Hebrew texts of about two thirds of the book were retrieved towards the end of the last century. Five manuscripts (A,B,C,D,E) of the 11th and 12th centuries were found in the Geniza of Old Cairo. The fragments of the Hebrew text of Ben Sira found at Qumran, cave 1 (1st cent. A.D.) and Masada (1st cent. B.C.) confirm the genuine character of the Geniza texts, although these were copied much later.

The original text of Ben Sira contained a conservative position regarding retribution, without mention of an afterlife. One of the features of the expanded text is inclusion of such a reference. The following examples will illustrate this point; the additions are noted by italics: — 6:4: "For a wicked soul shall destroy him that has it and makes him to be a joy to his enemies, *and shall lead him into the lot of the wicked.*" 6:22(23): "For the wisdom of doctrine is according to her name, and she is not manifest to many. *But with them to whom she is known, she continues even to the sight of God.*" 15:5: "*In the midst of the assembly ("of the Church" in the Old Latin version) she (i.e. Wisdom) shall open his mouth, and shall fill him with the spirit of wisdom and understanding, and shall clothe him with a robe of glory.*" In 21:10 (11) the short text, given in the RSV, reads: "The way of sinners is smoothly paved with stones, but at its end is the pit of Hades." Unless Sirach has changed his stance on Sheol (see R.A.F. MacKenzie's note) the reference intended by Hades in this text is to Sheol as the end of life, not as a place of punishment. The expanded text as found in the Old Latin is different. There the ending becomes: "and in their end is hell, *and darkness and pains.*" 24:9(14) in the short text reads: "From eternity, in the beginning, he created me (i.e. Wisdom), and for eternity I shall not cease to exist" (RSV). In the Old Latin the ending becomes: "*and unto the world to come I shall not cease to be.*" 24:22 (30): "*Those who work with my help shall not sin. Those who explain me (i.e. Wisdom) shall have life everlasting.*"

An explanation of the expanded text of Sirach is called for. One explanation is that Sirach's writing became a very popular one, and was used in circles that had passed beyond his conservative theology of retribution and the afterlife. In such circles the original Hebrew was updated, either by marginal glosses or insertions into the text, and reference made to divine visitation after death, to a judgment, and such like. Such an expanded Hebrew text, circulating together with the original shorter one, can explain the variant expanded versions. In 1951, in a doctoral dissertation on the matter presented to the Pontifical Biblical Commission in Rome, Conleth Kearns, O.P., put forward the thesis that the origin of the expanded text is to be sought in Essene circles and originated there about 76 — 50 B.C. There are those who would say that this position has been confirmed by the Qumran finds.

4. HYMNS, PRAYERS AND LITURGICAL TEXTS.

Hymns, prayers and liturgical texts are found within a number of compositions of the Qumran community. In this section, however, we study only these genres having complete texts to themselves.

i. The Hymns (1QH).

The Hymn (in Hebrew *Hodayoth*) Scroll from cave 1 consists of 18 columns of text, with hymnic compositions, not separated from one another by space or heading. For this reason, the number of hymns originally intended is uncertain. The hymns are songs of praise or thanksgiving, spoken or sung by an individual. It is a matter of debate whether this "I" stands really for an individual or for the community, and how the distribution of hymns is to be made between individual and collective songs of praise. It is also uncertain whether all the hymns were composed by the same author. Some scholars believe that all the hymns were composed by the Teacher of Righteousness himself, the founder of the community. Others think that the hymns of the individual, as distinct from the collective ones, are from him. Whatever of these questions, the hymns contain deep religious feeling and express some of the central beliefs of the Qumran community.

The very first hymn is in praise of God the creator (1QH 1:7-11):

By thy wisdom [all things exist from] eternity,
and before creating them Thou knewest their works for ever and ever.

[Nothing] is done [without Thee]
And nothing is known unless Thou desire it.
Thou hast created all the spirits
[and hast established a statute] and law for all their works.
Thou hast spread out the heavens for Thy glory
and hast [appointed] all [their hosts] according to Thy will;
the mighty winds according to their laws
before they became angels [of holiness]
... and eternal spirits in their dominions ....
All things [exist] according to [Thy will]
and without Thee nothing is done (1QH 1:20; see also 1QS 11:11).

This all powerful God is both creator and master of good
and evil (1QH 15:13-19):

> I know that the inclination of every spirit
>   [is in Thy hand];
> Thou didst establish [all] its [ways] before ever creating it,
>   and how can any man change Thy words?
> Thou alone didst [create] the just
>   and establish him from the womb
>   for the time of goodwill,
> that he might hearken to Thy Covenant
>   and walk in all (Thy ways),
> and that [Thou mightest show Thyself great] to him
>   in the multitude of Thy mercies,
> and enlarge his straitened soul to eternal salvation,
>   to perpetual and unfailing peace
> Thou wilt raise up his glory
>   from among flesh.
>
> But the wicked Thou didst create
>   for [the time] of Thy [wrath],
> Thou didst vow them from the womb
>   to the Day of Massacre,
>   for they walk in the way which is not good.
> They have despised [Thy Covenant]
>   and their souls have loathed Thy [truth];

> they have taken no delight in all Thy commandments
> and have chosen that which Thou hatest.

In this same hymn he goes on to confess (1 QH 16:11-12):

> And I know that man is not righteous
>   except through Thee,
> and therefore I implore Thee
>   by the spirit which Thou hast given [me]
>   to perfect Thy [favours] to Thy servant [for ever],
> purifying me by Thy Holy Spirit,
>   and drawing me near to Thee by Thy grace
>   according to the abundance of Thy mercies.

This same belief and prayer is given greater length in another hymn (1QH 4:29-33):

> But what is flesh [to be worthy] of this?
> What is a creature of clay
>   for such great marvels to be done,
>   whereas he is in iniquity from the womb
>   and in guilty unfaithfulness until his old age?
> Righteousness, I know, is not of man,
>   nor is perfection of way of the son of man:
> to the Most High God belong all righteous deeds.
> The way of man is not established
>   except by the spirit which God created for him
>   to make perfect a way for the children of men,
> that all His creatures might know
>   the might of his power,
> and the abundance of his mercies,
>   towards all the sons of His grace
> (literally "sons of his good pleasure").

The members of the religious community enjoyed the company of the angels. This fundamental belief is thus expressed in another hymn (1QH 6:12-14):

> For Thou wilt bring Thy glorious [salvation]
>   to all the men of Thy Council,
>   to those who share a common lot
>   with the Angels of the Face.

And among them there shall be no mediator to [invoke Thee]
and no messenger [to make] reply.

ii. A Lamentation (4QapLam: or 4Q179).

In this text, preserved in several fragments, we have a
lamentation inspired by the biblical Book of Lamentations,
but quite distinct from it.

iii. Apocryphal Psalms (11QPs).

This Psalm Scroll from Qumran cave 11, edited in 1962
by J.A. Sanders, contains 42 of our canonical psalms and
together with these some apocryphal psalms and other
poetic pieces as well as a prose piece on David's compositions. The biblical psalms are not in their canonical
sequence and the other non-biblical poetic compositions are
intermingled with them. The manuscript itself, on paleo-
graphical grounds, is assigned to the first half of the first
century A.D. The date of the individual pieces, of course,
must each be determined on its own merits.

Of the four apocryphal psalms one (Ps 151 A,B) was
already known (although in a variant form) from the Greek
Septuagint translation and Latin rendering; two others
(Syriac Pss II and III, 11QPs[a] 154 and 11QPs[a] 155 respectively) existed in a Syriac translation, and the fourth is
related to the Greek version of Sirach 51:13-19, 30. Ps 151 is
on the election of David. It appears to combine two original
psalms, the amalgam already existing in Hebrew before
being translated into Greek. The apocryphal psalm, Syriac
II, is a hymn praising divine wisdom. The first editor of the
Qumran text believes that it might be proto-Essenian, or
Hasidic, from the period of the separation of the dissident
group. (Portions reproduced below p. 183.) The other psalm,
Syriac III, has little or nothing Essenian or proto-Essenian
about it. (See below, p.184.) A further non-canonical psalm
of the manuscript (11QPs[a]Plea), entitled "Plea for Deliverance" by the editor, is more rabbinical than Essene in its
language and concepts, even speaking of an "evil inclination" (line 15). (See below, p.184.) The text related to Sirach 51 is

a hymn in praise of wisdom. There is also a new, acrostic, psalm (11QPs[a] Zion) called by the editor "Apostrophe to Zion" (below p. 184f); then a hymn to the creator (11QPs[a] Creat), and finally the prose text on the number of David's Poems, which reads as follows:

> **27** David son of Jesse was wise and brilliant like the light of the sun; (he was) a scribe, intelligent and perfect in all his ways before God and men.
>
> YHWH gave him an intelligent and brilliant spirit and he wrote 3,600 psalms and 364 songs to sing before the altar for the daily perpetual sacrifice, for all the days of the year; and 52 songs for the Sabbath offerings; and 30 songs for the New Moons, for Feast days and for the Day of Atonement.
>
> In all, the songs which he uttered were 446, and 4 songs to make music on behalf of those stricken (by evil spirits).
>
> In all, they were 4,050.
>
> All these he uttered through prophecy which was given him from before the Most High.

iv. *The Blessings (1QSb).*

In this text we have a series of liturgical blessings which have been preserved as a second appendix to the Community Rule; (the first appendix is the Messianic Rule, considered above.) These blessings may have been intended for use in the messianic age of the future, although it is possible that they were actually used during a liturgy in anticipation of the messianic age. The blessings appear to be for a liturgy at which the new eschatological community will be inaugurated. The blessings are for (1) the faithful, (2) the high priest (possibly the Priestly Messiah), (3) the priests in general, (4) the prince of the congregation (possibly the Davidic Messiah). The blessings are to be recited by the Master or Guardian of the community. They are thus introduced respectively:

> (1) Words of blessing. The master shall bless them that fear [God and do] His will, that keep His command-

ments, and hold fast to His holy [Covenent], and walk perfectly [in all the ways of] His [truth]; whom He has chosen for an eternal Covenant which shall endure for ever.

(2) *(Introduction to blessing of the High Priest has been lost.).*

(3) Words of blessing. The M[aster shall bless] the sons of Zadok the Priests, whom God has chosen to confirm His Covenant for [ever, and to inquire] into all His precepts in the Midst of His people, and to instruct them as He commanded: who have established [His Covenant] on truth and watched over all His laws with righteousness and walked according to the way of His choice.

(4) The Master shall bless the Prince of the Congregation .... and shall renew for him the Covenant of the Community that he may establish the kingdom of His people for ever, [that he may judge the poor with righteousness and] dispense justice with [equity to the oppressed] of the land, and that he may walk perfectly before Him in all the ways [of truth], and that he may establish His holy Covenant at the time of the affliction of those who seek God.

v. The Words of the Heavenly Lights (4QDib Ham; or 4Q504-506).

In this text we have liturgical prayers for recitation on various days of the week. The texts on which they are preserved in Qumran were written about 150 B.C., indicating that the liturgical piece may well be pre-Essene or proto-Essene. We shall return to the text again (below pp. 178-181).

vi. A liturgical Prayer, possibly of Covenant Renewal (1Q34^{bis}).

This badly preserved text refers to the renewal of the Covenant and may have been part of the Pentecost liturgy. It speaks of creation, of man's rejection of God and of Covenant Renewal.

> .... we shall praise Thy name for ever [and ever]. For this hast Thou created us...
>
> But the seed of man did not understand all that Thou

caused them to inherit; they did not discern Thee in all Thy words and wickedly turned aside from every one. . . .

But in the time of Thy goodwill Thou didst choose for Thyself a people. Thou didst remember Thy Covenant and [granted] that they should be set apart for Thyself from among all the peoples as a holy thing. And Thou didst renew for them Thy Covenant [founded] on a glorious vision and the words of Thy Holy Spirit), on the works of Thy hands and the writing of Thy Right Hand, that they might know the foundations of glory and the steps towards eternity.

vii. *The Triumph of Righteousness (1Q27).*

This text, put together from fragments, is included in a section on liturgical texts, and it may well have originally been part of a sermon. It might also have formed part of an apocalyptic writing. Its theme is one familiar from the Qumran texts: the struggle between good and evil.

viii. *The Wicked and the Holy (4Q181).*

This is the title given by Geza Vermes to a text which its first editor J.M. Allegro left untitled. It deals with the destinies of the wicked and the elect. The following section of it merits citation:

In conformity with their congregation of uncleanness, [they are to be separated] as a community of wickedness until [wickedness] ends. In accordance with the mercies of God, according to His goodness and wonderful glory, He caused some of the sons of the world to draw near [Him] . . . to be counted with Him in the com[munity of the g]ods as a congregation of holiness in service for eternal life and [sharing] the lot of his holy ones . . . . . each, according to his lot which He has cast for . . . for eternal life.

ix. *Liturgical Curses (4Q280-282; 286-287).*

One of these curses is on Melchiresha, one of Satan's names in Qumran texts. Some of the fragments correspond to portions of the *Community Rule* and *War Rule*.

x. The Angelic Liturgy (4QShirShab).

Finally, in this section we may mention this text known as the Song of the Sabbath Sacrifice. It is preserved in two fragments and describes the divine worship in heaven. One piece of this same work was also found in Masada (see above p.   ). In the first fragment, the seven chief angels utter their blessing, and the object of their blessings seems to be the community of the saints, both heavenly and earthly "...[all who walk] uprightly ...... all the gods [who exalt] true knowledge ... all who eagerly do his will ... all who glorify Him ...". The second fragment contains a description of the divine Throne-Chariot, and is proof of the interest in this in early and pre-Christian Jewish mysticism. We shall return to the point again (below pp.192f).

5. MISCELLANEOUS COMPOSITIONS

i. The Copper Scroll (3Q15).

This scroll was found in cave 3 during excavations in 1952. The text, in this instance, is written not on parchment but rather is engraved on copper. It is in post-biblical Mishnaic Hebrew. In this it is unlike the other Hebrew manuscripts from the Qumran caves. It is unlikely that this scroll is a product of the Qumran scriptorium. It was probably written elsewhere, and not by a trained scribe, and was deposited in the cave for safekeeping.

The scroll is a list of real or imaginary treasures, said to be deposited in over sixty hiding places. The caches are said to be gold, silver, aromatics and manuscripts. The amount said to have been deposited is immense. It has been reckoned that the total amount of precious metal must have added to sixty-five tons of silver and twenty-six tons of gold.

Scholars are divided as to whether the treasures in question were real or imaginary. Some opt for the latter alternative, chiefly by reason of the very size of the caches. The Copper Scroll, then, would be a work of fiction. Others think that the treasures were real, and represented either the fortunes of the Essene sect or of the temple of Jerusalem.

ii. *Horoscopes (4Q186).*

In Cave 4 of Qumran two texts with horoscopes have been identified, one in Hebrew, the other in Aramaic. Contrary to the regular practice, the Hebrew text runs from left to right, and together with the "square" Hebrew script, regular in later Old Testament times, it also uses the older "Phoenician" script as well as letters borrowed from the Greek alphabet. Special interest is shown in the person's physical features, with indication of his goodness or badness by the proportions of light and darkness in his make-up. It is not clear what purpose such horoscopes served. They may have been used to foretell the future in astrological fashion. But they may also have been no more than mere literary compositions, without astrological intent.

iii. *A Messianic Horoscope (4QMess ar).*

This Aramaic horoscope is concerned with the birth and physical features and the character of some important personage, most probably the Prince of the Congregation or the Royal Messiah. The following is a translation of a section of the imperfectly preserved text:

> . . . . And the hair will be red. And there will be lentils on . . . . and small birthmarks on his thigh . . . . . And then he will acquire wisdom and learn [understanding]. . . Counsel and prudence will be with him, and he will know the secrets of man. His wisdom will reach all the peoples, and he will know the secrets of all the living. And all their designs against him will come to nothing, and [his] rule over all the living will be great. His design [will succeed] for he is the Elect of God . . . .

5. PRAYER AND PRAYERS OF THE INTERTESTAMENTAL PERIOD

Prayer is as central to God's people as the covenant itself. Actual prayer-forms, both in verse and in prose, are recognized literary types which existed during the entire Old Testament period, from the pre-literary stage of the tradition onwards. The most commonly used forms are the prayer of intercession, the prayer of confession (which is a special type in itself) and the prayer of thanksgiving. Forms of such prayers may be either brief or long. Furthermore, the prayer form, like the speech or sermon, may be used as the vehicle for a particular theology, as in the case of Solomon's lengthy prayer at the dedication of the temple, as reported in 1 Kings 8:22-53, with its strong Deuteronomistic doctrine.

I. Early Post-Exilic Prayers

During the post-exilic period, from 500 to 200 B.C., the older prayers were brought together in collections for liturgical use, as in the Psalter, and new ones were composed. Even after earlier prayers had become regarded as sacred and canonical, new prayers continued to be composed for liturgical and extra-liturgical, and also most probably, private use.

Some prayers were composed as independent literary works and continued to circulate in this manner. Others, originally independent, could easily have come to be inserted into other works because it was believed they suited the context. Others still from the beginning seem to have been composed as parts of a larger composition. We have an example of the first kind in *The Prayer of Manasseh*. Examples of the second kind may be seen in Azariah's Prayer of Intercession in the Greek text of Daniel (Dan 3:25-45), the Song of the Three Children in Greek Daniel (Dan 3:52-90), probably in Daniel's Prayer of Petition in Dan 9:3-19, with its parallel in Baruch 1:15-3:8. Prayers such as that in Judith, chapter 9, were originally composed to stand as part of the larger work.

Some of the prayers we are considering may represent generally accepted Jewish theology and piety of their period. Others may be inspired to a greater or lesser degree by the beliefs and devotion of some particular group within Judaism, e.g. the Qumran covenanters (Essenes), the Pharisees. In some cases it is easy to discern the particular group within which a particular prayer was composed. In other cases, however, this is far from being the case, possibly for the reason that together with particular forms of devotion there remained alive in Israel a common liturgical tradition which continued to be unaffected by sectional or sectarian doctrine.

II. *Prayers from the Second and First Centuries B.C.*

A number of Jewish prayers seem to have been composed during the first half of the second century B.C. Some of those we find inserted in books of the Bible, whether in the Hebrew-Aramaic text, in deuterocanonical additions to this or in deuterocanonical books. We also find them in apocryphal works. It is also quite probable that no small amount of the prayers of the present Jewish *Prayer Book* originated in the second century, B.C., possibly even during the first part of it. We work at a disadvantage in the study of the prayers found in the Jewish *Prayer Book* firstly in that often we are able to trace their history in early and Mishnaic times only through their opening words and secondly by reason of the very real likelihood that the actual formulation of the prayer itself varied through the centuries. However, despite these limitations, the actual amount of information at our disposal has led specialists in this area to postulate the early date we have already noted for the origin of some of the prayers in question.

We are as yet in no position to state categorically what the central Jewish liturgical ritual and prayer formulae were during the second century B.C. and even during the century following. It is, however, quite conceivable that this was already fairly well established and that much of it passed over into the devotion of the different sections within Judaism when these arose.

We have already considered some of the prayers and hymns of the Qumran community. In the course of this chapter we shall have occasion to go over some of this material once again.

1.SIRACH'S PRAYER FOR THE DELIVERANCE OF ISRAEL (SIRACH 36:1-17) — ABOUT 180 B.C.

There is a noticeable lack of emotion in the 50 or 51 chapters that Jesus ben Sirach has given us in the book that bears his name, and, apart from this prayer, an equal lack of messianic expectations. The messianic content of the prayer in 36:1-17 is noteworthy likewise by reason of the very likely pre-Maccabean date of its origin. The piece ends with a petition to the Lord to listen to the prayer of his servants "according to the blessing of Aaron for thy people." By "the blessing of Aaron" the priestly blessing of Num 6:23-26 may be intended. Some scholars, however, prefer to see here a reference to the Eight Benedictions recited on the Day of Atonement by the High Priest according to the Mishnah (*Yoma* 7:1): "for the Law, for the Temple-Service, for the Thanksgiving, for the Forgiveness of Sin, and for the Temple separately, and for the Israelites separately, and for the priests separately; and for the rest a (general) prayer." The following is the full text of Ben Sirach's prayer:

36 Have mercy upon us, O Lord, the God of all, and look
   upon us,
 ² and cause the fear of thee to fall upon all the nations.
 ³ Lift up thy hand against foreign nations
   and let them see thy might.
 ⁴ As in us thou hast been sanctified before them,
   so in them be thou magnified before us;
 ⁵ and let them know thee, as we have known
   that there is no God but thee, O Lord.
 ⁶ Show signs anew, and work further wonders;
   make thy hand and thy right arm glorious.
 ⁷ Rouse thy anger and pour out thy wrath;
   destroy the adversary and wipe out the enemy.
 ⁸ Hasten the day, and remember the appointed time,
   and let people recount thy mighty deeds.
 ⁹ Let him who survives be consumed in the fiery wrath,
   and may those who harm thy people meet destruction.
¹⁰ Crush the heads of the rulers of the enemy,
   who say, "There is no one but ourselves."
¹¹ Gather all the tribes of Jacob, and give them their inheri
   tance, as at the beginning.
¹² Have mercy, O Lord, upon the people called by thy name,
   upon Israel, whom thou hast likened to a first-born son.
¹³ Have pity on the city of thy sanctuary,
   Jerusalem, the place of thy rest.
¹⁴ Fill Zion with the celebration of thy wondrous deeds,
   and the temple with thy glory.
¹⁵ Bear witness to those whom thou didst create in the beginning,
   and fulfil the prophecies spoken in thy name.
¹⁶ Reward those who wait for thee, and let thy prophets be
   found trustworthy.

17 Hearken, O Lord, to the prayer of thy servants,
according to the blessing of Aaron for thy people,
and all who are on the earth will know that thou art the
Lord, the God of the ages.

2. COMMUNAL LAMENT OF DANIEL 9:4-19; BARUCH 1:14—3:8.

It is quite possible that the passage in Daniel is not from
the same author as the rest of the work. The Hebrew is
different from that of the surrounding text and in this prayer
alone in the book is the sacred name "Yahweh" used. The
piece is probably an earlier, though post-exilic, liturgical
prayer, of the kind we find in Ezra 9:6-15, Neh 9:6(16)-37. Its
exact relationship to the text in Baruch is uncertain. Some
believe that the Baruch passage is directly dependent on
Daniel.

3. THE PRAYER OF AZARIAH (GREEK DANIEL 3:26-45).

This prayer is similar to that of Daniel 9:4-19. It is a
communal lament, even though placed on the lips of Azariah in the fiery furnace: the furnace into which Azariah,
with the other youths, was cast is but a symbol of the
purifying trials the people are undergoing. Both in this
prayer and in that of Daniel 9:4-19 the underlying theology
is that of the Book of Deuteronomy, theology not characteristic of the Book of Daniel itself. Although preserved only in
Greek, the prayer was probably composed originally in
Aramaic or Hebrew.

4. THE COMMUNAL LAMENT IN JUDITH, CHAPTER 9 — ABOUT 150 B.C.

The date to be assigned to the composition of the Book of
Judith is quite uncertain. Some would place it about 150
B.C. (as does John Craghan in volume 16 of this series).
Others would prefer a later date, say between 100 and 50

B.C. In chapter 9, the communal lament is an integral part of the work, even though it is presented as the personal prayer of Judith as she prepares herself to slay Holofernes. Judith's prayer makes direct reference to the sack of Shechem by Simeon (Gen 34), and also depends on the Book of Exodus, especially Exod chap. 15. The reader can consult John Craghan's commentary for further information.

5. THE PRAYER OF MANASSEH.

The Second Book of Chronicles (2 Chron 33:10-13) speaks of the repentance of the impious king Manasseh and of the prayer he addressed to God. Some verses later (vv. 18-19) we are told that the text of Manasseh's prayer may be found in two literary works: the Chronicles of the Kings of Judah and the Chronicles of the Seers. It was probably these references that led to the composition of the non-canonical text now known as "The Prayer (or "Repentance") of Manasseh." The text is preserved in the Greek Septuagint rendering, in the Latin Vulgate (as a non-canonical Appendix), in Syriac and other languages. The prayer was composed sometime during the intertestamental period (200 B.C. — A.D. 70). It has proved impossible to assign a more precise date. The piece is generally regarded as "a classic of penitential devotion" — "one of the finest pieces in the Apocrypha" in the words of Bruce Metzger. The text of this short apocryphal piece is given here in full.

> O Lord Almighty,
>   God of our fathers,
> of Abraham and Isaac and Jacob
>   and of their righteous posterity;
> 2 thou who hast made heaven and earth
>   with all their order,
> 3 who hast shackled the sea by thy
>   word of command,
>   who hast confined the deep
>   and sealed it with thy terrible and
>   glorious name;

⁴ at whom all things shudder,
    and tremble before thy power,
⁵ for thy glorious splendour cannot be
        borne,
    and the wrath of thy threat to sin-
        ners is irresistible;
⁶ yet immeasurable and unsearchable
        is thy promised mercy,
⁷ for thou art the Lord Most High,
    of great compassion, long-suffering,
        and very merciful,
    and repentest over the evils of men.
    Thou, O, Lord, according to thy great
        goodness
    hast promised repentance and for-
        giveness
    to those who have sinned against
        thee;
    and in the multitude of thy mercies
        thou hast appointed repentance for
            sinners,
        that they may be saved.
⁸ Therefore thou, O Lord, God of the
        righteous,
    hast not appointed repentance for
        the righteous.
    for Abraham and Isaac and Jacob,
        who did not sin against thee,
        but thou hast appointed repentance
        for me, who am a sinner.
⁹ For the sins I have committed are more in number than
        the sand of the sea; my transgressions are multiplied,
            O Lord, they are multiplied.
    I am unworthy to look up and see the height of heaven
        because of the multitude of my iniquities.
¹⁰ I am weighted down with many an iron fetter,
        so that I am rejected because of my sins,
        and I have no relief;
    for I have provoked thy wrath

and have done what is evil in thy sight,
   setting up abominations and multiplying offences.
[11] And now I bend the knee of my heart, beseeching thee for
   thy kindness.
[12] I have sinned, O Lord, I have sinned, and I know my
   transgressions.
[13] I earnestly beseech thee,
   forgive me, O Lord, forgive me!
   Do not destroy me with my transgressions!
Do not be angry with me for ever or lay up evil for me,
   do not condemn me to the depths of the earth.
For thou, O Lord, art the God of those who repent,
[14]   and in me thou wilt manifest thy goodness;
for, unworthy as I am, thou wilt save me in thy great
   mercy,
[15]   and I will praise thee continually all the days of my life.
For all the host of heaven sings thy praise,
   and thine is the glory for ever.
         Amen.

6. THE PRAYERS OF MORDECAI AND ESTHER (GREEK ESTHER 13;14)— SHORTLY BEFORE 114 B.C.

The Hebrew text of the Book of Esther leaves some questions unanswered and raises others. For instance it never mentions God and contains no prayer. It is probably to remedy these particular points that a prayer of Mordecai and another of Esther are introduced into the Greek rendering of the work. Some of these additions were probably made by a certain Lysimachus, an Alexandrian Jew who lived in Jerusalem and translated the Hebrew book of Esther into Greek about 114 B.C. as noted in the introduction to the section numbered Esth 11:1. Others were probably inserted later, either by Lysimachus or some one else.
   Mordecai's prayer (Greek Esther 13:9-17) contains elements that had by then become classical in Hebrew interces-

sion: God is called "Lord," "King" and "the Lord God of Abraham." He is the righteous God, who has created all things, has redeemed his people from Egypt, answers prayer and can save them in their present distress.

Esther in her prayer calls on God, Lord and King, to help her (Greek Esther 14:3-19). He took Israel out of the nations, and their ancestors from among them as an everlasting inheritance. She confesses her people's sin and calls on the Lord God of Abraham to save his people from the hands of evildoers.

7. THE PRAYER OF THE HIGH PRIEST SIMON (3 MACCABEES 2:2-20)— ABOUT 50 B.C.

Despite its title, 3 Maccabees does not deal with the Maccabees but with the plight of the Egyptian Jews under Ptolemy IV Philopator (221-203 B.C.). It was composed in Greek and in Alexandria, probably in the first century B.C., although some prefer a date in the first century A.D. The work tells how Ptolemy IV tried to enter the Holy of Holies in Jerusalem, but was miraculously repelled. This attempted profanation of the temple is the setting for the prayer of the High Priest Simon — most probably Simon II, son of Onias II and High Priest about 219—196 B.C. This, most probably, was also the High Priest praised so highly by Ben Sirach (Sirach chap. 50). Simon's prayer is in the classic Jewish form, after the pattern of Pss 105 and 106. It addresses God in terms of his power and his glory and speaks of the great deeds he has done in saving his people. The text of the prayer is as follows:

> **2** Then the high priest Simon, facing the sanctuary, bending his knees and extending his hands with calm dignity, prayed as follows: [2]"Lord, Lord, king of the heavens, and sovereign of all creation, holy among the holy ones, the only ruler, almighty, give attention to us who are suffering grievously from an impious and profane man, puffed up in his audacity and power. [3]For you,

the creator of all things and the governor of all, are a just Ruler, and you judge those who have done anything in insolence and arrogance. [4]You destroyed those who in the past committed injustice, among whom were even giants who trusted in their strength and boldness, whom you destroyed by bringing upon them a boundless flood. [5]You consumed with fire and sulphur the men of Sodom who acted arrogantly, who were notorious for their vices; and you made them an example to those who should come afterward. [6]You made known your mighty power by inflicting many and varied punishments on the audacious Pharaoh who had enslaved your holy people Israel. [7]And when he pursued them with chariots and a mass of troops, you overwhelmed him in the depths of the sea, but carried through safely those who had put their confidence in you, the Ruler over the whole creation. [8]And when they had seen works of your hands, they praised you, the Almighty. [9]You, O King, when you had created the boundless and immeasurable earth, chose this city and sanctified this place for your name, though you have no need of anything; and when you had glorified it by your magnificent manifestation, you made it a firm foundation for the glory of your great and honored name. [10]And because you love the house of Israel, you promised that if we should have reverses, and tribulation should overtake us, you would listen to our petition when we come to this place and pray. [11]And indeed you are faithful and true. [12]And because oftentimes when our fathers were oppressed you helped them in their humiliation and rescued them from great evils, [13]see now, O holy King, that because of our many and great sins we are crushed with suffering, subjected to our enemies, and overtaken by helplessness. [14]In our downfall this audacious and profane man undertakes to violate the holy place on earth dedicated to your glorious name. [15]For your dwelling, the heaven of heavens, is unapproachable by man. [16]But because you graciously bestowed your glory upon your people Israel, you sanctified this place. [17]Do not punish

us for the defilement committed by these men, or call us
to account for this profanation, lest the transgressors
boast in their wrath or exalt in the arrogance of their
tongue, saying, [18]"We have trampled down the house of
the sanctuary as offensive houses are trampled down.'
[19]Wipe away our sins and disperse our errors, and reveal
your mercy at this hour. [20]Speedily let your mercies overtake us, and put praises in the mouth of those who are
downcast and broken in spirit, and give us peace."

8. THE PRAYER OF THE PRIEST ELEAZAR (3 MACCABEES 6:2-15).

In the overall structure of 3 Maccabees, Eleazar the priest
prays after Ptolemy IV has ordered cruel and unusual punishments against the Jews in Egypt in a final effort to make
them forsake their religion. Eleazar is presented as "famous
among the priests of the country," i.e. of Egypt. He may
have been a priest of the Jewish temple at Leontopolis. Like
the preceding prayer of Simon, this one also is typically
Jewish in form and style, with a doxology and thanksgiving
for God's earlier interventions in Israel's favour. The reason
for God's expected intervention in the new crisis is from
sheer divine mercy, not any merit on Israel's part. The text
of the prayer is as follows:

> Then a certain Eleazar, famous among the priests of
> the country, who had attained a ripe old age and through-
> out his life had been adorned with every virtue, directed
> the elders around him to cease calling upon the holy God
> and prayed as follows: [2]"King of great power, Almighty
> God Most High, governing all creation with mercy, [3]look
> upon the descendants of Abraham, O Father, upon the
> children of the sainted Jacob, a people of your conse-
> crated portion who are perishing as foreigners in a for-
> eign land. [4]Pharaoh with his abundance of chariots, the
> former ruler of this Egypt, exalted with lawless insolence
> and boastful tongue, you destroyed together with his
> arrogant army by drowning them in the sea, manifesting

the light of your mercy upon the nation of Israel. ⁵Sennacherib exulting in his countless forces, oppressive king of the Assyrians, who had already gained control of the whole world by the spear and was lifted up against your holy city, speaking grievous words with boasting and insolence, you, O Lord, broke in pieces, showing your power to many nations. ⁶The three companions in Babylon who had voluntarily surrendered their lives to the flames so as not to serve vain things, you rescued unharmed, even to a hair, moistening the fiery furnace with dew and turning the flame against all their enemies. ⁷Daniel, who through envious slanders was cast down into the ground to lions as food for wild beasts, you brought up to the light unharmed. ⁸And Jonah, wasting away in the belly of a huge, sea-borne monster, you, Father, watched over and restored unharmed to all his family. ⁹And now, you who hate insolence, all-merciful and protector of all, reveal yourself quickly to those of the nation of Israel — who are being outrageously treated by the abominable and lawless Gentiles. ¹⁰Even if our lives have become entangled in impieties in our exile, rescue us from the hand of the enemy, and destroy us, Lord, by whatever fate you choose. ¹¹Let not the vain-minded praise their vanities at the destruction of your beloved people, saying, 'Not even their god has rescued them.' ¹²But you, O Eternal One, who have all might and all power, watch over us now and have mercy upon us who by the senseless insolence of the lawless are being deprived of life in the manner of traitors. ¹³And let the Gentiles cower today in fear of your invincible might, O honored One, who have power to save the nation of Jacob. ¹⁴The whole throng of infants and their parents entreat you with tears. ¹⁵Let it be shown to all the Gentiles that you are with us, O Lord, and have not turned your face from us; but just as you have said, 'Not even when they were in the land of their enemies did I neglect them,' so accomplish it, O Lord."

9. THE SONG OF THE THREE YOUTHS (GREEK DANIEL 3:51-90).

This addition in the Greek text of Daniel is a litany-psalm, similar to Ps 136. It is composed of two parts, vv. 52-56 and 57-90, distinguished from one another both by content and the form of the responsory. The first part is a hymn in praise of the God of Israel who resides in his holy temple, that is in heaven. The second part, known as the *Benedicite* from the opening word of the Latin translation, calls on all created beings, in the order of their creation, to praise the Lord. The date of composition of the pieces is quite uncertain.

10. PROTOTYPE OF THE *SHEMONEH ESREH* IN THE HEBREW TEXT OF SIRACH 51:12 — EARLY 2ND CENTURY B.C.

In a first appendix to the book of Sirach we have an individual psalm of thanksgiving (Sirach 51:1-12). This is followed by an acrostic in which Ben Sirach speaks of his personal experience. In between these in the Hebrew Text, but not in the Greek or in any other translation (Syriac or Latin), we have a prayer, reminiscent of Ps 117:1-4 and especially of Ps 136.

Since the prayer is found only in the Hebrew and not in the Greek, and since it fits its present context badly , it is generally accepted today that it was not part of the original work and that it is not from the pen of Ben Sirach. However, it is also generally agreed that the prayer is very old and most probably pre-Maccabean (before 170 B.C.) since it prays for the sons of Zadok who no longer held the office of high priest after Menelaus had purchased that honour for himself in 172 B.C.

This prayer is especially interesting because of its close similarities with the classical Jewish prayer known as *Shemoneh Esreh* or "The Eighteen Benedictions"(see below, pp. 199-203). It is given here in the translation of S. Schechter and

C. Taylor, with slight modernization of the endings in
"....eth."

> **12** O give thanks unto the Lord for he is good, For his
> mercy endures for ever. [2]O give thanks unto the God of
> praises, For his mercy endures for ever. [3]O give thanks
> unto him that keeps Israel, For his mercy endures for ever
> [4]O give thanks unto him that forms all, For his mercy
> endures for ever [5]O give thanks unto him that redeems
> Israel, For his mercy endures for ever. [6]O give thanks
> unto him that gathers the outcasts of Israel, For his mercy
> endures for ever. [7]O give thanks unto him that builds his
> city and his sanctuary, For his mercy endures for ever. [8]O
> give thanks unto him that makes the horn of the house of
> David to bud, for his mercy endures for ever. [9]O give
> thanks unto him that chose the sons of Zadok to be
> priests, For his mercy endures for ever. [10]O give thanks
> unto the Shield of Abraham, For his mercy endures for
> ever. [11]O give thanks unto the Rock of Isaac, For his
> mercy endures for ever. [12]O give thanks unto the Mighty
> One of Jacob, For his mercy endures for ever. [13]O give
> thanks unto him that chose Zion, For his mercy endures
> for ever. [14]O give thanks unto the King of the kings of
> kings, For his mercy endures for ever. [15]And he will lift up
> the horn of his people. A praise for all his saints; Even for
> the children of Israel, a people near unto him. Praise ye
> the Lord.

11. THE LITURGY OF THE HEAVENLY LIGHTS

Among the Qumran Scrolls there have been found several
fragments representing at least three manuscripts of a work
entitled "Words of the Heavenly Lights." The oldest of these
manuscripts has been dated to about 150 B.C., the next to
70-60 B.C. and the third to about A.D. 50. The earliest date
of the first manuscript and the absence from the work of
specifically sectarian ideas indicates that we are most probably in the presence of a work from the Hasidim of the

earliest and pre-Essene stage of Qumran literature. The work probably represents an aspect of the priestly liturgy, a liturgy which the Qumran community, the Sons of Zadok, had inherited.

The manuscripts appear to enshrine a liturgical rite. The mysterious title "The Words of the Heavenly Lights" has not yet been satisfactorily explained. The prayers and the hymns included in the composition, however, appear to have been intended for various days of the week. One of them mentions "the fourth day" (Wednesday) and appears to have been a prayer for use on this day. Another has as heading: "Hymns for the Sabbath Day." Before these hymns we have a long penitential prayer which can be presumed to have been intended for the preceding day, Friday. The entire text was probably part of a liturgy honouring the different days of the week and recalling the great events that occurred in each according to the creation narrative of Genesis or later Jewish tradition.

A liturgy having to do with light or the heavenly lights is associated with the priests, the sons of Levi, in a number of texts with levitical affiliations. Speaking of Aaron, the Book of Ecclesiasticus (Ben Sirach) 45:17 says: "In his commandments he (i.e. God) gave him authority in statutes and judgments, to teach Jacob his testimonies, and to enlighten Israel with his law." The author is thinking more of the contemporary priests, sons of Aaron, than of Moses' brother himself. In *The Testament of Levi* 4:3, speaking to his sons ("the sons of Levi") the patriarch says: "The light of knowledge shalt thou light up in Jacob, and as the sun shalt thou be to all the seed of Israel." And when writing of the Levitical or Priestly Messiah yet to come (*Test. Levi* 18:1-4), the same document speaks again in terms of light: "And his star shall arise in the heaven as of a king, lighting up the light of knowledge as the sun the day. And he shall be magnified in the world. And he shall remove all darkness from under heaven."

The fourth day was that on which the heavenly lights were created according to Genesis 1:14-19. It was the most important day of the calendar followed by the Qumran community, the day on which each of the three seasons of this calendar began, the day on which the feasts of Passover and Tabernacles, with its octave day, fell. The imperfectly preserved text of the "Liturgy of the heavenly lights" for this day is as follows (4Q504 DibHam^a col. VII) — (translation by author):

> Prayer of the Fourth Day. Remember, Lord ..... He (it?) has been sanctified in glory....(Face) to face you have been seen in our midst ... We have heard your holy words .... so that we might believe for ever. You have made a covenant with us at Horeb, with all these statutes and judgments .... good and holy....

In another fragment (folio 4) of the same work we read:

> These things we know because you have graciously given us a holy spirit. Have pity on us and recall not against us the iniquities of the forebears in all their evil behaviour. Redeem us and pardon our iniquity and our sin ..... a law which you have commanded through Moses ... a kingdom of priests and a holy nation...which you have chosen. Circumcise the foreskin of our heart .... strengthen our hearts to do .... to walk in your ways.

The following text (4Q504 DibHam^a, 8 recto) from the same liturgy may have been intended for Sunday:

> Recall, O Lord, ... you live for ever ..... Adam, our father, you formed in the likeness of your glory .... You breathed into his nostrils the breath of life, and with intelligence and knowledge you filled him ..... Over the Garden of Eden which you planted you gave him dominion ... and to walk in the land of glory ....

The following prayer was probably intended for Friday, a day dedicated to penance in Qumran; it occurs in the manuscript immediately before a piece entitled: "Hymns for the Sabbath Day," It reads as follows in G. Vermes' translation:

> 5 [they forsook] the fount of living waters and served a strange god in their land. Also, their land was ravaged

by their enemies; for Thy fury and the heat of Thy wrath overflowed, together with the fire of Thy jealousy, making of it a desert where no man came nor went. Yet notwithstanding all this, Thou didst not reject the seed of Jacob neither didst Thou cast away Israel to destruction, breaking Thy Covenant with them. For Thou alone art a living God and there is none beside Thee. Thou didst remember Thy Covenant, Thou who didst rescue us in the presence of all the nations, and didst not forsake us amid the nations.

For Thou hast shed Thy Holy Spirit upon us, bringing upon us Thy blessings, that we might seek Thee in our distress [and mur]mur (prayers) in the ordeal of Thy chastisement. We have entered into distress, have been [stri]cken and tried by the fury of the oppressor. For we also have tired God with our iniquity, we have wearied the Rock with [our] sins. [But] in order that we may profit, Thou has not wearied us who leadest [us] in the way in [which we must walk. But] we have not heeded . . .

6 [Thou hast taken away] all our transgressions and hast purified us of our sin for Thine own sake. Thine, Thine is righteousness, O Lord, for it is Thou who hast done all this! Now, on the day when our heart is humble, we expiate our iniquity and the iniquity of our fathers, together with our unfaithfulness and rebellion. We have not rejected Thy trials and scourges; our soul has not despised them to the point of breaking Thy Covenant despite all the distress of our soul. For Thou, who has sent our enemies against us, strengthenest our heart that we may recount Thy mighty deeds to everlasting generations. We pray Thee O Lord, since Thou workest marvels from everlasting to everlasting, to let Thine anger and wrath turn away from us. Look on [our affliction] and trouble and distress, and deliver Thy people Israel [from all] the lands, near and far, [to which Thou hast banished them], every man who is inscribed in the Book of life . . . serve Thee and give thanks to [Thy holy Name] . . .

7 who deliverest us from all distress. Amen! [Amen!]

12. SOLOMON'S PRAYER FOR WISDOM (WISDOM CHAP. 9) — ABOUT 50 B.C.

Although the text has been excellently treated of by James Reese in another volume in this series (vol. 20, pp. 100-106), I believe that "Solomon's" prayer for wisdom merits inclusion here. It is the prayer not merely of the king of Israel but of everyman, called by divine design to be king in his own domain. The wisdom of which the text speaks was with God at the creation of the universe and only by each individual's participation in this divine wisdom can he or she come to understand the meaning of the created order and the purpose of human existence. The text is as follows:

9 "O God of my fathers and Lord of mercy, who hast made all things by thy word, 2and by thy wisdom hast formed man, to have dominion over the creatures thou has made, 3and rule the world in holiness and righteousness, and pronounce judgment in uprightness of soul, 4give me the wisdom that sits by thy throne, and do not reject me from among thy servants. 5For I am thy slave and the son of thy maidservant, a man who is weak and short-lived, with little understanding of judgment and laws; 6for even if one is perfect among the sons of men, yet without the wisdom that comes from thee he will be regarded as nothing. 7Thou hast chosen me to be king of thy people and to be judge over thy sons and daughters. 8Thou hast given command to build a temple on thy holy mountain, and an altar in the city of thy habitation, a copy of the holy tent which thou didst prepare from the beginning. 9With thee is wisdom, who knows thy works and was present when thou didst make the world, and who understands what is pleasing in thy sight and what is right according to thy commandments. 10Send her forth from the holy heavens, and from the throne of thy glory send her, that she may be with me and toil, and that I may learn what is pleasing to thee. 11For she knows and understands all things, and she will guide me wisely in my actions and guard me with her glory. 12Then my works will be acceptable, and I shall judge thy people justly,

III. Psalms and Canticles

1. PSALMS AND CANTICLES IN THE QUMRAN TEXTS (11Q PS)

In the chapter dealing with the literature of the Qumran community we have given brief consideration to the contents of the Psalms Scroll from Qumran Cave 11. Since the non-canonical psalms and canticles of this scroll have little or nothing of the peculiar features of the Qumran sect about them, we may in this section consider these same compositions from the point of view of the continuity of psalm composition in Israel. The apocryphal psalm known as Syriac II(11QPs^a 154) may well be a very old composition. As we noted above, the first editor of the Qumran text thinks that it might in fact be proto-Essenian or Hasidic, from the early days of the Qumran community. It is a hymn in praise of wisdom, and extols meditation on the Law:

> For to make known the glory of the Lord
>   is Wisdom given,
> And for recounting his many deeds
>   she is revealed to man:
> To make known to simple folk his might,
>   and to explain to simple folk his greatness,
> Those far from her gates,
>   those who stray from her portals.
>   . . . .
> From the gates of the righteous is heard her voice,
>   and from the assembly of the pious her song.
> When they eat with satiety she is cited,
>   and when they drink in community together,
> Their meditation is on the Law of the Most High,
>   their words on making known his might.
> How far from the wicked is her word,
>   from all haughty men to know her (11QPs^a 154, 5-8, 12-15).

Psalm Syriac III(11QPs^{a}155) has nothing sectarian about it. It could command assent from any of the various forms of Judaism during the intertestamental period.

> May the Judge of Truth remove from me the rewards of evil.
> O Lord, judge me not according to my sins;
>> for no man living is righteous before thee.
> Grant me understanding, O Lord, in thy Law,
>> and teach me thine ordinances,
> That many may hear of thy deeds
>> and peoples may honour thy glory.
> Remember me and forget me not,
>> and lead me not into situations too hard for me.

In a further non-canonical psalm (known as 11QPs^{a}Plea) we have a touching plea for deliverance, with a prayer to be spared from the power of "the evil inclination": a designation for the power of evil within humans which became common in rabbinic literature. The psalm opens as follows:

> Surely a maggot cannot praise thee
>> nor a grave-worm recount thy loving kindness.
> But the living can praise thee,
>> (even) all those who stumble can laud thee (11QPs^{a}Plea 1-2).

In a later passage we read:

> When I remember thy might my heart is brave,
>> and upon thy mercies do I lean.
> Forgive my sin, O Lord,
>> and purify me from my iniquity.
> Vouchsafe me a spirit of faith and knowledge,
>> and let me not be dishonoured in ruin.
> Let not Satan rule over me,
>> nor an unclean spirit;
> Neither let pain nor the evil inclination
>> take possession of my bones. (11QPs^{a}Plea 12-16).

Tender love for the Holy City is manifest in the acrostic psalm known as "Apostrophe to Zion" (11QPs^a Zion). It opens as follows:

> I remember thee for blessing, O Zion;
>> with all my might I have loved thee.
>> May thy memory be blessed for ever!

Great is the hope, O Zion:
   that peace and thy longed-for salvation will come.
Generation after generation will dwell in thee
   and generations of saints will be thy splendour:
Those who yearn for the day of thy salvation
   that they may rejoice in the greatness of thy glory.
On (the) abundance of thy glory they are nourished
   and in thy splendid squares will they toddle.
The merits of thy prophets will thou remember,
   and in the deeds of thy pious ones wilt thou glory
                    (11QPs^aZion 1-6).

2. THE PSALMS OF SOLOMON

Some hundred years after the foundation of the Qumran community, and possibly after the composition of the non-canonical psalms just now considered, another group of psalms was composed in Palestine. These are the compositions known as *The Psalms of Solomon*, a collection of eighteen psalms composed in the style of the poems found in the canonical Psalter. Themes running through the *Psalms of Solomon* are the need to praise God for his goodness, the righteousness of God, God's continuous help, the destruction of sinners, life for those who fear the Lord. Frequent references are made to "the pious" (the Hebrew original of which would be *Hasidim*) and sinners.

The position of the *Psalms of Solomon* on the question of the afterlife is not quite clear. Some scholars have seen references to the resurrection in some passages, e.g. Pss Sol. 3:16 (12), 15:15 (13), to which others add Pss Sol. 13:9, 14:2-3, 6. Ps. Sol. 3 says that the sinner falls and rises no more; he shall not be remembered when the righteous is visited. The Psalm thus ends: "But they that fear the Lord shall rise to life eternal. And their life (shall be) in the light of the Lord, and shall come to an end no more." Unfortunately, we do not have sufficient context in this to warrant the conclusion that there is reference to the resurrection rather than eternal life without belief in a resurrection. Ps. Sol. 15 speaks of the reward of the righteous and the punishment which awaits the wicked. The psalm ends with the following words: "And sinners shall perish for ever in the day of the Lord's judgment, when God visits the earth with his judgment. But they that fear the Lord shall find mercy therein, and shall live by the compassion of their God; but sinners shall perish for ever" (15:14 (12)f.) Once again, the statement is too general to warrant the conclusion that the reference is to the resurrection. There may be a reference to eternal life in Ps. Sol. 14:2, 6-7 (5, 9-10): "The pious of the Lord shall live by it (i.e. the Law) for ever; the Paradise of the Lord, the trees of life, are his pious ones; their planting is rooted for ever.... Therefore their inheritance (i.e. of sinners and transgressors) is Sheol and darkness and destruction, and they shall not be found in the day when the righteous obtain mercy; but the pious of the Lord shall inherit life in gladness."

Two well-known psalms of the Pss of Sol. (Pss 17, 18) speak of the advent of the Messiah. The most important of these is Ps. Sol. 17. Part of this is a historical review. In Ps Sol. 17:6-8 (5f.) there appears to be an attack on the Hasmonean dynasty, which had reached an all-time low when the Romans were called into the scene of Palestinian politics. The passage runs:

> Thou, O Lord, didst choose David (to be) king over Israel, and swaredst to him touching his seed that never should his kingdom fail before thee. But, for our sins, sinners rose up against us; they assailed us and thrust us out; what thou hast not promised to them, they took away from us with violence. They in no wise glorified Thy honourable name; they set a (worldly) monarchy in place of (that which was) their excellency; they laid waste the throne of David in tumultuous arrogance.

In vv. 23-30 (21-27) we have a prayer for the coming of the Messiah, followed by a partial description of his work:

23 21 Behold, O Lord, and raise up unto them their king, the
son of David,
At the time in the which Thou seest, O God, that he
may reign over Israel Thy servant.

24 22 And gird him with strength, that he may shatter
unrighteous rulers,

25   And that he may purge Jerusalem from nations that
trample (her) down to destruction.

23   Wisely, righteously he shall thrust out sinners from
(the) inheritance.
He shall destroy the pride of the sinner as a potter's vessel.

24   With a rod of iron he shall break in pieces all their substance,

27   He shall destroy the godless nations with the word of his
mouth;

25   At his rebuke nations shall flee before him,
And he shall reprove sinners for the thoughts of their
heart.

28 26 And he shall gather together a holy people, whom he shall
lead in righteousness,
And he shall judge the tribes of the people that has been
sanctified by the Lord his God.

29 27 And he shall not suffer unrighteousness to lodge any
more in their midst,
Nor shall there dwell with them any man that knoweth
wickedness,

30   For he shall know them, that they are all sons of their God.

A little further on we read (vv. 32-41 (30-36):

32 30 And he shall have the heathen nations to serve him under
his yoke;
And he shall glorify the Lord in a place to be seen of (?)
all the earth;

33   And he shall purge Jerusalem, making it holy as of old:

34 31 So that nations shall come from the ends of the earth to
see his glory,
Bringing as gifts her sons who had fainted,

35   And to see the glory of the Lord, wherewith God hath
glorified her.

32   And he (shall be) a righteous king, taught of God, over them,

36 And there shall be no unrighteousness in his days in their midst,
        For all shall be holy and their king the anointed of the Lord.

37 33 For he shall not put his trust in horse and rider and bow,
        Nor shall he multiply for himself gold and silver for war,
        Nor shall he gather confidence from (?) a multitude (?) for the day of battle.

38 34 The Lord Himself is his king, the hope of him that is mighty through (his) hope in God.
        All nations (shall be) in fear before him,

39 35 For he will smite the earth with the word of his mouth for ever.

40 He will bless the people of the Lord with wisdom and gladness,

41 36 And he himself (will be) pure from sin, so that he may rule a great people.
        He will rebuke rulers, and remove sinners by the might of his word;

It is generally agreed that the Pss of Sol. were composed about 50 B.C., between Pompey's conquest of Palestine in 65 B.C. and some time after he had been slain at Mount Cassius near the Pelusium [Egypt] in 48 B.C. Reference to this latter event is seen in Ps. Sol 2:30:31: "And I had not long to wait before God showed me the insolent one slain on the mountains of Egypt. Esteemed of less account than the least, on land and sea; his body [,too,] borne hither and thither on the billows with such insolence, with none to bury [him], because He had rejected him with dishonour."

There may have been more than one author for these psalms. Some scholars have made attempts to associate the composition with one or other of the known religious groups in Palestine, e.g. Pharisees, Hasidim, Essenes, Qumran community. The evidence of the Psalms themselves scarcely permits so definite a conclusion. It seems, however, that the Psalms were composed in Palestine and most probably in Hebrew.

IV. Early Jewish Mystical Testimonies

The term "mysticism" is one more of the words which require explanation before being used. In general one may say that mysticism, Jewish as well as Christian, may be defined as that aspect of religious experience in which one's mind is in direct encounter with God — or at least is believed to be in such a direct relationship.

The best-known form of Jewish mysticism is that known as the *kabbalah*, which flourished from the twelfth century onwards. The literature of this form of Jewish religious experience is, of course, much too recent for consideration in this work devoted to the intertestamental period. However, Jewish esoteric teachings and mystical practices can be traced back beyond this to early Christian and, indeed, pre-Christian times. The mystical teaching of the earlier period is found in the *hekaloth* literature. Two early forms of this Jewish mysticism are known as the *Ma'aseh Bereshith* and *Ma'aseh Merkabah*. The *hekaloth* (the Hebrew word is the plural form of *hekal*, meaning "Hall," or "palace") are the heavenly halls or palaces, the upper world which extends throughout the seven palaces in the *araboth*, i.e. the uppermost of the seven heavens. The mystics devoted to this form of union with God were interested in what existed and occurred in these palaces: the angelic hosts that fill the *hekaloth*, but especially the Throne-Chariot (in Hebrew *merkabah*), the rivers of fire that flow in front of the Chariot, various details of the Chariot, but above all else were they interested in the vision of the One enthroned on the Chariot (cf. Ezek 1:26). This form of mysticism is known principally through the *hekaloth* literature which was composed mostly during the third to the sixth centuries.

During the early Christian centuries the two principal forms of Jewish mysticism were the *Ma'aseh Merkabah* (literally: "The work of the Chariot"), and *Ma'aseh Bereshith* (literally: "The work of Creation"). Both were concerned with esoteric mystic speculations, the former on the divine chariot as described in the Book of Ezekiel (Ezek 1,

10), the latter on the creation of the world as narrated in the opening chapter of Genesis. Even though the word *merkabah*, the Hebrew for "chariot," is not used in the Book of Ezekiel at all, in substance these chapters do speak of God enthroned above a form of throne which can be described as a chariot and which was so called in Judaism before the Christian era.

Although the Rabbis tended to frown on all forms of mysticism, there is evidence for the existence of *Merkabah* mysticism in the first and second centuries of our era, and this even among rabbis held in high repute as pillars of the reorganization after the fall of Jerusalem. Evidence for the practice of both *Merkabah* and *Bereshith* forms of mysti-cism can be gathered from the Mishnah which records a prohibition to have the Creation narrative expounded to less than two persons and the Chariot narrative (*Merkabah*) even to one on his own, unless he was a scholar versed in the subject (Mishnah, *Hagigah* 2:1). It was also considered inadvisable to use the *Merkabah* sections of Ezekiel in the synagogue as readings from the Prophets, although this caution was not universally followed (Mishnah, *Megillah* 4:10).

However, despite its anti-mystical bias rabbinic tradition itself records that some of its most revered founders were devotees of mysticism, notably R. Johanan ben Zakkai, Bar Azzai, Ben Zoma, Elisha ben Avuhah, Aher and Rabbi Akiba. These are reported as having entered Paradise and of having had a mystical experience of the Godhead. Of these, Rabbi Akiba alone is said to have remained unscathed (literally); of the others, one died, another was smitten (mentally), another forsook Judaism, apparently for Gnosticism.

It is now recognized by scholars that these forms of mysticism with the special interest in Genesis 1 and the Chariot sections of Ezekiel existed before the Christian era. This holds especially for the interest in the texts of Ezekiel: the figures, the living animals and wonders surrounding the divine throne, and the throne itself. It may well have existed a full two hundred years before our era. In fact it may partly explain the interest shown by the apocalyptic writers in otherworldly journeys and the marvels of the extraterrestrial realms. Writing on this matter, Gershom Scholem, the leading authority on Jewish mysticism, says: "Not only the revelation of the end of time and its awesome terrors, but also the structure of the hidden world and its inhabitants: heaven, the Garden of Eden, and Gehinnom, angels and evil spirits, and the fate of the souls of this hidden world ......, revelations concerning the Throne of Glory and its Occupant ..... establish a link between this (Apocalyptic) literature and the much later writers concerning the *ma'aseh bereshith* and the *ma'aseh merkabah.*"

It may be possible to trace the origins of this *Merkabah* mysticism or interest as far back as the Book of Chronicles, since in 1 Chron 28:18 *merkabah* seems to be used in a technical sense. In this text David is reported as having given to Solomon the plan for the golden *chariot* (*merkabah*) of the cherubim that spread their wings over the ark of the covenant of the Lord. The author of Chronicles is thinking of the Ark of the Covenant and may have described it as the golden chariot under the influence of Ezekiel (Ezek 1:10; 43:3-4).

The first clear use of the term "chariot" (*merkabah*) in a technical sense is found in the Book of Ben Sirach (Sirach 49:8), composed about 180 B.C., and translated into Greek by his grandson over half a century later. In this particular text there is a slight difference between the Greek and the extant Hebrew text. The Hebrew, which can be presumed to be the original, is thus rendered by the *New American Bible*: "Ezekiel beheld the vision and described the different creatures of the chariot." The Hebrew word *znym*, rendered as "creatures" in NAB, literally means "kinds", "sorts", or in later Hebrew "qualities." The rendering given probably coresponds to the meaning originally intended, i.e. the living creatures of Ezekiel's vision, although it might include as well the other peculiarities of the divine throne as described by Ezekiel, i.e. the fire, the wheels, etc., all of which were objects of keen interest for devotees of *Merkabah* mysticism.

In a text from Qumran we have further clear evidence that this form of mysticism existed before the Christian era. The text in question is 4QShirShabb and has been summarily described above (p. 163) in the chapter dealing with the literature of Qumran. It is part of a composite text, the first section of which is entitled "The Song of the Sabbath Sacrifice." In this, seven heavenly princes, i.e. angels, are said to utter blessings on certain groups or individuals, apparently of the Qumran Community. The prayer formula probably derives from the belief that the heavenly, angelic, liturgy and that of the Community on earth were at one and united in divine praise. Interest in the heavenly Chariot, then, could have been intended as an aid to the devotion of the members of the community.

The manuscript with this text is dated paleographically to about 50 B.C. The peculiar theology and terminology it uses has led scholars to regard it as the product of the community itself, in which authority was held by the Sons of Zadok. It may be that *merkabah* interest and mysticism were handed down in priestly circles, from those surrounding Ezekiel, through those of Ben Sirach's day to the Sons of Zadok of Qumran. I here reproduce the Qumran text, in the translation of Geza Vermes which differs somewhat from that of the piece's first editor John Strugnell.

THE DIVINE THRONE-CHARIOT

...the [ministers] of the Glorious Face in the abode of [the gods] of knowledge fall down before Him, [and the Cheru]bim utter blessings. And as they rise up, there is a divine small voice ... and loud praise; (there is) a divine [small] voice as they fold their wings.

The Cherubim bless the image of the Throne-Chariot above the firmament, and they praise the [majesty] of the fiery firmament beneath the seat of His glory. And between the turning wheels, Angels of Holiness come and go, as it were a fiery vision of most holy spirits; and about them (flow) seeming rivulets of fire, like gleaming bronze, a radiance of many gorgeous colours, of marvellous pigments magnificently mingled.

The spirits of the Living God move perpetually with the glory of the wonderful Chariot. The small voice of blessing accompanies the tumult as they depart, and on the path of their return they worship the Holy One. Ascending, they rise marvellously; settling, they [stay] still. The sound of joyful praise is silenced and there is a small voice of blessing in all the camp of God. And a voice of praise [resounds] from the midst of all their divisions in [worship of] ... and each one in his place, all their numbered ones sing hymns of praise.

V. The Prayers of Rabbinic Judaism

The present Jewish liturgy contains certain rites and prayers the origins of which most probably go back to Maccabean or even pre-Maccabean times. Although these have come down to us through transmission within Rabbinic Judaism, in origin they would, in that case, ante-date the emergence of the sects and thus probably represent mainstream Judaism, even though some Pharisaic or rabbinic elements were probably added in the course of transmission.

Our earliest true Jewish Prayer Books date only from the ninth and tenth century, i.e. the *Seder Rav Amram Gaon* (9th cent.) and the *Siddur Saadiah Gaon* (10th cent.). The actual beginnings of the *Prayer Book*, however, are somewhat earlier than this, but are still reasonably late since the writing of Prayer Books was permitted only after the completion of the Talmud in the seventh century or so. During the talmudic and the earlier period it was understood that prayer was to be recited by heart, not from a book. The writing down of the texts of blessings and prayers was regarded as forbidden. A rabbinic dictum expressed it thus: "Writers of blessings are (like) those who burn the Torah."

Fortunately for the purposes of dating, earlier Jewish sources such as the Mishnah and Tosefta contain the opening words of well-known prayers, which are still found as the incipits of prayers in the Jewish *Prayer Book*. This fact would seem to indicate that such prayers have been faithfully transmitted, at least with regard to essentials, down through the centuries. The most one can expect with regard to fidelity in this question must concern the essentials, since earlier rabbinic tradition did not believe in the verbatim repetition of prayer formulae. The formula could vary while the essential elements were retained. In fact it was not only permitted, but even advised, to vary the formula used in addressing God.

In this section we consider some of the traditional Jewish prayers that either originated in intertestamental times or at least are based on prayers and prayer practice from that same age.

1. THE *SHEMA'* AND ITS ACCOMPANYING BENEDICTIONS.

The *Shema'* is Israel's profession of faith par excellence. It is a Credo rather than a prayer in the proper sense. It gets its name from its opening word: "Hear (O Israel) . . . .", and consists of the following three biblical texts: Deuteronomy 6:4-9 (Hear, O Israel", on the divine unity), Deuteronomy 11:13-21 (on the rewards and punishments following obedience and disobedience to God's commands; on inscribing the commandments on the doorposts), and Numbers 15:37-41 (on the wearing of tassels to remind one of the commandments). These central biblical texts were accompanied by Benedictions. In the present-day Jewish *Prayer Book* these are as follows: The opening words of the morning benedictions before the *Shema* are: "Who formest light . . . ." (*Yoṣer'or*) and "With abounding love. . . ." (*'Ahabah rabba*). The morning Benediction after it begins: "True and firm . . . ." (*'Emet we-yaṣṣib*). The evening Benedictions before the *Shema'* are: ("Who at Thy word bringest the evening twilight . . . ." (*Ma'arib 'arabim*) and "With everlasting love. . . ." (*'Ahabat 'olam*) and after it "True and everlasting. . . . ." (*'Emet we-'emunah*) and "Cause us to lie down . . . . ." (*Hashkibenu*).

The practice of reciting the *Shema'* probably goes back to

the mid-second century B.C. at least. The Nash Papyrus with the text of Deut 6:4-6 and the Ten Commandments dates from approximately 150 B.C. The Mishnah (*Tamid* 5:1) says that in the Temple (and hence before A.D. 70) all three portions of the *Shema'* were recited together with the Ten Commandments. The same Mishnah text also makes explicit reference to the Benediction *'Emet we-yassib* after the *Shema'* and to another Benediction recited before the *Shema'* which was later identified with *'Ahabah Rabba*. It was probably the recitation of the *Shema'* Josephus had in mind when he says (*Ant.* 4, 8, 13, §212) that Moses ordained that twice a day (when the day begins and when the hour of sleep comes on) the Jews should acknowledge before God the bounties he had bestowed on them in delivering them from Egypt.

As noted above, in the present-day Jewish *Prayer Book* seven Benedictions accompany the *Shema'*, the opening words of which have been given. The Mishnah (*Berakoth* 1:4), codified in its present form about A.D. 200, specifies that in the mornings one recited two Benedictions before the *Shema'* and one after it, and in the evenings two before and two after, and further (*Berakoth* 2:2; cf. *Tamid* 5:1) specifies that the Benediction after the *Shema'* is that beginning *'Emet wa-yassib* — the incipit of the prayer still used in this position in the Morning Service. Only four benedictions for the *Shema'* are required by the Mishnah text. It could well be that the present-day seven Benediction custom is the expansion of an earlier four (cf. Ps 119:164 — "seven times daily shall I praise you") and that the individual Benedictions have been somewhat expanded. Apart from this, however, the four Benedictions are probably in essence as they were about A.D. 200, and indeed perhaps in pre-Christian times.

We shall now consider the Benedictions separately.

The first Benediction is known as the *Yoṣer* or *Yoṣer 'or* ("Former of Light"). In the course of a study of the Synagogue liturgy in the first century Paul P. Levertoff maintains that probably the earliest form of the prayer was as follows:

> Blessed are thou, O Lord our God, King of the World, Former of Light and Creator of darkness, maker of peace and Creator of all things; who gives light in mercy to the earth and to those who live thereon, and in his goodness renews every day, continually, the work of creation. Let a new light shine over Zion and thy Messiah's light over us.

This, however, is a reconstruction. The form of the prayer in the present-day Jewish *Daily Prayer Book* is as follows (in Philip Birnbaum's translation):

> Blessed art thou, Lord, our God, King of the universe, who formest light and createst darkness, who makest peace and createst all things. In mercy thou givest light to the earth and to those who dwell on it; in thy goodness thou renewest the work of creation (in Hebrew: *ma'aseh bereshith*) every day, constantly. How great are thy works, O Lord! In wisdom thou hast made them all; the earth is full of thy creations. Thou alone, O King, hast ever been exalted, lauded and glorified and extolled from days of old. Eternal God, show us thy great mercy! Thou art Lord of our strength, our defending Stronghold, our saving Shield, our Protection.

The text of this blessing in the *Prayer Book* goes on for five more paragraphs and has all the appearance of having being expanded in transmission. Its closing words are:

> O cause a new light to shine upon Zion, and may we all be worthy soon to enjoy its brightness. Blessed art thou, O Lord, Creator of the Lights.

One interesting section of this prayer in the *Prayer Book*, and apparently inserted into its present position, is a text linking Isa 6:3 with Ezekiel 3:12 and the Chariot of Ezekiel. We have, thus, in this prayer a combination of the *ma'aseh Bereshith* with the *ma'aseh Merkabah*.

Speaking of the praises rendered by the heavenly angels, the prayer says:

They all open their mouth with holiness and purity, and song and melody, while they bless and praise, glorify and reverence, sanctify and acclaim:

The name of the great, mighty and revered God and King; holy is he. They all accept the rule of the kingdom of heaven, one from the other, granting permission to one another to hallow their creator. In serene spirit, with pure speech and sacred melody, they exclaim in unison and with reverence:
Holy, holy, holy, is the Lord of hosts;
The whole earth is full of his glory.
Then the celestial ofannim (cf. Ezekiel chap. 1, 3, 10; literally: "Wheels") and the holy beings (*hayyoth*; Ezekiel chaps. 1, 3, 10, 14; RSV: "living creatures), rising with a loud sound towards the Seraphim, respond and praise and say: Blessed be the glory of the Lord from his abode.

Although this is an insertion in its present context, it is a very old piece of Jewish liturgy, and shall be considered further at a later stage; (see below pp. 203-205).

The second prayer before the *Shema'* is known from its opening words as *'Ahabah Rabba*. It is a most beautiful prayer and very probably was recited in the first century B.C. in much the same form which it now has in the *Daily Prayer Book*. This runs as follows:

With a great love hast thou loved us, Lord our God; great and abundant mercy hast thou bestowed upon us. Our Father, Our King, for the sake of our forebears who trusted in thee, whom thou didst teach laws of life, be gracious to us and teach us likewise. Our Father, merciful Father, thou who art ever compassionate, have pity on us and inspire us to understand and discern, to perceive, learn and teach, to observe, do and fulfil gladly all the teachings of thy Torah. Enlighten our eyes in thy Torah; attach our heart to thy commandments; unite our heart to love and reverence thy name, so that we may never be put to shame. In thy holy, great and revered name we trust — may we thrill with joy over thy salvation. O bring us home in peace from the four corners of the earth, and make us walk upright to our land, for thou art the God who performs triumphs. Thou hast chosen us from all peoples and nations, and hast forever brought us near to thy truly great name, that we may eagerly praise and acclaim thy Oneness. Blessed art thou, O Lord, who hast graciously chosen thy people Israel.

The opening words of *'Emet we-yaṣṣib* ("True and constant"), the benediction recited after the *Shema'*, are found in the Mishnah (*Berakoth* 2:2; *Tamid* 5:1). Its earliest form may not have differed very much from that found in the present-day *Daily Prayer Book*, which is as follows:

True and certain, established and enduring, right and steadfast, beloved and precious, pleasant and sweet, revered and glorious, correct and acceptable, good and beautiful is this faith to us forever and ever. True it is that the eternal God is our King, the Stronghold of Jacob and our saving Shield. He exists throughout all generations; his name endures; his throne is firm; his kingdom and his truth are forever established. His words are living and enduring, faithful and precious, forever and for all eternity, as for our fathers so also for us, for our children and future generations, and for all generations of the seed of Israel his servants.

The second Benediction, the *Hashkibenu*, after the *Shema'* of the Evening Synagogue service, although possibly only later inserted into its present context, may well be an old prayer. The text of the Jewish *Prayer Book* (in P. Birnbaum's translation) is as follows:

Grant, Lord our God, that we lie down in peace, and that we rise again, O our King, to life. Spread over us thy shelter of peace, and direct us with good counsel of thy own. Save us for thy name's sake; shield us, and remove from us every enemy and pestilence, sword and famine and grief: remove the adversary from before us and from behind us; shelter us in the shadow of thy wings; for thou art our protecting and saving God; thou art indeed a gracious and merciful God and King. Guard thou our going out and our coming in, for life and peace, henceforth and forever. Blessed art thou, O Lord, who guardest thy people Israel forever.

By the second century A.D. the composition of the *Shema'* was already a matter of reflection. A tradition handed down in the name of R. Joshua ben Karha (about A.D. 140-165) said that in the *Shema'* Deut 6:4-9 with its command to love the Lord came before Deut 11:13.21 (with the emphasis on the commands) "so that a man may first take on him the yoke of the kingdom of heaven, and afterwards take on the yoke of the commandments" (Mishnah, *Berakoth* 2:2).

2. THE *SHEMONEH ESREH* OR THE EIGHTEEN BENEDICTIONS

The *Shemoneh Esreh* (literally in Hebrew: "The Eighteen"), the Eighteen Benedictions, is also known in Hebrew simply as *Hat-tephillah* — "The Prayer" — the Jewish prayer par excellence. Since it was recited standing it is also known in Hebrew as the *Amidah*. It had to be recited thrice daily by every Israelite, including women, slaves and children.

Jewish tradition maintains that the Eighteen Benedictions were arranged in their order in the time of Rabban Gamaliel (II) at Yabneh (cf. Babylonian Talmud, *Berakoth* 28b), thus giving us a date from the end of the first century A.D. Certain references to the fall of Jerusalem indicate that the Eighteen Blessings attained their present form after A.D. 70. It is quite clear, however, that by A.D. 70-100 the prayer was already known as "The Eighteen (Benedictions)", and that by then also the basic contents of the individual blessings were fixed. In fact we can say that in its essentials this prayer must be older than A.D. 70, and indeed that it pre-dates the Christian era. This position is corroborated by the similarities between the *Shemoneh Esreh* and the prayer in the Hebrew text of Sirach 51:12 which we have considered already (above pp. 177f).

There are two recensions of the Eighteen Blessings, the Babylonian and the Palestinian. In the former the number is actually nineteen, not eighteen, even though the prayer retains its original title. The anomaly is due to the interpolation of an extra number (actually a curse) in no. 12 "against the heretics", which included, but was not restricted to, Judaeo-Christians.

The Palestinian Recension has also this insertion but has retained the number 18 by omitting a specific prayer for the Messiah, still found in the other recension.

While both recensions are quite similar to one another, it is generally maintained that the Palestinian is the older, although not quite the same as that being used in the first century A.D. It is given here in Solomon Schechter's translation of the text found in the last century in the Cairo Geniza.

    I. Blessed art thou, O Lord,
        Our God and God of our fathers,
        God of Abraham, God of Isaac, and God of Jacob,
        Great, mighty, and awesome God,
        God Most High, creator of heaven and earth,
        Our shield and shield of our fathers,
        Our refuge in every generation.
        Blessed art thou, O Lord, shield of Abraham.

    II. Thou art mighty — humbling the haughty,
        Powerful — calling to judgment the arrogant,
        Eternal — preserving the dead;
        Causing the wind to blow and the dew to fall,
        Sustaining the living, resurrecting the dead —

    III. Thou art holy and thy name is awesome
        And there is no god beside thee.
        Blessed art thou, O Lord, the Holy God.

    IV. Graciously favour us, our Father, with understanding
        from thee,
        And discernment and insight out of thy Torah.

Blessed art thou, O Lord, gracious bestower of
understanding.

V. Turn us to thee, O Lord, and we shall return,
Restore our days as of old.
Blessed art thou, O Lord, who desires repentance.

VI. Forgive us, our Father, for we have sinned against thee.
Erase and blot out our transgressions from before thine eyes,
For thou art abundantly compassionate.
Blessed art thou, O Lord, who forgives readily .

VII. Behold our afflictions and defend our cause,
And redeem us for thy name's sake.
Blessed art thou, O Lord, Redeemer of Israel.

VIII. Heal us, O Lord our God, of the pain in our hearts,
Remove grief and sighing from us
And cause our wounds to be healed.
Blessed art thou, O Lord, who heals the sick of Israel his
people.

IX. Bless this year for us, O Lord our God,
And may its harvest be abundant.
Hasten the time of our deliverance.
Provide dew and rain for the earth
And satiate thy world from thy storehouses of goodness,
And bestow a blessing upon the work of our hands.
Blessed art thou, O Lord, who blesses the years.

X. Blow a blast upon the great *sofar* for our freedom,
And raise a banner for the ingathering of our exiles.
Blessed art thou, O Lord, who gathers the dispersed of his
people Israel.

XI. Restore our judges as of old,
And our leaders as in days of yore,
And reign over us — thou alone.
Blessed art thou, O Lord, Lover of justice.

XII. May there be no hope for the apostates,
      And speedily uproot the kingdom of arrogance in our
         own day.
      May the Nazarenes and the *minim* [sectarians] perish in
         an instant.
      May they be blotted out of the book of living,
      And not be written with the righteous.
      Blessed art thou, O Lord, who subdues the arrogant.

XIII. Show abundant compassion to the righteous converts,
      And give us a good reward together with those who do
         thy will.
      Blessed art thou, O Lord, Stay of the righteous.

XIV. Have compassion, O Lord our God, in thine abundant
         mercy,
      On Israel thy people,
      And on Jerusalem thy city,
      And on Zion, the abode of thy glory,
      And upon the royal seed of David, thy justly anointed.
      Blessed art thou, O Lord, God of David, Rebuilder of
         Jerusalem.

XV.   Hear, O Lord our God, the voice of our prayers,
      And have compassion upon us,
      For thou art a gracious and compassionate God.
      Blessed art thou, O Lord, who hears prayer.

XVI. May it be thy will, O Lord our God, to dwell in Zion.
      And may thy servants worship thee in Jerusalem.
      Blessed art thou, O Lord, for it is thou whom we worship
         in reverence.

XVII. We thank thee,
      Our God and God of our fathers,
      For all of the goodness, the lovingkindness, and the mercies
      With which thou has requited us, and our fathers before us.
      For when we say, 'our foot slips';
      Thy mercy, O Lord, holds us up.

Blessed art thou, O Lord, to whom it is good to give
thanks.

XVIII. Bestow thy peace
Upon Israel thy people,
And upon thy city,
And upon thine inheritance,
And bless us all, together.
Blessed art thou, O Lord, Maker of peace.

In the Babylonian Recension no. 14 reads much as in the Palestinian, but with a greater influence from the events of A.D. 70:

> And to Jerusalem, thy city, return with mercy and dwell in its midst as thou hast spoken; and build it soon in our days to be an everlasting building; and raise up quickly in its midst the throne of David. Blessed are thou, Lord, who buildest Jerusalem.

No. 15 in the Babylonian Recension is an explicit prayer for the advent of the Messiah. It reads:

> Cause the shoot of David to shoot forth quickly, and raise up his horn by thy salvation. For we wait on thy salvation all the day. Blessed art thou, Lord, who causeth the horn of salvation to shoot forth.

Although this text is absent from the Palestinian Recension it is very probable that it formed an original part of the *Shemoneh Esreh*: since in these Benedictions we find all the elements of Israel's future hope, it is only to be expected that they should also have contained an explicit prayer for the Messiah and for the messianic redemption.

3. THE *QEDUSHSHAH*.

The *Qedushshah* (the Hebrew for "Sanctification") is the angelic "sanctification" of the divine name. This sanctification has its roots in the theophanies of Isaiah and Ezekiel and the core of the prayer in question consists in the recitation of two verses from the biblical accounts of these theophanies, i.e. Isa 6:3 ("Holy, holy, holy, is the Lord of hosts;

the whole earth is full of his glory"), and Ezek 3:12 ("Blessed be the glory of the Lord from his place").

The present-day Jewish *Prayer Book* has three prayers which belong to the *Qedushshah* type, i.e. one found in the third of the Eighteen Benedictions, the other in the Benediction *Yoser* (the first Benediction before the recitation of the *Shema‘*) and the third known as the *Qedushshah de-Sidra*. From the tractate *Berakoth* 5, 9c of the Palestinian Talmud we have clear evidence for the existence of the first of these during the Talmudic period, even though the form of the *Qedushshah* being used then does not appear to correspond to those now in use. This does not mean that the second *Qedushshah*, i.e. that to the *Yoser* Benediction of the *Shema‘*, did not then exist. It most probably did, and possibly even earlier. In a text from the Tosefta (*Berakoth* 1,9) from the end of the Mishnaic period (and about A.D. 180) mention is also made of the *Qedushshah*, and in a context dealing with the Benedictions accompanying the recitation of the *Shema‘*. In the course of the discussion it is said:

> R. Judah (A.D. 135-210) used to respond together with him who pronounced the Benediction: "Holy, holy, holy, is the Lord of hosts; the whole earth is full of his glory," and "Blessed be the glory of the Lord out of his place."

Modern authorities on the subject are divided as to which of the two *Qedushshah*'s this refers, to that of the Eighteen Benedictions or to that accompanying the *Shema‘*. Joseph Heinemann thinks that there is reason to believe that *both* forms of the *Quedushshah* came into being during, or even before, the Mishnaic period (i.e. A.D. 1-200), the only question being to what extent either had been accepted as an integral part of the statutory worship in all places during this period.

We print here, in Birnbaum's translation, the text of these various *Qedushshah* prayers from the Jewish *Daily Prayer Book*.

i. *The Qedushshah to the Shema' Benediction Yoṣer.*

Be thou blessed, our Stronghold, our King, and Redeemer, Creator of holy beings; praised be thy name forever, our King, Creator of ministering angels, all of whom stand in the heights of the universe and reverently proclaim in unison, aloud, the words of the living God and everlasting King. All of them are beloved, all of them are pure, all of them are mighty; they all perform with awe and reverence the will of their Creator; they all open their mouth with holiness and purity, with song and melody, while they bless and praise, glorify and reverence, sanctify and acclaim—

The name of the great, mighty and revered God and King; holy is he. They all accept the rule of the kingdom of heaven, one from the other, granting permission to one another to hallow their Creator. In serene spirit, with pure speech and sacred melody, they all exclaim in unison and with reverence:

Holy, holy, holy is the Lord of hosts;
The whole earth is full of his glory.

Then the celestial ofannim and the holy beings, rising with a loud sound toward the seraphim, respond with praise and say:

Blessed be the glory of the Lord from his abode.

To the blessed God they offer melodies; to the King, the living and eternal God, they utter hymns and praises. Truly, he alone performs mighty acts and creates new things; he is a warrior who sows justice, produces triumphs, and creates healing. Revered in renown, Lord of wonders, in his goodness he renews the creation every day, constantly, as it is said. "He makes the great lights; truly, his mercy endures forever." O cause a new light to shine upon Zion, and may we all be worthy soon to enjoy its brightness. Blessed art thou, O Lord, Creator of the lights.

ii. The Qedushshah of the Eighteen Benedictions.

The third of the Eighteen Benedictions in the Palestinian Recension reads thus: "Thou art holy and thy name is awesome and there is no god beside. Blessed art thou, O Lord, the Holy God." The *Qedushshah* for this blessing is as follows:

> We sanctify thy name in this world even as they sanctify it in the highest heavens, as it is written by thy prophet: "They keep calling to one another:
>> Holy, holy, holy is the Lord of hosts;
>> The whole earth is full of his glory."
>
> Those opposite to them say: Blessed —
> Blessed be the glory of the Lord from his abode.
> And in all thy holy Scriptures it is written:
>> The Lord shall reign forever,
>> Your God, O Zion, for all generations.
>> Praise the Lord!

iii. The Qedushshah de-Sidra

There is a third form of the *Qedushshah* in the Jewish *Daily Prayer Book*. It is that known as the *Qedushshah de-sidra*. The origins of this *Qedushshah* lay in the school house — the *Beth Ha-midrash* — and it was only later incorporated into liturgical texts. Like other *Beth Midrash* prayers this one gives thanks for the Torah, requests that God may enlighten the believers' minds to understand it, and prays for the coming of redemption and of the kingdom of God. The *Prayer Book* text of this *Qedushshah* is as follows:

> Thou, holy God, art enthroned amidst the praises of Israel. They keep calling to one another: "Holy, holy, holy is the Lord of hosts; the whole earth is full of his glory." *They receive it from one another, and say: "Holy in the highest heavens, his divine abode; holy upon earth, his work of might; holy forever and to all eternity is the Lord of hosts; the whole earth is full of his radiant glory."* Then a wind lifted me up, and I heard behind me a mighty sound: "Blessed be the glory of the Lord from his abode."

Then a wind lifted me up and I heard behind me a great moving sound of those who uttered praises, saying, "Blessed be the glory of the Lord from the place of his divine abode." The Lord shall reign forever and ever. *The Lord's kingship is established forever and to all eternity.*

Lord God of Abraham, Isaac and Israel our fathers, keep the mind and purpose of thy people ever in this spirit, and direct their heart to thyself. He, being merciful, forgives iniquity, and does not destroy; frequently he turns his anger away, and does not stir up all his wrath. For thou, O Lord, art good and forgiving, and exceedingly kind to all who call upon thee. Thy righteousness is eternal, and thy Torah is truth. Thou wilt show grace to Jacob, love to Abraham, as thou hast sworn to our fathers from days of old. Blessed be the Lord who day by day bears our burden; God is ever our salvation. The Lord of hosts is with us; the God of Jacob is our stronghold. Lord of hosts, happy is the man who trusts in thee. O Lord, save us; may the King answer us when we call.

Blessed be our God who has created us for his glory, and has separated us from those who go astray; who has given us the Torah of truth and planted eternal life in our midst. May he open our heart to his Torah; may he set in our heart love and reverence for him to do his will and serve him with a perfect heart, so that we shall not labor in vain, nor rear children for disaster. May it be thy will, Lord our God and God of our fathers, that we keep thy laws in this world, and thus be worthy to live to see and share the happiness and blessing in the Messianic days and in the life of the world to come. So that my soul may sing praise to thee, and not be silent; Lord my God, I will thank thee forever. Blessed is the man who trusts in the Lord; the Lord will be his protection. Trust in the Lord forever and ever, for the Lord God is an everlasting stronghold. Those who know thy name put their trust in thee, for thou hast not forsaken those who seek thee, O Lord.[7]

The Lord was pleased, because of his righteousness, to render the Torah great and glorious.

4. THE KADDISH.

Another very popular Jewish prayer is that known as the *Kaddish*. It is found in a number of forms in the present-day synagogue service. It is accepted by students of Jewish liturgy that the *Kaddish* is a very old prayer, dating back at least to Tannaitic times, that is to the first two Christian centuries. It becomes problematic when we try to determine the form under which it then circulated. It appears that we can say it existed at least in its basic skeletal form: "Magnified and sanctified be his great name .... and may his kingdom come ... May his great name be blessed for ever and ever."

We have no indication that this prayer formed part of the congregational service during the Mishnaic period (A.D. 10-200). It appears rather that it was used at the conclusion of the public sermon.

One unique feature about this prayer is that it was in Aramaic, not in Hebrew, the usual language for prayer. The use of Aramaic may have been connected with its association with the sermon, which was also in Aramaic.

The *Kaddish* of the modern Jewish Daily *Prayer Book* has three forms: the whole (or complete) *Kaddish*, the half-*Kaddish*, and the "Scholars'" *Kaddish* (*Qaddish de-Rabbanan*), to which a fourth form, the Mourners' *Kaddish*, may be added.

We here give the texts of these various forms. The reader will notice that the essential, unchanging, element in them all is the opening section, here printed in italics.

i. *The Complete Kaddish.*

> *Glorified and sanctified be God's great name throughout the world which he has created according to his will. May he establish his kingdom in your life-time and during your days, and within the life of the entire house of Israel, speedily and soon; and say, Amen.*
>
> May his great name be blessed forever and to all eternity. Blessed and praised, glorified and exalted, extolled and honoured, adored and lauded be the name of the Holy

One, blessed be he, beyond all the blessings and hymns, praises and consolations that are ever spoken in the world; and say, Amen.

May the prayers and supplications of the whole house of Israel be accepted by their Father who is in heaven; and say, Amen.
May there be abundant peace from heaven, and life, for us and for all Israel; and say, Amen.
He who creates peace in his celestial heights, may he create peace for us and for all Israel; and say, Amen.

ii. The "Half" Kaddish
The "Half" Kaddish consists of the same prayer just given, with the exception of the concluding passage — from "May the prayers. . . . " to the end.

iii. The "Scholars'"
Kaddish (*Kaddish de-Rabbinan*) consists of the whole *Kaddish* with the section "May the prayers and supplications. . ." being substituted by the following:

(We pray) for Israel, for our teachers and their disciples and the disciples of their disciples, and for all who study the Torah here and everywhere. May they have abundant peace, lovingkindness, ample sustenance and salvation from their Father in heaven; and say, Amen.

The prayer then continues as in the whole *Kaddish*: "May there be abundant peace from heaven . . . . . "

iv. The Mourners' Kaddish
The Mourners' Kaddish contains the text of the Whole *Kaddish*, with the exception of the petition "May the prayers and supplications. . . . . . .".

Apart from its interest as a form of early Jewish non-liturgical prayer, the *Kaddish* is of interest by reason of its very close relationship to the "Our Father," particularly as given in the Gospel of Matthew (Mat 6:9-13). It would be vain to attempt to reconstruct a "primitive" form of the prayer for Tannaitic, much less for New Testament, times since it was of the nature of such prayers not to have fixed formulae.

6. THE LITERATURE OF HELLENISTIC JUDAISM

In this chapter we shall consider Jewish literature in the Greek language, whether composed in Palestine or in the Diaspora. It would be unwise, and unwarranted by the evidence, to set up too great a distinction between the two, just as it would be to set Diaspora Judaism too sharply over against that of Palestine. While it is clear that the religion, culture and literature of the Jews in the Greek-speaking regions outside of the homeland had a development somewhat different from that of the Hebrew or Aramaic-speaking Jews of Palestine, there was also a bond of union among them, and a factor of no small importance in this bonding must have been the use of the Greek language both in Palestine itself as well as in the lands of their dispersion.

The conquest of the East by Alexander the Great brought Greek culture to practically all the nations that were incorporated into the new kingdoms that came into being after his death. The old civilizations of Babylon, Persia, Syria, Egypt and Palestine could not remain unaffected by the new state of affairs.

Archeology has shown that the influence of Greek civilization was already felt in Palestine before Alexander. Its pace would naturally have accelerated after Palestine became formally part of the Greek world. The battle of Ipsus (Phrygia) in 301 put Ptolemy in control of Egypt and Palestine, with Seleucus in charge of the remaining lands of Syria and of Babylon. The country remained under Egyptian rule until about 200 B.C., when control of the area was ceded to the Seleucid monarch Antiochus III.

In one sense the imposition of Greek rule helped to activate the native traditions of the old civilizations now conquered. We have noted above in the first chapter (p. 31) the collection of the ancient Babylonian traditions made by the Chaldean priest Berossus and dedicated to the Seleucid ruler Antiochus I (281-261 B.C.). The three-volume work was in Greek and appropriately entitled *Babyloniaca*. In that same third century the Egyptian priest Manetho performed a like task with regard to Egyptian tradition, in the work bearing the title *Aegyptiaca*. It is possible that Phoenician traditions received like treatment.

The composition of works in Greek, and probably by Jews, appears to have begun in Palestine as early as in Babylonia or Egypt, if not earlier. We can probably put the beginnings of this new age of literary compositions in the Greek language at about 300 B.C. and are in a position to trace it down to the end of the era covered in this volume. The purpose of these works written by Jews in the Greek language was varied. In part it must have been to inform the Greek-speaking non-Jewish world of Jewish traditions and to defend the Jews against pagan calumnies and false accusations. On other occasions the motive was simply to provide a philo-Hellene Jewish community with reading material of a religious, and sometimes of a secular nature.

With the exception of the writings of Josephus and Philo, the former a representative of Palestinian and the latter of Diaspora Judaism, and naturally the biblical translations, all these Greek products of Judaism have been lost, or are known only through the fragments preserved by ancient writers, whether Jewish, pagan or Christian, such as Josephus Flavius, Alexander Polyhistor, Eusebius of Caesarea, Origen and Clement of Alexandria — to mention the more important.

We shall here work our way through this Hellenistic Jewish literature, for the great part following a chronological order.

1. Pseudo-Hecataeus of Abdera
— about 312 B.C.

In his treatise *Against Apion* (I,22 §§183-205 and elsewhere) Josephus gives a number of excerpts on Jewish history from a work he attributes to Hecataeus of Abdera —a well-known pagan Greek historian of the late fourth-early third century B.C. Modern scholarship is divided as to whether the excerpts are derived from the pagan writer Hecataeus or rather from a Jewish writer, presumably pseudonymous. The passages cited by Josephus, and the contents of the work as given by him, show such an acquaintance with Jewish affairs that the work may well be from the pen of a Jew rather than of a pagan, the work may even have been composed by a Jerusalem priest who became a soldier and joined the army of Alexander the Great as it marched towards the Red Sea. A date of about 300 B.C. would suit for the composition of this work on the history of the Jews. Together with the excerpts given by Josephus in *Against Apion* I,22 §§183-205, there may also be an excerpt from it in the same work I, 7, 23, §§213-215 and also in *The Letter of Aristeas* 83-120.

There are other texts given by Josephus (*Against Apion* II, 4, §§43-47; *Antiquities I, 7, 1* §159; 12, 2, 4 §38) and in *The Letter of Aristeas* (12-27, 31), Clement of Alexandria (*Stromata* 5, 113, 1-2) and Origen (*Contra Celsum* 1, 15b). These excerpts are scarcely from the Pseudo-Hecataeus just mentioned. They are probably drawn from the works of one or more pseudonymous writers. Among the excerpts from Hecataeus given by Josephus in his work *Against Apion* the following may be cited:

> Among these (who wished to accompany Ptolemy to Egypt after his victory at the battle of Gaza, 312 B.C.) was

Ezechias (=Onias?), a chief priest of the Jews, a man of about sixty-six years of age, highly esteemed by his countrymen, intellectual, and moreover an able speaker and unsurpassed as a man of business. Yet (he adds) the total number of Jewish priests who receive a tithe of the revenue and administer public affairs is about fifteen hundred (I, 22 §187).

The Jews were already noted for their devotion to their laws. In Hecataeus' words:

And (so he says), neither the slander of their neighbours and foreign visitors, to which as a nation they are exposed, nor the frequent outrages of Persian kings and satraps can shake their determination; for these laws, naked and defenceless, they face torture and death in its most terrible form, rather than repudiate the faith of their ancestors (I, 22 §§190-191).

2. Pseudo-Eupolemus
— probably a Samaritan; about 300 B.C.

The work entitled *On the Jews* was excerpted from by the Greek historian Alexander Polyhistor and attributed to the Jewish writer Eupolemus, who flourished about 150 B.C. (see no. 9 below). Polyhistor's excerpts were reproduced by Eusebius in *Praeparatio Evangelica* (book 9,17; see also 9, 18, 2). It is now recognized that the text is not from the well-known Jewish writer Eupolemus but rather from a Samaritan who wrote about 300 B.C.

In the extant texts we find the biblical account of Genesis combined with apocryphal lore, with Jewish, Greek and probably also with Babylonian legends.

The city of Babylon is said to have been first founded by those who escaped the Flood. Enoch, not the Egyptians, is said to have been the first who discovered astrology. Methusaleh, Enoch's son, is said to have learned all things through the angels of God, "and thus we gained our knowledge."

This is the kind of lore we find in the Enochic writings and is found also in the *Genesis Apocryphon* found at Qumran (see p. 147 above). Abraham, Pseudo-Eupolemus further tells us, was trained in astrology, which he taught first to the Phoenicians and later to the Egyptians. Abraham is also presented as having lived for some time with the Egyptian priests at Heliopolis.

In the retelling of Genesis chapter 14 we read that "being entertained as a guest in the city of Argarizim (=*Har Garizim*, Mount Gerizim), which may be translated as Mount of the Most High, he (Abraham) received gifts from Melchizedek, who was its priest of God and its king." In this passage, what the Bible recounts of Salem (presumably Jerusalem, and so understood in Jewish tradition) has been transferred to the holy mount of the Samaritans.

3. The Greek Septuagint Translation of the Pentateuch — about 250 B.C.

The translation of the Pentateuch from Hebrew into Greek must be reckoned as one of the major achievements in the history of Jewish Hellenistic literature. The account given in the *Letter of Aristeas* of how this translation came to be made is well known: Ptolemy king of Egypt (Ptolemy II Philadelphus, 285-246 B.C.) wanted a Greek translation of the books of Moses for his library at Alexandria. He requested Eleazar, said to have been High Priest at Jerusalem, to send to him in Alexandria seventy-two men (six from each tribe) of exemplary life, possessing skill in the law and with ability to translate. The men sent are said to have had proficiency both in the literature of the Jews and of the Greeks.

It is generally agreed today that the legend of the origin of the Septuagint contained in the *Letter of Aristeas* can be disregarded. The letter itself was composed about 150-100 B.C. and is of scant historical value. However, the legend seems to have some historical basis and it is now agreed that

the Torah was translated from Hebrew into Greek in the
third century, about 250 B.C. or so. It was already used by
the Jewish author Demetrius, who wrote in Greek between
222 and 205, but was probably a native Palestinian.

It is not altogether certain for whom this translation of
the Torah was first intended. That it was for the Ptolemys'
library at Alexandria seems unlikely. Many believe that it
originated to serve the needs of the Jewish community in
Alexandria. The view has also been put forward (by Moses
Gaster in particular) that the work originated not in Alexandria but in Palestine. It could have been originally intended
for a Palestinian readership, or both a Palestinian and
Alexandrian Greek-speaking community.

According to the tradition found in the Letter of Aristeas,
the translation was made by Palestinian scholars, proficient
both in Jewish and Greek learning. While by reason of the
nature of the evidence it seems impossible to determine
whether the translators were Alexandrian or Palestinian
Jews, the balance of probability would seem to indicate that
the translation reflects Palestinian Jewish learning, just as
the basic Hebrew text used was one current in the third
century, and probably in Palestine. In some cases the translation deviated from the text that was later to become
standard and official in Judaism, a fact that would necessi-
tate corrections or revisions of the original Septuagint rendering both in Palestine and Egypt to have it better conform
to the authoritative Hebrew text. We shall return to this
point below.

4. Later Greek Translations of the Scriptures — 250 - 100 B.C.

It appears that by 132 B.C. or so, not only the Law but
also the Prophets and parts at least of the third section of the
Jewish canon of scripture, the Writings that is, had been
translated into Greek. This much we can apparently gather
from the words of Jesus Ben Sirach's grandson in the pref-
ace which he has put to his translation of his grandfather's

work: "For what was originally expressed in Hebrew does not have exactly the same sense when translated into another language. Not only this work (i.e. his translation of Jesus Ben Sirach), but even the law itself, the prophecies, and the rest of the books differ not a little as originally expressed."

The greater part of the Former and Latter Prophets may well have been translated between 250 and 200 B.C.

From a colophon appended to the end of the Greek translation of the Book of Esther we learn both the translator's name and the date the rendering was made. The colophon reads:

> In the fourth year of the reign of Ptolemy and Cleopatra, Dositheus, who said he was a priest and a Levite, and Ptolemy his son brought to Egypt the preceding Letter of Purim, which they said was genuine and had been translated by Lysimachus the son of Ptolemy, one of the residents of Jerusalem.

The Ptolemy in question is generally taken to be Ptolemy VIII (or X, Latyrus, Soter II) and his fourth year as 113-112 B.C. However, some opt for Ptolemy XII and Cleopatra V and the fourth year as 78-77 B.C. The Letter of Purim referred to is the entire Book of Esther, recently translated into Greek. Dositheus and his son Ptolemy were probably Alexandrian Jews who had resided for some time in Jerusalem. They would have come on the Book of Esther there and Lysimachus, Ptolemy's son and grandson of Dositheus, translated it. It may also have been Lysimachus who composed or added the *Additions to Esther*, which are six in all and total 107 verses. These were probably composed to supply a religious element that is lacking in the original Hebrew, where neither God nor religious practices are ever mentioned. In the Additions, on the contrary, frequent mention is made of God, of the divine election of Abraham and Israel and of prayer.

The deuterocanonical *Letter of Jeremiah* is found in Roman Catholic Bibles as chapter six of the Book of Baruch. It was originally an independent work. (See Jerome

Kodell, O.S.B. in vol. 14, pp. 211-212 of this series.) The original may have been composed about 300 B.C., whether in Hebrew or Aramaic is uncertain. It must have been translated into Greek by 100 B.C. at the latest since fragments of this translation (with portions of vv. 43-44) dated to about 100 B.C. have been found in Cave 7 of Qumran.

The evidence yielded by both these Greek translations is limited but none the less significant in that both are intimately connected with Jerusalem and Palestine rather than with the Diaspora. Lysimachus, the translator of the Book of Esther, had resided at Jerusalem and probably translated the work there. The earliest evidence we have for the use of the Greek translation of the *Letter of Jeremiah* comes from Palestine. This Palestinian interest in the Greek translation and the use of the work in Palestine will continue right down to the end of the period studied in this book.

5. *Later Jewish Revisions of the Greek Translations*

The evidence provided by the Qumran manuscripts concerning the use of the Hebrew text of the Bible current before the reorganization of Judaism at Jamnia after the fall of Jerusalem in A.D. 70, shows that actually three forms of the Hebrew text were in use: one closely related to the Masoretic Text which became the official text of Judaism, another of the kind presumed to stand behind the Greek Septuagint rendering and a third of the kind used by the Samaritans and still preserved in the Samaritan Pentateuch. As Judaism came to accept more and more the text now known as Masoretic, the Greek translations were judged in the light of this. More than once recensions of the Greek were made to bring the rendering into line with the Hebrew text recognized as standard and most acceptable.

Our evidence for the early text of the Septuagint and of the recensional work on it comes from fragment and manuscript finds in Egypt and Palestine. From Egypt we have the papyrus fragment Fuad 266 with Deut 31:36-32:7, probably from the middle of the second century B.C. We also have the papyrus Greek 458 of the John Rylands Library of Manchester University, with parts of Deut 22:24-24:3; 25:1-3; 26:12, 17, 19; 28:31-33 — apparently also from the mid-second century B.C.

The continued interest in the Greek text in Palestine is clear from Qumran fragments of this rendering. We have fragments of three such manuscripts from Cave 4: a papyrus scroll with parts of Lev 2-5 (4QLXXLev^b), a leather scroll with Lev 26:2-16 (4QLXXLev^a), a leather scroll with fragments of Num 3:30-4:14 (4QLXXNum). These Qumran fragments date from the second century B.C. to about the turn of the era. From the Naḥal Ḥeber of the Dead Sea area have come substantial fragments of a leather scroll with the Greek rendering of the Minor Prophets, to be dated to the first century A.D. The Qumran fragments of the Greek rendering of Numbers have been seen to represent what was earlier called "the Lucianic Recension" (named from the Christian Antiochene priest and martyr Lucian, who is supposed to have made a recension of the Greek Bible). This "proto-Lucianic" recension represented at Qumran is now recognized as a deliberate recension carried out during the second and first century B.C. in an attempt to bring the Greek rendering from Egypt into line with the Hebrew manuscripts then current and recognized as authoritative in Palestine.

The Greek text of the Minor Prophets scroll represents another early recension of the Septuagint, one earlier called "Theodotionic" and now known as "Proto-Theodotionic." This recension has certain very definite principles in approaching its task of bringing the earlier Greek (Septuagint) rendering into line with the Hebrew. From the fact that it renders the words *gam* and *wegam* of the Hebrew text by the Greek *kaige* it is commonly known as the *kaige* Recension. It has, however, a number of other identifying features besides. Fidelity to the Hebrew text, particularly in the form this was taking on in rabbinic Judaism, was however of paramount importance.

In these texts from the Dead Sea area we have evidence of the continuing interest on the part of Palestinian Jewish scholars in the Greek text. This continued and produced further development of the Theodotionic recension along the principles of Rabbinic rules of interpretation.

A virtuoso attempt to revise the Septuagint along the lines of rabbinic interpretation, in particular those of Rabbi Akiba, was made by Aquila, a Jewish proselyte from Pontus who flourished during the reign of the Emperor Hadrian and worked under the guidance of Rabbi Akiba (martyred A.D. 135). He wanted to have the same Greek word reproduce the same Hebrew one, with little attention to the context and sometimes less to grammar, and intelligibility. This was because, following on Akiba's principles, he believed that there was significance in every iota and tittle of the Hebrew text. The best known example of Aquila's style of rendering is Gen 1:1 in which he translates the Hebrew *'et*, — which in itself can mean "with" or merely be the sign of the accusative, and thus untranslatable — with the Greek *syn*, which can only mean "with." Following his principles on this word and on some other matters, Aquila thus renders Gen 1:1: "In the sum (or "chief point") God created with the heaven and with the earth....."!!!

6. Demetrius
— 222-205 B.C.

The writer Demetrius is mentioned by Josephus (*Against Apion* I, 23, § 218) who apparently believed he was a pagan. Demetrius wrote a work on Jewish chronology from Abraham to the Exodus under the title: "Concerning the Kings of the Jews."

He wrote during the reign of Ptolemy IV (222-205 B.C.). It is generally accepted that he published his work in Alexandria. However, the possibility that he was Palestinian and that he published his work in Palestine cannot be ruled out.

All that remains of the work are fragments preserved in the writings of Josephus and Eusebius. The work used the Septuagint Greek translation, the first writing known to do so. Demetrius remains faithful to the Greek biblical text and has few midrashic embellishments.

7. *The Saga of the Tobiads*
— *about 170 B.C.*

The early second century B.C. saw an intensification of Hellenism in Jerusalem and in Judea, a process that ultimately led to the persecution of Antiochus IV Epiphanes in 167-164 B.C. and to the Maccabean revolt. It is probably as a result of this movement, and through no mere accident, that we have a concentration of Jewish Hellenistic writings during the mid-second century B.C.

In this process of Hellenization the Tobiads played a very important role. They were a rich Jewish family of the Transjordan who had intermarried with the high priestly family in Jerusalem. Best known among them was Joseph the son of Tobias who had by sheer astuteness succeeded in becoming chief tax farmer of Syria and Palestine for the Egyptian king.

In *Antiquities* (12, 4, 1-11, §§154-236) Josephus records the saga of the Tobiads. This must have existed as a written work, not merely as oral tradition and would appear to have been composed in the pre-Maccabean era, and prior to 171 B.C. It is also to be supposed that the work was in Greek as the Tobiads were leaders in the Hellenization movement.

The saga has nothing religious about it. It recounts the adventures of John the Tobiad and especially of his son Hyrcanus in the court of Ptolemy of Egypt. The intended readership of the work can be presumed to have been Palestinian Jews, and presumably not those of the pious type.

8. *Artapanus*
— *second century B.C.*

Artapanus' work *Concerning the Jews* is known to us only through excerpts in the Church Fathers, principally

Clement of Alexandria (*Stromata*) and Eusebius (*Praeparatio Evangelica*). He methodically embellishes, or rewrites, the biblical account to glorify the Jewish people and to show that the Egyptians were indebted to them for all useful knowledge and information. Abraham is said to have taught astrology to the Pharaoh Pharethothes. Joseph introduced better cultivation of land. Moses was the real founder of all culture and in fact of the worship of the gods in Egypt. The Exodus from Egypt is also narrated with some embellishment.

9. Eupolemus
— 158/157 B.C.

Eupolemus is mentioned as a writer on Jewish history by Josephus and by Eusebius. Excerpts from his work have been preserved by Eusebius and Clement of Alexandria. The title of his work seems to have been *The Kings of Judea*, even though two other titles are given in relation to it, e.g. *The Prophecy of Elijah*, which was more likely only a section of it.

This writer is probably to be identified with Eupolemus, the son of John, the son of Accos, who according to 1 Macc 8:17 and 2 Macc 4:11 was sent together with Jason son of Eleazar on an embassy to Rome in 161 B.C. to negotiate a treaty between the resurgent Hasmoneans and the Roman Republic. Evidently Eupolemus was a friend of the Jewish ruler Judas Maccabee and a gifted diplomat as well, since he succeeded in his mission. He may have been a priest since he speaks at length in his writing of Solomon's temple. He composed his work in the year 158/157 B.C.

The extant fragments of the book treat of Jewish history from Moses to the fall of Jerusalem. Eupolemus was concerned in his writing to show that the Jewish people went back further in their origins than the Greeks. He was also interested in biblical chronology. He added considerably to the account given in the biblical text. Solomon is said to have sent a pillar of gold to Suron king of Phoenicia which was set up in Tyre in the temple of Zeus. King Jonachin (Jehoiochin) is presented as having attempted to have Jeremiah burned alive. On the conquest of Jerusalem Nebuchadezzar is said to have sent the gold, silver and brass of the temple to Babylon; not, however, the ark and the tablets: these Jeremiah retained. This story about Jeremiah and the custody of the ark (contrary to Jer 3:16; 39:14; 40:4) is also found in the roughly contemporary passage 2 Macc 2:4-8.

10. Aristolulus
— 200-150 B.C.

Aristolulus was one of the most renowned and influential Jews in Egypt in the mid-second century B.C. He is probably the Aristobulus to whom the letter in 2 Maccabees was addressed (cf. 2 Mac 1:10), and in that passage he is said to be of the family of anointed priests and teacher of Ptolemy the king — presumably Philometer VI (181-145 B.C.). Fragments of his work called *An Explanation of the Mosaic Laws* are given by Clement of Alexandria (*Stromata* 1, 15; 5:14) and Eusebius (*Praeparatio Evangelica* 8,9; 13,12; *Historia Ecclesiastica* 7:32). The surviving fragments contain expositions of sections of the Books of Genesis and Exodus.

His approach to the scriptures is allegorical. In one section of the work he asserts that portions of the Pentateuch were rendered into Greek before the entire work was translated in the days of Ptolemy Philadelphus and that these portions were used by the Greek philosophers Pythagoras, Socrates and Plato and formed the basis of their philosophical teachings. In one of the fragments Aristolulus discusses the Hebrew calendar and establishes that the Passover always falls immediately after the vernal equinox.

11. Jason of Cyrene
— between 160 and 150 B.C.

In the introduction to his work, which comes after the prefatory letters (2 Mac 1:1-2:18), the author of 2 Maccabees tells us that in his writing he is attempting to condense into one volume what had been set forth by Jason of Cyrene in five.

Since 2 Maccabees ends with the defeat of the Syrian general Nicanor soon after the death of Judas Maccabee in 160 B.C., we may presume that Jason's five-volume work also came so far and that his history was composed soon after 160 B.C. Since the author of 2 Maccabees presents himself as an epitomist, we can presume that most, if not all, it contains, including its theology, was in Jason's volumes.

Jason seems to have used the work of Eupolemus, to whom the Epitomist once refers casually in 2 Mac 4:11 in the identification of a certain John who had been sent to Rome on a diplomatic mission. There this John is identified through his son Eupolemus — a very unusual manner of identification. Jason himself was probably the same person as the Jason son of Eleazar who in 1 Mac 8:17 is said to have been sent to Rome on a delicate diplomatic mission together with Eupolemus the son of John.

The fact that he was known as of Cyrene links Jason with the Diaspora. He may have composed his work in Alexandria. However, the theology of 2 Maccabees, which is presumably also that of Jason, is much closer to that of the Hasidim or of nascent Pharisaism than to that of Alexandria. This would tend to argue for a basic Palestinian origin, which in turn would suit the evidence which associates Jason and his father closely with Judas Maccabee and Palestine. (On Jason see also John Collins in volume 15, pp. 259-262, of this series.)

12. The Acts of Judas Maccabee
— about 150 B.C.

Judas Maccabee died in action against the Syrians in 160 B.C. After recounting his death and burial, the author of 1 Maccabees writes: "Now the rest of the acts of Judas, and the wars and the brave deeds that he did, and his greatness, have not been recorded, for they were many" (1 Mac 9:22).

This statement, contrary to first impressions, seems to affirm the sparseness of the record of Judas' life rather than its non-existence. The author may be contrasting the meagre record of Judas's deeds with the more elaborate account of John Hyrcanus' deeds available in the chronicles of his high priesthood (cf. 1 Mac 16:23-24).

Scholars believe that the *Acts of Judas* was in fact one of the sources used by the author of 1 Maccabees, and also by the author of 2 Maccabees, or by Jason in his original five-volume history.

The *Acts of Judas* were probably written in Greek, not in Hebrew or Aramaic, and this despite the nationalism of Judas Maccabee. The campaign of the Maccabees against the Greeks was political rather than cultural, and even after the destruction of the Greek cities which were the power bases of Hellenism the Hellenistic cultural influenced continued. As Victor Tcherikover says in his book *Hellenistic Civilization and the Jews:*

> It is very doubtful if the destruction of these (Greek) cities caused much damage to the condition of Greek civilization in the Orient; it was the Syrian population which suffered in the Hasmonean wars, not Greek culture. Hellenism did not come to an end in Palestine owing to the destruction of the cities — it merely lost its political importance. Moreover, the same state which had destroyed the Greek urban communities was itself prepared to follow in the footsteps of the conquered and to adopt the Hellenistic customs of the Orient, and the Hellenism of the Hasmoneans may have been no whit inferior to that of the Syrian population of the Greek cities.

13. Theodotus of Shechem, a Samaritan — second century B.C.

Eusebius in his work *Praeparatio Evangelica* (9, 22), quoting the pagan historian Alexander Polyhistor, gives excerpts from an epic on Shechem and the rape of Dinah

(Genesis 34) said to have been composed by a certain Theodotus, a personage otherwise unknown. The exact title of
the epic is not recorded. As a poet, Theodotus is rated highly
by scholars, and as far better than other known Jewish
writers such as Philo the Elder (no. 14 below) or Ezechielus
(no. 15 below). The subject of the epic would seem to
indicate that he was a Samaritan, as does his contrast of
Shechem with Jerusalem, to the detriment of the latter city.
He may, in fact, have been polemicizing in the epic against
Philo the Elder, his contemporary, who is known to have
written in praise of Jerusalem.

The fragment of a mere forty-seven lines opens as follows
with the praises of Shechem (in Theodotus' words, Sikimia):

> Rich was the land, well watered, browsed by goats,
> Not far from the field to city was the road
> No leafy copse the weary wanderer found;
> Yet from it two strong mountains close at hand,
> With grass and forest trees abounding, rise,
> Midway a narrow path runs up the vale,
> Beneath whose further slopes the sacred town
> of Sikimia mid sparkling streams is seen
> Deep down the mountain's side, around whose base
> E'en from the summit runs the well-built wall
>   (translation by E.H. Gifford).

Theodotus' text goes on to recount Jacob's arrival at the
land administered by Emmor and his son Sychem, Jacob's
journey to Laban, Dinah's beauty and attractiveness, the
revenge of Dinah by Symeon and Levi, and the pillaging of
the town. Little, if anything, is added to the account of these
events given in the biblical text.

14. Philo the Elder, Epic Poet
— about 170 B.C.

Philo the Elder is the author of a Greek epic entitled *On
Jerusalem*. Of the original lengthy work only twenty-four
lines survive, preserved in Eusebius' *Praeparatio Evangelica*

(9,20; 24; 37). Philo, the author of this epic, is probably to be identified with Philo the Elder mentioned by Josephus and Clement of Alexandria between Demetrius and Eupolemus. The extant fragments are very obscure and hard to interpret. The subject of the first fragment is Abraham, and probably the sacrifice of Isaac. The second speaks of Joseph and the third praises the springs and the water pipes of Jerusalem. Since Philo is mentioned between Demetrius and Eupolemus by Josephus and Clement, his floruit was probably about 170 B.C.

15. Ezechielus, the Tragic Poet
— second or early first century B.C.

Eusebius (*Praeparatio Evangelica* 9, 28), citing from Polyhistor, speaks of Ezechielus (or Ezekiel) "the writer of tragedies," and quotes from a work of his entitled *Exagoge* ("The Exodus"). The play begins with a long soliloquy by Moses, telling how the Jews came to Egypt, how they were oppressed, etc. The author follows the biblical account of the Book of Exodus closely, and in the extant fragments this goes as far as the events by the waters of Elim, where there were (so we are told) 12 springs of water and 70 palm trees. The vocabulary reflects that of the Septuagint. In some places the author departs from the biblical text and adds either from his own imagination or from Jewish haggadic tradition, e.g. in the section dealing with a certain Chum to whom Zipporah makes reply (lines 66ff.), a dream of Moses concerning his vision of Mount Sinai (68-82), details concerning the destruction of the Egyptians (lines 193-242), the number of springs and palm trees at Elim and the appearance of the wonderful bird there (lines 254-269).

16. Greek Esdras (1 or 3 Esdras)
— about 150-100 B.C.

This book, found in the Greek Septuagint Bible, begins abruptly with the great passover celebrated by king Josiah and goes on to narrate biblical history as far as the account of Ezra's public reading of the law (as found in Neh 7:73-8:12). It reproduces the substance of 2 Chr 35:1-36:23, the whole of the Book of Ezra and Neh 7:38-8:12. There are many differences between its account and that of the biblical books and the section in 1 (3) Esdras 3:1-5:6 with the story of the three young men in the court of Darius has no parallel in the Bible. The work is not a translation of the Masoretic text of the books in question, and is quite independent of the Greek Septuagint translation. It can be taken to represent an independent Greek translation and adaptation of the books in question, or of related Hebrew or Aramaic texts. In the *Antiquities* Josephus uses 1 (3) Esdras rather than the canonical books for the period covered by them. He may have regarded it as canonical and authoritative.

The purpose of the composition was to stress the contribution made by Josiah, Zerubbabel and Ezra to restoration of true Israelite worship.

The precise date of composition is uncertain, but it probably was between 150 and 100 B.C.

17. The Sibylline Oracles of Egyptian Judaism, Book III — about 150 B.C.

Of the Collection of Sibylline Oracles, only books 3-5 are Jewish. The others are Christian. The bulk of book III is very old — from about the middle of the second century B.C. — although there are some later additions. Authors are not united as to how the book should be divided. Its main contents are as follows: verses 1-45: Jewish hatred of idolatry; 46-96: the reign of the Holy King and the destruction of the wicked, the destruction of Beliar (these 50 verses are apparently later than the main body of Sib. book III); 97-349: description of the fall of the tower of Babel, lists of kingdoms and a review of world history; 350-488: a collection of various oracles from different dates with many place

names of Asia Minor. This latter collection may be connected with the Erythrean Sybil (in Ionis). We have Jewish
material again from 489 onward, as follows: 489-573: a series
of Jewish oracles against the nations; 574 to the end: on the
Jewish temple.

We can go deeper into the work and discern certain
patterns in it. John Collins has made a special study of
Sibyllines III and isolates in the writing four oracles, each of
which enlightens us on the eschatological views of its
author. All four oracles follow a certain pattern: sin, punishment, salvation — generally through the advent of a king or
kingdom. The oracles are as follows: verses 162-195: the
crimes of the Romans bring about a period of tribulation,
which will last until the time of the seventh king of Egypt. (ii)
verses 196-294 (in the historical account of the Babylonian
exile): idolatry leads to disaster, exile, destruction of the
temple. After the sending of a king there is restoration,
particularly of the temple. (iii) verses 546-656: idolatry will
eventually lead to disaster, materialising in the invasion of
Egypt by the king from Asia and by strife among the Greeks.
A king comes from the sun. The sequel to this is not elabo-
rated. (iv) verses 657-808: the opposition to the Jewish
temples will lead to cosmic disorder, followed by the exaltation of the Jewish temple and the establishment of an eternal
kingdom.

Salvation, or the messianic reign, is expected in the reign
of the seventh king (presumably the seventh Greek king),
who would either be Ptolemy Philometer (180-145 B.C.) or
Ptolemy VIII Euergetes (145-116 B.C.). The agent of salvation was regarded as being a Greek king, not the son of
David. In the final oracles the traditional Jewish pattern of
the end time is evident: march of the Gentiles against the
Jewish temple, cosmic disasters, the exaltation of the temple
followed by an eternal kingdom.

John Collins also thinks that the emphasis on the Jerusalem Temple in *Sibyllines* III may be due to the fact that its
authorship is in some way connected with the Temple of
Onias at Leontopolis, where the Zadokite Onias may have

kept alive a conservative form of temple-oriented eschatology. This would have been somewhat similar to what the Zadokite monks at Qumran had done, even though these had broken with the actual temple of Jerusalem and looked forward to a temple at the end time. John Collins finds a positive argument, among others, in favour of associating the theology of the *Third Book of the Sibyllines* with the Onias Temple in the fact that the degree of emphasis on the temple found in *Sibyllines* III is not paralleled in any other intertestamental Egyptian Jewish work. This would appear, in John Collins' opinion, to indicate that the author of the *Third Book of Sibyllines* had some connection with the Jerusalem Temple.

18. Third Maccabees
— first century B.C.

The title of this book is a misnomer since it treats of the sufferings of the Egyptian Jews under Ptolemy IV Philopator (221-203 B.C.) rather than of the persecution of the Palestinian Jews under Antiochus IV at the time of the Maccabees. It describes how Ptolemy IV attempted to enter the holy of holies in the temple in Jerusalem and how he was miraculously repelled (1:1 — 2:24). Then, on his return to Egypt he revenges his humiliation on the Jewish community there and attempts to impose the pagan cult of Dionysius on them. He even orders punishment and death on all who refuse to forsake Judaism (2:25-5:51). However, after Eleazar an aged priest prays for his people, the king repents and becomes the protector of the Jews.

The work was written in Greek by an Alexandrian Jew in the first century B.C. and is preserved in Greek, Syriac and Armenian.

The teaching of the book represents orthodox Judaism, stressing devotion to the Law of Moses and temple worship, and the special status of the Jews as God's chosen people.

19. The Letter of Aristeas
— about 100 B.C.

This work is remembered for the legend it contains on the translation of the Pentateuch from Hebrew into Greek (see no. 3 above). Although the letter casts light on the author's interests and theological views, still the content seems to be fairly meagre. There is emphasis on the Law. The work has conventional ethical teaching, with stress on trust in God. "The highest good in life is to know that God is the Lord of the universe and that in our finest achievements it is not we who attain success but God who by his power brings all things to fulfilment and leads us to the goal" (§195). The author's interest in the Jerusalem temple is evident from his detailed description of it: the temple itself including the arrangements for the water supply (§§ 83-91), the ministration of the priests and of Eleazar in particular (§§ 92-99), the Akra or citadel (§§ 100-104). We also are given a brief description of Jerusalem (§§ 105-106), and a description of the country districts of Palestine (§§ 107-120).

20. Philo Judaeus
— about 25 B.C. to A.D. 50.

No treatment of Hellenistic Judaism would be complete without mention at least of the best-known figure of all its writers, namely the philosopher Philo Judaeus.

The only known date in Philo's life is A.D. 40, when as an old man he headed a delegation of the Jewish community of Alexandria to the Roman Emperor Gaius Caligula. Philo is known principally through his numerous writings. These are variously classed into groups. Here we arrange them according to the classification of the Philonic specialist Samuel Sandmel.

In the first class we can put "Miscellaneous Writings," sometimes called "historical writings." These are works of a non-biblical character and can be listed as follows: (1)

Hypothetica, (2) *That every good man is free* (which contains Philo's account of the Essenes), (3) *On the Contemplative Life* (with an account of the *Therapeutae*, the Jewish monks living near Lake Mareotis in the neighbourhood of Alexandria), (4) *Against Flaccus* (who was appointed Roman Prefect in Alexandria A.D. 32). There were pogroms against the Jews in the city A.D. 38. (5) *The Legation to Gaius*, A.D. 40, headed by Philo himself.

The second class can be headed "The Exposition of the Law," and comprises treatises on biblical matters. These treatises are: (1) *On the Life of Moses*, (2) *On the Creation of the World*, (3) *Concerning Abraham*, (4) *On Joseph*, (5) *On the Decalogue*, (6) *On the Special Laws (e.g. the Festivals)*, (7) *On the Virtues*, (8) *On Rewards and Punishments*.

The third class of writings is entitled "The Allegory of the Laws." Different in style from the preceding section these treatises on biblical matters begin with a series of biblical verses, which shape the content. All the works in this category are expositions on biblical passages from Gen 2:1-3, 5-14 as far as Gen 37:7-10. The treatises are as follows: (1) *Allegories of the Laws* I-III (Gen 2:1-3:1), (2) *On the Cherubim*, (3) *On the Sacrifice of Abel and Cain*, (4) *That the Worst is wont to attack the better* (Gen 4:8), (5) *On the Posterity of Cain* (Gen 4:16), (6) *On the Giants* (Gen 6:1-4), (7) *On the Unchangeableness of God* (Gen 6:4-12), (8) *On Farming* (Gen 9:20-21), (9) *On Drunkness* (Gen 9:20-29), (10) *On Sobriety* (Gen 9:24-27), (11) *On the Confusion of Tongues* (Gen 11:1-9), (12) *On the Migration of Abraham* (Gen 12:1-3), (13) *Who is Heir of things divine?* (Gen 15:2-18), (14) *On Mating for the Purpose of Education* (Gen 16:1-6), (15) *On Flight and Finding* (Gen 16:9, 11-12), (16) *On the Change of Names* (Gen 17:1-5, 15-22), (17) *On Dreams* (Gen 27:12-15), (18) *On Dreams* II (Gen 37:7-10).

The fourth class of writings can be entitled: "Questions and Answers on Genesis and Exodus." In these we are first given a brief literal exegesis of the text, followed by an elaborate philosophical explanation, frequently flowing into allegorical interpretation.

Even though he does treat of the literal meaning of the

texts in his "Questions and Answers," Philo's chief interest is in the allegorical interpretation of the scriptures. The titles of his works show that his thought centered around, or flowed from, the sacred text. However, he can be studied both as a philosopher and exegete. Central to his teaching on God's relationship to the world is his doctrine of the *Logos*. The term itself occurs repeatedly in his works but is never defined. In *Who is Heir of Things Divine?*, chapter 42 (§ 206) the *Logos* says of itself: "I stand between the Lord and you; I am neither uncreated like God nor created like you, but midway between the two extremes, a hostage on both sides." It is a matter of debate whether Philo considered the *Logos* as a reality, as a distinct entity having real existence, or as no more than an abstraction.

It can be presumed that Philo's exegesis and philosophy did not originate with himself, that the way at least was prepared for them in the Jewish learning of Alexandria. However, we have no clear evidence of such a preparation. We are also in the dark concerning Philo's relationship to Palestinian Judaism and to the first-century Palestinian Rabbis, although there are indications that Philo did visit Palestine and kept some contact with Judaism there.

21. The Fourth Book of Maccabees — first century A.D.

4 Maccabees is a philosophical treatise that could be entitled: "On the Supremacy of Reason over the Emotions." It opens with the words: "The subject that I am about to discuss is most philosophical, that is, whether devout reason is sovereign over the emotions." First there is a philosophical introduction (1:1-3:18) in which the author tells us that he is about to demonstrate his point best "from the noble bravery of those who died for the sake of virtue, Eleazar and the seven brothers and their mother" (1:8). The author of this work belongs to the Stoic tradition, combining its principles with those of Judaism. He then moves on to the

story of the Maccabean martyrs, referring to the High Priest Onias III, "that noble and good man", and to Apollonius' attempt on the treasury of the temple (3:19-4:14). After this there follows (5:1-7:23) a detailed account of the martyrdom of Eleazar, "leader of the flock ..., of priestly family , learned in the law, advanced in age" (5:4) after which is narrated the martyrdom of the seven brothers (8:1-12:19). The author then gives a philosophical interpretation of the events (13:1-14:10), followed by an account of the martyrdom of the mother of the seven (14:11-17:1) and the author's panegyric of her (17:2-18). To this brave woman, the real heroine of the story, the author reserves the closing oration, one in which she expatiates on the principles that guided her life. Her words are addressed to her children, by which all God-fearing Jews, not merely the seven martyrs are intended.

Despite the author's Stoic ideas and language, his theology is genuinely Jewish. The work is noteworthy for its twin doctrine of martyrdom and the afterlife. With regard to the former, the author takes martyrdom as a substitutionary atonement that expiates the nation's sin and purifies the land. Thus, for instance, the author himself in 1:11 on the martyrs: "They became the cause of the downfall of tyranny over their nation. By their endurance they conquered the tyrant, and thus their native land was purified through them." The dying Eleazar prays to God: "Be merciful to your people and let our punishment suffice for them. Make my blood their purification, and take my life in exchange (*antipsychon* in Greek; cf. Mark 10:45) for theirs" (6:28-29). In an exhortation the eldest brothers says to the others: "Fight the sacred and noble battle for religion (cf. 2 Tim 4:7). Thereby the just Providence of our ancestors may become merciful to our nation and take vengeance on the accursed tyrant" (9:23-24). And in the author's panegyric on the mother we read the following (17:18-22):

> **17** The tyrant himself and all his council marveled at their endurance, **18**because of which they now stand before the divine throne and live through blessed eternity.

[19]For Moses says, "All who are consecrated are under your hands." [20]These, then, who have been consecrated for the sake of God, are honored, not only with this honor, but also by the fact that because of them our enemies did not rule over our nation, [21]the tyrant was punished, and the homeland purified — they having become, as it were, a ransom for the sin of our nation. [22]And through the blood of these devout ones and their death as an expiation, divine Providence preserved Israel that previously had been afflicted.

As examples in faith and endurance the martyrs can look to Aaron, Isaac ("and by reason like that of Isaac he [Eleazar] rendered the many-headed rack ineffective," 7:14), the three youths in Assyria in the ordeal of the furnace (13:9), the father (i.e. Abraham) "by whose hand Isaac would have submitted to being slain for the sake of religion" (13:12), while Abraham himself was willing to sacrifice Isaac (14:20). This is developed more fully in 16:20: "For his (God's) sake also our father Abraham was zealous to sacrifice his son Isaac, the ancestor of our nation; and when Isaac saw his father's hand wielding a sword and descending upon him, he did not cower." Daniel and the three young men in the furnace are again mentioned in 16:21, and Abel, Isaac ("who was offered as a burnt offering"), Joseph, Phineas, Hananiah, Azariah, Mishael, Daniel in the lions' den in the mother's final discourse.

Unlike 2 Maccabees, with the doctrine of bodily resurrection (2 Macc chap 7), in 4 Maccabees there is question of a happy immortality, not bodily resurrection, for the martyrs. The martyrs have command of their emotions "since they believe that they, like our patriarchs Abraham and Isaac and Jacob, do not die to God, but live in God." Similarly in 16:25: "They knew also that those who die for the sake of God live for God, as do Abraham and Isaac and Jacob and all the patriarchs" (cf. also Mark 12:26, Luke 20:38, Rom 6:10, 14:8, Gal 2:19). The brothers about to be martyred console and strengthen themselves with the words: "Let us not fear him who thinks he is killing us, for great is the

struggle of the soul and the danger of eternal torment lying
before those who transgress the commandment of God (cf.
Matt 10:28, Luke 12:4) ... For if we so die, Abraham and
Isaac and Jacob will welcome us, and all the fathers will
praise us" (13:14-15, 17-18). As Eleazar says: "The Fathers
(i.e. Patriarchs) will receive me as pure, as one who does not
fear your violence even to death" (5:37).

Their belief, as is thus clear, was in a happy immortality
after death. In her final discourse the mother reminds her
children of the scripture texts with which their father used to
confirm the faith of his children. It is interesting that three of
those (Prov 3:18, Ezek 37:2-3, Deut 32:29 with 30:20) were
understood in rabbinic Judaism as implying the doctrine of
the bodily resurrection. In this discourse they are probably
used as basis for belief in a happy immortality. The mother's
words are (18:6-19):

> **6** The mother of the seven sons expressed also these
> principles to her children: 7"I was a pure virgin and did
> not go outside my father's house, but I guarded the rib
> from which woman was made. 8No seducer corrupted me
> on a desert plain, nor did the destroyer, the deceitful
> serpent, defile the purity of my virginity. 9In the time of
> my maturity I remained with my husband, and when
> these sons had grown up their father died. A happy man
> was he, who lived out his life with good children, and did
> not have the grief of bereavement. 10While he was still
> with you, he taught you the law and the prophets. 11He
> read to you about Abel slain by Cain, and Isaac who was
> offered as a burnt offering, and of Joseph in prison. 12He
> told you of the zeal of Phineas, and he taught you about
> Hananiah, Azariah, and Mishael in the fire. 13He praised
> Daniel in the den of the lions and blessed him. 14He
> reminded you of the scripture of Isaiah, which says, 'Even
> though you go through the fire, the flame shall not con-
> sume you.' 15He sang to you songs of the psalmist David,
> who said, 'Many are the afflictions of the righteous.' 16He
> recounted to you Solomon's proverb, 'There is a tree of
> life for those who do his will.' 17He confirmed the saying

of Ezekiel, 'Shall these dry bones live?' [18]For he did not forget to teach you the song that Moses taught, which says, [19]"I kill and I make alive: this is your life and the length of your days.'"

Four Maccabees was evidently composed in the Jewish Diaspora and in Greek. Exactly where and when this happened are matters of debate. Some think it was composed in Egypt, probably in Alexandria. Others opt for Antioch on the Orontes, since the work is regarded as being in the florid Asiatic style and early Christian tradition located the martyrdom in question at Antioch (see also 4 Mac 5:1). The work was possibly composed as an oration to be delivered at a festival commemorating the martyrs or at the Feast of the Dedication of the Temple (cf. 1:10, 3:19, 14:9 and John 10:22).

The date of composition is during or after the period A.D. 20-54 when Cilicia was joined to Syria and Phoenicia (see 4:2). Some scholars would assign its composition to the reign of Caligula (A.D. 37-41), who proposed to violate the Temple of Jerusalem (see 4:5-14). Others, on the belief that the emphasis laid on martyrdom is due to the events of A.D. 70, date the work to the period A.D. 70-135.

22. Sibylline Oracles Book IV
— about A.D. 80.

The *Fourth Book of the Sibylline Oracles* appears to be a unity, from a single author. The plan of this work is fairly simple. First we have a description of God as the source of inspiration (lines 1-23), followed by a picture of the joy of the righteous and the fate of the wicked (24-46). Next the author gives a sketch of the history of the ten generations of the world, but breaks off into a series of oracles against various countries and towns after two generations (47-51). The book ends with an eschatological passage (152-192), within which we have an exhortation to repentance (162-178). From internal references the book can be dated to

about A.D. 80: lines 107-8 speak of the restoration of Laodi-
cea after the earthquake (of A.D. 60); 115-118 speak of
internal struggles in Jerusalem during the siege (in A.D. 69);
125-6 speak of the destruction of the temple (A.D. 70);
119-24 speak of the disappearance of Nero, the expectation
of his return, and the struggles of A.D. 76. There has been
doubt as to whether the book is a Jewish or Christian
composition, arguments for the latter being drawn from the
books attitude on temples (line 28), sacrifices (29), mention
of the folly of the Jews (117) and the emphasis on repentance
(168). The work, however, is generally taken to have been
composed by a Jew.

23. Josephus, Flavius
— born A.D. 38; died after A.D. 100.

Josephus himself (*Life* 2) tells us that he was descended
from the Hasmoneans and belonged to a priestly family of
the first course (*mishmeret*) of Jehoiarib. He must have been
well educated in his youth. He himself tells us that he was, in
fact, so renowned for his knowledge of the Torah that the
high priests and leading men of Jerusalem used to consult
him on points of halakah. His early training was, apparently, that proper to a member of a priestly family. He also
tells us that from the age of 16 to 19 years he was with a
certain ascetic named Bannus in the desert. This man was
probably an Essene, though not necessarily so. Then in his
nineteenth year he began to govern his life by the rules of the
Pharisees. We can presume that his connections with the
priestly class remained close since in A.D. 64, at the age of
26, he was sent on a mission to Rome to secure the release of
certain priests who had been sent there to answer for some
offences they were accused of. Two years later he found
himself commander of the anti-Roman forces in Galilee at
the outbreak of the Jewish war. He surrendered to the
Romans and succeeded in winning Vespasian's favour.
After the capture of Jerusalem he left his native soil never to
return. He went to Alexandria and later to Rome. The exact

date of his death is unknown but it probably was after A.D. 100.

All of Josephus' four extant works are important sources for Jewish history and tradition. The first to be composed was *The Jewish War* — an account of the war of the Jews against the Romans. Josephus himself tells us that he wrote two versions of this. The first one was in his own vernacular, i.e. Aramaic, and composed for "the up-country barbarians", i.e. the Aramaic-speaking Jews of the Parthian kingdom, especially those of Babylon. This edition is lost. The extant Greek version is an adaptation by Josephus himself of the Aramaic work. It was published about A.D. 78, when Josephus was about 40 years old. The next work to be published was *The Jewish Antiquities*, about sixteen years later (A.D. 94 or so). It appears that soon before publication of *The Antiquities* Justus of Tiberias had published his history of the Jewish War, with serious accusation of misconduct during the war in Galilee directed against Josephus. It is possible that Josephus' third and autobiographical work, the *Life*, was published at the same time as the *Antiquities* and as a reply to Justus. Some scholars, however, maintain that the *Life* was published about A.D. 96, and may have appeared together with a second edition of the *Antiquities* which appeared between A.D. 93/94 and 100. Josephus' final extant work to be published was *Against Apion*, or to give its original title, *On the Antiquity of the Jews*. In the first part of this work Josephus sets out to refute the detractions and contentions of anti-Semitic writings. In the course of doing so he excerpts from a large number of works no longer extant. In the second part Josephus gives his positive defence of the Jewish people, setting forth the inner value of Judaism and its superiority over Hellenism. In this we have a rather full presentation of Jewish halakah as known to Josephus.

The person and works of Josephus provide a fitting end for this survey of Jewish Hellenistic literature. He himself has provided in his excerpts witness to the richness of this literature over the entire intertestamental period. In his day this literature was still extant. For us now most of it is

known only in title or in excerpts. Apart from his importance as a historian and as a source for Jewish history, he
·also provided us with much information on Jewish haggadah and halakah..

Although he avows more than once in the *Antiquities* (i.e.
Ant. 1,1, 3 §17; 10, 10, 6 §218) that he gives his readers the
biblical text without addition or omission, it has long been
recognized that he does add to the text and that one of the
sources of his additions was Jewish midrash. Some of those
are paralleled in other known Jewish sources, while some
others are as yet otherwise unknown. Noteworthy additions
in Josephus' works are the midrashim on the birth, infancy
and on certain episodes in the life of Moses (*Ant.* 2, chapters
9-10, §§ 201-253). There is an expanded account of Abraham's sacrifice of Isaac (*Ant.* 1, ch. 13, §§ 222-236). The
place of the sacrifice is given as Mount Moriah (the Morian
Mount), "the mount whereon king David later erected the
temple." Isaac's age is given as 25 years and in his readiness
he is said to have rushed to the altar and his doom. Together
with the cases in which Josephus either transmits or refash-
ions earlier Jewish midrashim, there are others in which
he appears to give his own interpretation of biblical history.
Josephus was himself, most probably, an interpreter of
scripture and a creative haggadic midrashist.

With regard to the Jewish halakah presented by Josephus
in book four of the *Antiquities* and in his other work,
Against Apion — a number of those are not in agreement
with otherwise known Jewish *halakoth*. They probably
represent halakah that were in existence in Josephus' day,
among the priestly class perhaps, but have since been lost.

Attempts have been made to link Josephus and his midrash (haggadic and halakic) with one or other of the three
religious groups mentioned by himself, namely the Sadducees, the Essenes and the Pharisees, but so far without
notable success. He had contacts with all three and in many
instances went his own way and was something of an oppor-
tunist. Possibly the deepest influence on him was the earliest
— his training as member of a priestly family.

7. THE LITERATURE OF RABBINIC JUDAISM, AND PHARISAISM

In this the final chapter of the survey of the literature of the intertestamental period we intend to treat of the literature of rabbinic Judaism and of the relationship of the rabbinic tradition with Pharisaism. And just as we began our survey by going back beyond the accepted starting point, 200 B.C., by some three hundred years, so too in this chapter we shall come down beyond A.D. 100 to the end of the Mishnaic or Tannaitic period of Judaism about A.D. 200, and in some respects beyond this again into the fifth century A.D. The reason for this is that neither history in general nor the history of literature in particular can be easily divided into periods. The intertestamental period itself was heir to an earlier tradition, a tradition which helps us understand it. So, too, does the Jewish tradition consigned to writing only after the intertestamental period throw light on the religious thought and practice of the earlier age.

1. Some Definitions and History.

The earliest age of rabbinic tradition proper is known as the tannaitic, the Age of the Tannaim. It covers the time

between the deaths of Hillel and Shammai and the end of
the generation which produced the Mishnah, that is roughly
from about the years 10 to 200 of our era.

A *tanna* was a rabbinic sage or teacher of this period. The
word itself comes from the Aramaic verb *t^{e}ne* or *t^{e}na'*, "to
repeat," "to do a second time," and since teaching was
through repetition it also means, "to teach," "study," especially the branches or items of the rabbinic tradition, as for
instance *Mishnah* or *Baraita*. The verb also meant "to
report a tradition," since all this was part of the process.

The Hebrew word corresponding to the Aramaic *t^{e}ne* or *t^e-
na'* is *shanah* (the Hebrew letter *shin* in certain words corresponding to the Aramaic *t* or *tau*), from which vero the noun
Mishnah is derived, just as *midrash* is derived from *darash*.
The term *mishnah* has a variety of meanings. It is most
commonly met as a designation for the official collection of
Jewish laws, finalized about A.D. 180. We shall treat of this
work in detail a little later. The Jews themselves, however,
use the term *mishnah* for the individual paragraphs which
comprise this large work. The collection itself they would,
then, designate by the plural *Mishnayoth*.

The word *baraita*, used a few lines back, is another Aramaic term and means literally "external," "foreign, not
belonging to." It is feminine in form and intended to go with
an Aramaic noun meaning "teaching" (*matnita*). A *baraita*
is an item of tannaitic teaching not included in the official
Mishnah. A number of such *baraitot* (plural of *baraita*)
were considered important enough to be remembered and
transmitted in rabbinic tradition and are recorded in the
commentaries on the Mishnah which we have in the
Talmuds.

The *Tosefta* (the Aramaic word for "addition" or "supplement") is a collection of such *baraitot*. As a compilation it
presupposes the Mishnah, the plan of which it follows as a
general rule. Needless to say, it contains material not found
in the Mishnah, although much of its contents actually
repeats what we have in the Mishnah.

The compilation of the Mishnah ended about A.D. 200,

and with it the age of the Tannaim. The Mishnah achieved official status as the Jewish law code. But it, too, now needed commentary and this it received in the rabbinic schools of both Palestine and Babylon during the centuries following on the completion of the Mishnah. This commentary is known as *gemara*, which derives from a verb *gemar*, the primary meaning of which is "to end," "complete," but which came to mean "learn a tradition by heart." *Gemara* is thus the "learning of the oral tradition," or simply "the tradition" itself. This oral instruction (*gemara*) of both Babylonian and Palestinian Jewish academies of learning in due time came to be consigned to writing together with the Mishnah. This is what we have in both Talmuds: the Babylonian Talmud and Palestinian Talmud, the compilation of which was completed in the fifth century. The Talmuds are composed in a combination of Hebrew and of Aramaic, the Aramaic respectively of the Babylonian and Palestinian dialects. They contain the discussions of the schools and range over a wide area of legal and non-legal lore, of midrash both halakic and haggadic.

While the rabbinic period itself is reckoned as having begun with the demise of Hillel and Shammai, about A.D. 10, the first generation of Tannaim is regarded as having begun with the fall of Jerusalem in A.D. 70. The destruction of the Holy City and the temple with the defeat of the First Jewish Revolt, and the crushing of the Second Jewish Revolt, that of Bar Cochba (or Bar Cosiba, to use his real name) in A.D. 135, are events of capital importance in the development of rabbinic Judaism. In rabbinic tradition the period of transmission of the oral law, that known as "The Pairs," came to an end with Hillel and Shammai, about the end of the first decade of our era. The following six decades or so saw the discussion on legal matters between their respective schools. Then came the disastrous war with Rome and the destruction of Jerusalem. With this begins the period of reconstruction and consolidation and the real emergence of rabbinism as the guiding force in Judaism. The father of this new stage in rabbinism was Rabbi Joha-

nan ben Zakkai who established a flourishing centre of
Jewish learning at Jabneh (Jamnia) near Joppe (Jaffa). His
student Eliezer ben Hyrcanus founded a school at Lydda,
also in Judea. During the period between the two wars
(A.D. 70 - 132) Judea was the centre of Jewish learning. Two
of the leading scholars during this period were R. Akiba and
R. Ishmael, whom we shall consider in somewhat more
detail later. The Second Revolt forced the Jewish population and the Jewish teachers to move from Judea to Galilee,
where they founded schools — principally at Usha, Tiberias, She'arim and Sepphoris. It was in these schools that the
work on the development of the tradition and the compilation of the Mishnah and other tannaitic works was carried
on. The process would be continued in later centuries by
Amora'im, the successors of the Tannaim. It was these
teachers who gave us the two Talmuds, the Palestinian and
the Babylonian, this latter a reminder that the Babylonian
Jewish academies had become by this stage as active and
renowned as the Palestinian.

2. Rabbinic Midrash

In our opening chapter we had something to say on the
nature of *midrash* and the presence of this phenomenon
already in the Bible itself. The term and the reality *midrash*
belong in a very special way to rabbinic Jewish literature,
which in a sense can be regarded as almost entirely
midrashic.

What *midrash* is has already been considered. What was
said concerning it within the Bible holds good for rabbinic
midrash also. It is a complex phenomenon. Basically it
concerns a manner of regarding the scriptures. It has its
starting point in the scriptures. It is concerned not with what
the original meaning of the sacred text was but with the
message it contains for a later generation of believers. A
message the Bible must have, since it is God's inspired word
addressing itself to his people. *Midrash* implies actualiza-
tion, updating, making relevant. *Midrash* is an attitude of

mind with which one approaches the sacred text. It is the process, too, of seeking out the meaning of the inspired word in accord with this special attitude of reverence and of faith. It is also the result of this interpretation and investigation. Finally, *midrash* can also designate the works, the compilations, the written texts in which this special interpretation is now enshrined.

Rabbinic *midrash* is of two kinds, in accord with the manner in which the sacred text is approached. The central concern of Jewish life was *halakah* (from the Hebrew verb *halak*, meaning "to walk," "to go"), that is the law or laws governing their life as Jews, and mainly the laws not found in the Bible. The bulk of Jewish tradition is about this *halakah* and the attempts to derive such *halakah* from the Bible is known as *midrash halakah*. The other, the non-halakic section of rabbinic tradition, is called *haggadah* (from the verb *higgid*, meaning "to recount," "narrate"). *Midrash haggadah* is the name given to this other form of *midrash*. The term *haggadah*, however, is not always confined to a non-halakic interpretation of the Bible; it can be used at times with the meaning of legend, an embellishment of a narrative, or such like. *Haggadoth* (plural of *haggadah*) of this kind are often found as part of a free, midrashic, non-halakic interpretation of the scriptures

The actual, midrashic interpretation of the scriptures was carried out in different settings and served different functions in the Jewish community, whether as formal expositions in the schools, or as homilies in the synagogues, or as compositions in the form of homilies. Therefore, we have different forms of rabbinic *midrashim*, such as expository *midrashim*, homiletic *midrashim*, and such like. We shall treat of these individual *midrashim* later in this chapter.

3. Rules Governing Rabbinic Midrashic Interpretation.

Given the complexity of *midrash* it would seem nigh well impossible to formulate rules governing its operation. It derives from an attitude of the believer confronting the sacred text regarded as God's inspired and inspiring word, a voice calling for response in the here and now. This, however, does not mean that *midrash* is without any laws at all governing it. The midrashic approach is, to begin with, determined by the believer's underlying convictions, and these can conceivably lead to contradictory results. A Christian believer accepting that the fulfilment of the Law and the Prophets has come with Christ will differ from a Jew in the midrashic understanding of the Bible. A Saul would have read Deut 21:23 ("... for a hanged man is accursed by God...") before the events on the road to Damascus in a manner quite different from the Christian understanding of it. The central beliefs of the Qumran community determined their form of interpretation. Within each community in which the midrashic process was operative, a certain manner of interpreting given texts and passages must have evolved. A tradition of interpretation would have developed even though the laws governing such interpretation need not have been explicitly formulated.

To curb overvivid imagination, and particularly to serve as an aid in the development of halakic interpretation, certain norms were drawn up in time. A list of seven is attributed to the great teacher Hillel. These were hardly invented by him, but are rather a compilation of the main lines of procedure customary towards the turn of the era —principally in halakic interpretation of the scriptures. Hillel's first rule is known as *Kal wa homer* — inference *a minori ad maius*, from the less important to the more important. His second rule, *Gezerah Shawah*, is inference by analogy. Next comes a rule for constructing a family of related biblical halakic texts (*binyan 'ab mikkatub 'ehad*), when the texts are many. This is followed (no. 4) by a rule for a similar deduction from only two biblical passages. Rule no. 5 is called "The General and the Particular and the Particular and the General," i.e. detailed determination of the one case by means of the other. Then (no. 6) we have a rule on exposition by means of another similar passage, and finally (no. 7) exegesis from the context. These rules would have been used to invoke biblical support for already existing halakah rather than to establish new ways. In rabbinic tradition precedent and prescription meant more than reasoning and midrashic deduction.

Hillel's rules are in the main sober, and reasonable. So, too, presumably was his general approach to biblical interpretation. The stand taken by Rabbi Akiba, who had his floruit in the generation preceding A.D. 130, was quite different. Akiba and his very influential school practiced "atomistic" exegesis, interpreting sentences, clauses, phrases and even individual words independently of the context in which they were found. Thus, for instance, if Num 15:31 says of an individual transgressor: "He shall certainly be cut off" (literally: "cutting he shall be cut off"), for Akiba the repetition implied that the transgressor shall be cut off twice — in this life and in the world to come. In the preceding chapter we have already considered a little of Akiba's influence on the Greek translation of Aquila. Akiba's contemporary, R. Ishmael, and his school took up position against this cavalier treatment of the biblical text. R. Ishmael formulated the principle that "the Bible speaks human language"; it should be interpreted according to the canons of ordinary speech. Thirteen rules of intepretation are attributed to R. Ishmael. His hermeneutical rules, however, are in the main only developments of Hillel's seven, apart from the last one which establishes that "when two verses of scripture contradict one another, the contradiction is removed by a third verse."

From actual rabbinical practice rather than from any set of rules scholars have been able to ascertain certain devices used in haggadic *midrash* as found in the targums and the *midrashim*. The exposition thereby was drawing out as much riches as possible from the biblical text. One is the exploitation of the twofold or manifold sense of a word (*tartey mashma'*), i.e. to play on the double or multiplicity of meaning found in a number of Hebrew words. Another device is that of reading the consonants of the Hebrew word in a different combination, or with different vowels, from the accepted one (*'al tiqre*). Then there is the haggadic equivalent of the *gezerah shawah* of Hillel's list, that is the bringing together of related passages to effect a fuller understanding of a doctrine or tradition. This principle played a major part in the building up of rabbinic haggadic tradition.

4. The Mishnah

The Mishnah is a collection of Jewish halakah arranged in its present form in six major divisions, known as Orders (in Hebrew *sedarim*). These six Orders of the Mishnah are as follows: (1) *Zera'im* ("Seeds"), dealing with religious laws on agricultural matters, (2) *Mo'ed* ("Feast," lit. "Appointed time"), dealing with the laws of the Sabbath and of Festivals; (3) *Nashim* ("Women"), dealing with the laws on marriage, divorce, and family relationships; (4) *Nezikim* ("Damages") dealing with civil and criminal statutes and court procedures; (5) *Kodashim* ("Sacred Matters"), dealing with the laws of sacrifice and the temple cult; (6) *Toharot* ("purities"), dealing with laws of ritual uncleanness.

Each of these Six Orders has within it a number of tractates or treatises, varying from seven to thirteen, totalling sixty-three treatises in all.

Thus in the first Division or Order *Zera'im* we have the following treatises: *Berakoth* ("Benedictions"), *Peah* ("Gleanings"), *Demai* ("Produce not certainly tithed"), *Kila'im* ("Diverse Kinds"), *Shebi'ith* ("The Seventh Year"), *Terumoth* ("Heave-Offerings"), *Ma'aseroth* ("Tithes"), *Ma'aser Sheni* ("The Second Tithe"), *Hallah* ("Dough Offering"), *Orlah* ("The Fruit of the Young Tree"), and *Bikkurim* ("First-fruits").

The first tractate *Berakoth* gives rules concerning the times and manner of saying the two most important Jewish prayers, the *Shema'* ("Hear, O Israel," see above, pp.194-199) and the *Eighteen Benedictions* (see above pp. 199-203) but other forms of prayer as well, such as the grace to be said over different kinds of food, and concerning ejaculatory prayers. The reason for the inclusion of this tractate in a division devoted to Seeds probably lies in the fact that while the other tractates deal with the dues of the priests and levites to be paid before a crop becomes free for common use, so does this tractate deal with what a person should render to God before his other work and his meals.

The opening words of *Berakoth* and of the Mishnah concern the obligation of reciting the *Shema'*, the Jewish prayer that had to be recited twice daily — in the morning and in the evening. The discussion concerns the time the obligation to recite it begins and ends, and provides us with an example of the Jewish post-exilic principle of "making a hedge about the law" (*Aboth* 1:1), i.e. adding new laws and restrictions so as to keep a person far removed from breaking the law itself. The text begins thus:

> From what time in the evening may the *Shema'* be recited? From the time when the priests enter (the Temple) to eat of their Heave-offering (Num 18:8-20) until the end of the first watch (=third or fourth hour of the night). So R. Eliezer. But the Sages say: Until midnight. Rabban Gamaliel says: 'Until the rise of dawn.... Moreover, wheresoever the Sages prescribe "Until midnight" the duty of fulfilment lasts until the rise of dawn'... Why then have the Sages said: Until midnight? To keep a man far from transgression.

The second tractate *Peah*, "Gleanings" deals with the biblical laws (Lev. 19:9, 10; 23:22, Deut 24:19-21) which permit the poor to glean in the fields and vineyards and from the olive trees. It also treats of the "Poorman's Tithe" (Deut 14:28-29) which takes the place of the Second Tithe on certain years. The tractate opens on a spiritual note:

> These are things for which no measure is prescribed: *Peah*, First-fruits, the Festal Offering (cf. Deut 16:16), deeds of loving-kindness and the study of the law. These are things whose fruits a man enjoys in this world while the capital is laid up for him in the world to come:

honouring father and mother, deeds of loving-kindness, making peace between a man and his fellow; and the study of the Law is equal to them all.

The question confronted in the Tractate *Demai*, "Produce not certainly tithed," is the principle that produce should not be used until the tithe on it had been paid. Since the "uninstructed," sometimes called the "people of the land" or in Hebrew the *am ha-ares* or *amme ha-ares* (the plural form), were under suspicion of not giving tithe of their produce, the scrupulous observer of the law, especially the *Haber* or "Associate," needed directives about what his relations with the *am ha-ares* should be and what he should do with regard to produce purchased on which it could be suspected that tithes had not been paid. It was necessary to determine what was subject to tithe and what was not.

> The rules about *demai*-produce do not apply rigidly to wild figs, jujube fruit, hawthorn berries, white figs, sycamore figs. . . .(*Demai* 1:1).
>   Tithe must everywhere be given from these things as being *demai*-produce: fig-cake, dates, carobs, rice, and cummin. . . . (*Demai* 2:1).

Rabbinic tradition recalled that rules about *demai*-produce had been laid down by the Jewish ruler and High Priest John Hyrcanus, 135-105 B.C. (*Sotah* 9:10, *Ma'aser Sheni* 5:15).

The tractate *Shebi'ith*, "The Seventh Year," has as subject the law in Exod 23:10-11; Lev 25:2-7, 20-22; Deut 15:1-3 forbidding the cultivation of land in the seventh year. Chapter 10 treats of Deut 15:1ff. saying that the Seventh Year cancelled loans: "any loan whether it is secured by bond or not." In this context we are informed regarding the famous *prozbul* enactment of Hillel:

> (A loan secured by) a *prozbul* is not cancelled (by the Seventh Year). This is one of the things that Hillel the Elder ordained. When he saw that the people refrained from giving loans one to another and transgressed what is written in the law, *Beware that there be not a base*

thought in thine heart (Deut 15:9), Hillel ordained the *prozbul.*

This is the formula of the prozbul: 'I affirm to you, such-a-one and such-a-one, the judges in such-a-place, that, touching any debt due to me, I will collect it when-soever I will.' And the judges sign below, or the witnesses. . . . .

An ante-dated *prozbul* is valid, but if post-dated it is not valid. . . (*Shebi'ith* 10:3-5) (see above p. 108).

The sixth tractate, *Terumoth*, "Heave-offerings," concerns the portion of the harvest which Israelites must give to priests. This practice is already stipulated in the Bible: Num 18:19; Deut. 18:4. The next treatise has the title *Ma'aseroth*, "Tithes," tithes in general which also includes the Heave-offering. Apart from the Heave-offering, there were three other forms of tithes: (a) the First (or Levitic) Tithe, spoken of in Num 18:21, to be given (as the names suggests) to the levite, who in turn must tithe it, giving a tenth thereof to a priest (Lev 18:26, "Heave-offering of Tithe"). (b) Then there was the Second Tithe to be consumed by the owner in Jerusalem (Deut 14:22-27) or converted into money to be taken to Jerusalem, where it would be reconverted into food. (c) Finally there was the Poorman's Tithe (Deut 14:28-29; 26:12) which takes the place of the Second Tithe in the third and sixth years of a seven year cycle — in the later and rabbinic understanding of the biblical texts. The next tractate in the Mishnah, *Ma'aser Sheni*, "Second Tithe," with its special consideration of the Second Tithe shows the importance tithing had in the Pharisaic and rabbinic tradition. The tractate that follows is related in subject matter. It is called *Halla*, "Dough-offering," and is biblically based in Num 15:18-21 (cf. Ezek 44:30; Neh 10:37):

". . . .when you come into the land to which I bring you, and when you eat of the food of the land, you shall present an offering to the Lord. Of the first of your coarse meal you shall present a cake (*ḥallah*) as an offering. . . .".

After this comes the tractate *Orlah*, "The First of Young Trees" (literally: "Uncircumcision"), based on the law of Lev 19:23-24 which forbids the use of the fruit of young trees. The final tractate in this Order of the Mishnah is *Bikkurim*, "First-Fruits" which contains laws and casuistry in connection with Deut 26:1ff. and related halakic passages of the Bible.

The Second Order, *Mo'ed*, "Set Feasts" opens with a tractate of the Sabbath (*Shabbath*). The other tractates are *Erubin* ("The Fusion of Sabbath Limits"), *Pesachim* ("The Feast of Passover"), *Shakalim* ("The Shekel Dues"), *Yoma* ("The Day of Atonement"), *Sukka* ("The Feast of Tabernacles"), *Yom Tob* or *Betzah* ("Festival Days"), *Ta'anith* ("Days of Fasting"), *Megillah* ("The Scroll of Esther"), *Rosh ha-Shanah* ("Feast of the New Year"), *Mo'ed Katan* ("Mid-Festival Days"), *Hagigah* ("The Festal Offering").

The tractate on the Sabbath is one of the longest in the Mishnah. Laws governing Sabbath observance are already present in the Bible and the day was becoming more central and sacred as a sign of the covenant ever since the exile. Much of the Sabbath tractate concerns the interpretation of biblical laws and the deduction of further laws through casuistry. The main classes of work forbidden on the Sabbath were reduced to thirty-nine as we read in *Shabbath* 7:2:

> The main classes of work are forty save one: sowing, ploughing, reaping, binding sheaves, threshing, winnowing, cleansing crops, grinding, sifting, kneading, baking, shearing wool, washing or beating or dyeing it, spinning, weaving, making two loops, weaving two threads, separating two threads, tying (a knot), loosening (a knot), sewing two stitches, tearing in order to sew two stitches, hunting a gazelle, slaughtering or flaying or salting or curing its skin, scraping it or cutting it up, writing two letters, erasing in order to write two letters, building, pulling down, putting out a fire, lighting a fire, striking with a hammer and taking out aught from one domain into another. These are the main classes of work: forty save one.

These can be further spelt out. Thus, for instance, in *Shabbath* 9:5:

> (He is culpable) (of violating the Sabbath) that takes out (on the Sabbath) enough wood to cook the smallest egg, or spices enough to flavour a light egg...

The obligation of Sabbath rest was, however, only one among a number of religious obligations. In case of collision of obligations, it was necessary to determine which had precedence. Already biblical law had stated that the daily burnt offering (the *tamid*) was to be offered on the sabbath and indeed with a special Sabbath sacrifice (cf. Num 28:9-10). It became a matter of debate in later Jewish halakah which of two obligations took precedence. Qumran halakah seems to have given precedence in most things to the Sabbath obligation with the exception of the Sabbath burnt offering (cf. Qumran *Damascus Document* 11:17-18, above pp. 130f). That the Passover obligation, in strictly defined manner, takes precedence over the Sabbath is a decree attributed to Hillel. Circumcision also took precedence. The following texts of the Mishnah bear on the subject:

> These acts pertaining to the Passover-offering override the Sabbath: slaughtering it, tossing its blood, scraping its entrails, and burning its fat pieces. But the roasting of it and rinsing its entrails do not override the Sabbath. Carrying it (to the Temple) and bringing it from outside to within the Sabbath limit, and cutting of a wen (from the carcase) do not override the Sabbath. R. Eliezer says: They do override it. (Mishnah, *Pesachim* 6:1).
>
> They may perform on the Sabbath all things that are needful for circumcision..... (Mishnah, *Shabbath* 19:2).

The tractate *Shekalim* deals with the half-shekel (see Exod. 30:13-15) due to the temple from every Israelite from "twenty years old and upward," to be payed before the 1st of Nisan every year. The tractate *Yoma* contains rules for the

Day of Atonement. *Sukka* regulates the Feast of Tabernacles. Part of the ceremonies was the carrying of water in procession from the pool of Siloam to the Temple:

> "The rites of the Water-libation continue seven days" —what was the manner of this? They used to fill a golden flagon holding three *logs* (=about one and a half pints) with water from Siloam. When they reached the Water Gate they blew (on the *shofar*) a sustained, a quavering and another sustained blast... (Mishnah, *Sukka* 4:9).

The *Tosefta* while attending to the name of the gate and the drawing of water brings together biblical traditions on water and the midrash developed around these:

> Whence is the name "Water Gate"? It is so called because through it they take the flask of water used for the libation at the Feast. R. Eliezer ben Jacob (probably about A.D. 70; but possibly about A.D. 150) says of it: The waters are dripping (Ezek 47:2), intimating that water oozing and rising, as if from the flask, will in future days come forth from under the threshold of the Temple... (*The text goes on to interpret Ezek 47:3-5*). It may be other fountains will be mixed with them, as we learn from the Scripture, *In that day shall there be a fountain opened to the house of David, and to the inhabitants of Jerusalem, for sin and for uncleanness.* (Zech 13:1)

(*An interpretation of Ezek 47:8, 9, 10, 11, 12 follows. The text then interprets midrashically Num 21:17-20*):

> So the well, which was with Israel in the wilderness, was like a rock of the size of a *kebara* (= a small round vessel), and was oozing out and rising as from the mouth of this flask (unused for the drawing of the water at the Feast), travelling with them up the mountains and going down with them to the valleys. Wherever Israel encamped it (i.e. the well) encamped opposite them before the door of the Tabernacle. The princes of Israel with their staves surrounded it, and said over it this song, "Spring up, O well, sing ye to it." Then the waters bubbled forth, and

rose on high like a pillar; and every one drew out the staff of his tribe and family, as it is said, "*The well which the princes digged, which the nobles of the people delved, with the sceptre and with their staves*" (Num 21:18). *And from Mattanah to Nahaliel; and from Nahaliel to Bamoth; and from Bamoth to the valley,* etc. — going round every camp of the Lord...; and it made mighty streams, as it said, "*And streams overflowed*" (Ps 78:20).

The tractate *Pesachim* treats of various laws governing the Feast of Passover, but also dwells on its religious significance. After the second cup has been mixed, the son asked his father to teach him concerning the significance of the Feast.

And according to the understanding of the son his father instructs him. He begins with the disgrace and ends with the glory; and he expounds from *A wandering Aramean was my father*..... (Deut 26:5ff.) until he finishes the whole section.... (*Pesachim* 10:4).

A little later we read:

In every generation a man must so regard himself as if he came forth himself out of Egypt, for it is written, *And thou shalt tell thy son in that day saying, It is because of that which the Lord did for me when I came forth out of Egypt* (Exod 13:8). Therefore are we bound to give thanks, to praise, to glorify, to honour, to exalt, and to bless him who wrought these wonders for our fathers and for us. He brought us out from bondage to freedom, from sorrow to gladness, and from mourning to a Festival-day, and from darkness to great light, and from servitude to redemption; so let us say before him the *Hallelujah* (*Pesachim* 10:5).

The third Order *Nashim* ("Women"), has seven tractates, dealing with very central issues in Jewish life: *Yebamoth* ("Sisters-in-law"), *Ketuboth* ("Marriage Deeds"), *Nedarim* ("Vows"), *Nazir* ("The Nazirite Vow"), *Sotah* ("The suspected Adultress"), *Gittin* ("Bills of Divorce") and *Kiddu-*

shin ("Betrothals"). Most of these had already behind them certain items of biblical law, and of course, centuries of Jewish practice. These tractates tell us much about Jewish customs and social life: e.g. "The father has control over his daughter as touching her betrothal whether it is effected by money, by writ, or by intercourse (whereby betrothal is effected); and he has tne right to aught found by her and to the work of her hands, and (the right) to set aside her vows (cf. Num 30:5,16), and receive her bill of divorce..." (*Ketuboth* 4:4). Down through biblical times vows and oaths had been part of Jewish life and legislation. A tractate is devoted to each in the Mishnah — vows in the Order *Nashim*, Oaths in the Order *Nezikin*, "Damages." The difference between the two lay in this: that the vow forbade certain things to be used (it was made, e.g. with the formula, "Let such a thing be forbidden to me or to you"), while the oath forbade the one who swore it to do a certain thing, which in itself was not forbidden (it was made, e.g. with the formula "I swear that I will not eat such-a-thing"). The tractate *Nedarim* is based on Num 30:3-16 and Deut 23:22-24. It treats of the practice of making vows that had become common, of the various formulae being used, of the validity and annulment of vows, and of dispensation from them. The rules try to cope with an existing situation, and also counsel against the habit of taking vows for trivial reasons.

> If a man said to his fellow, *Konam* or *Konah* or *Konas*, these are substitutes for *Korban*, an Offering (i.e. a thing as forbidden to him for common use as a temple offering). (If he said), *Kerek* or *Herekh* or *Heref*, these are substitutes for *Herem*, a devoted thing.....(*Nedarim* 1:2).
>
> If he said, "May what I eat of thine be "not *hullin*" (i.e. not free for common use, but a Hallowed Thing) (or) "not valid as food", (or) "not clean," (or) "unclean," (or) "Remnant and Refuse," it is forbidden to him. (If he said, "May it be to me") 'as the lamb' (i.e. the Daily Whole-offering, Num 28:1-9), (or) 'as the (Temple-)sheds', (or) 'as the wood (for burning on the Altar', (or) 'as the Fire-

offerings,' (or) 'as the Altar' (or) 'as the Sanctuary,' (or) 'as Jerusalem', or if he vowed by any of the utensils of the Altar, although he did not utter (the word) *Korban*, an offering, it is a vow as binding as if he had uttered the word *Korban*. R. Judah says: If he said, ('May it be) Jerusalem!,' he has said naught. (*Nedarim* 1:3).

Then there were those who in vowing used the key words but understood them in a sense different from that of their religious context, in a manner that would leave them free of obligation, for example:

> If a man vowed and used the word *herem*, but said, 'In my vow I meant only a *herem* (net) of the sea,' or if he vowed and used the word *Korban*, but said, 'in my vow I meant only the *Korbans* (gifts) of kings'; ... or '*Konam* be any benefit I have of my wife!' but said, 'I vowed only (to abstain) from my first wife whom I divorced' — touching all such vows they need not seek (release from the Sages); but if they seek it they should punish them and apply the more stringent ruling. So R. Meir. But the Sages say: They open for them a door (to repentance) from another side, but instruct them so that they shall not behave themselves lightly in what concerns vows (*Nedarim* 1:5; Danby's translation).

The Fourth Order, *Nezikin*, Damages, deals first of all with various problems relating to property in three tractates, which were originally one: *Baba Kamma* ("The First Gate"), *Baba Metzia* ("The Middle Gate"), and *Baba Bathra* ("The Last Gate"). Next comes the tractate *Sanhedrin* ("The Sanhedrin"), dealing with the constitution and procedure of courts of law, and especially with the execution of capital punishment. Next comes the tractate *Makkoth*, ("stripes"), which treats of the manner of applying the law against false witnesses (Deut. 19:19), with the cities of Refuge, and with the administration of the "forty stripes" (Deut 25:2-3), whence the tractate's name. Next comes *Shebuoth* ("Oaths"), then the tractate *Eduyoth* ("Testimonies"), which contains a hundred selected *halakoth* on unrelated topics, to which are added the thirty cases where, by way of exception to its general practice, the school of Hillel adopted a more stringent attitude than the School of Shammai on debated questions of halakah. Most of the contents of this tractate are repeated elsewhere in the Mishnah. Next comes the tractate *Abodah Zarah* ("Idolatry"). Then comes *Aboth*, with its series of sayings from eminent teachers of the Law (sixty of them are named) between 300 B.C. or so and A.D. 200. Finally in this fourth Order comes the tractate *Horayoth* ("Decisions"), which on the basis of Lev 4:1-21, deals with occasions when individuals or the majority of the people have been led into transgression by a wrongful decision of the Sanhedrin.

The number liable to the Forty Strokes (in reality Forty-save-one) was quite high. The Mishnah, *Makkoth* 3:1-2, gives a long list which is still not exhaustive:

> These are they that are to be scourged: he that has connexion with his sister, his father's sister, his mother's sister, his brother's wife, his father's brother's wife or a menstruant (listed in Lev 20:17-21); a High Priest that married a widow, a common priest that married a woman that was divorced....; an Israelite that married a bastard....;....an unclean person who ate Hallowed things, or that entered the Temple while he was unclean (cf. Num 5:2), or that ate the fat or the blood (cf. Exod 29:24); ....or that ate at Passover what was leavened.....
>
> How many stripes do they inflict on a man? Forty save one, for it is written, *By number forty* (Deut 25:2-3); (that is to say) a number near forty. R. Judah says: He suffers the forty stripes in full. And where does he suffer the added one? Between the shoulders (*Makkoth* 3:10).
>
> How do they scourge him? They bind his two hands to a pillar on either side, and the minister of the synagogue lays hold on his garments... so that he bares his chest. A stone is set behind him on which the minister of the synagogue stands with a strip of calf-hide in his hand, doubled and redoubled, and two (other) straps that rise

and fall (are fastened) thereto. . . . He gives him one-third of the stripes in front and two-thirds behind; and he may not strike him when he is standing or when he is sitting, but only when he is bending low, for it is written, *The judge shall cause him to lie down* (Deut 25:2). And he that smites, smites with his one hand with all his might (*Makkoth* 3:12-13).

The Fifth Order, *Kodashim* ("Hallowed Things"), has eleven tractates, as follows: *Zebahim* ("Animal Offerings"), *Menahoth* ("Meal Offerings"), *Hullin* ("Animals killed for food") (not in sacrifice), *Bekhoroth* ("Firstlings"), *Arakhin* ("Vows of Valuation"), *Temorah* ("The Substituted Offering"), *Kerithoth* ("Extirpation"), *Meilah* ("Sacrilege"), *Tamid* ("The Daily Whole-Offerings"), *Middoth* ("The Measurements of the Temple", as it was before the destruction in A.D. 70), and finally *Kinnim* ("The Bird-Offerings").

Tohoroth, "Cleannesses," the sixth and final Order of the Mishnah, treats of cleanness and uncleanness, issues central to Rabbinic Judaism. In fact, it deals with the latter rather than the former, and "cleanness" in this context is a euphemism for its opposite.

It contains twelve tractates. The first, *Kelim* ("Vessels" "Utensils"), is the longest in the entire Mishnah, and treats of vessels and utensils susceptible to impurity. The next, *Oholoth* ("Tents", "Overshadowing") is on the ritual impurity which arises from the overshadowing of a dead person. *Nega'im* ("Leprosy-signs"), deals with leprosy, *Parah*, contains regulations and casuistry on the matter of the Red Heifer, and the regulations of Num 19:1-22. The tractate *Tohoroth*, within the Order which bears the same name, is mainly on the conditions which render food unclean. The next, *Mikwaoth* ("Immersion-Pools"), is on the pools for ritual immersion. The tractate *Niddah* ("The Menstruant") concerns the uncleanness involved in menstruation. The tractate *Makshirim* ("Predisposers"), is on the fluids rendering food susceptible of uncleanness. *Zabim* ("They that suffer a flux"), is on uncleanness from gonorrhea. The next tractate *Tebul Yom* ("He that immersed himself that day"), is on the uncleanness, lasting until sunset, of one who has gone through the required immersion during the day. *Yadaim* ("Hands") is on the uncleanness of unwashed hands and the manner of having them rendered ritually clean. The final tractate *Uktzin* ("Stalks"), is on the uncleanness transferred by the stalks of husks of fruits or plants.

5. *Tannaitic Midrashim*

The Tannaitic *Midrashim* are midrashic expositions, mainly halakic, on the last four books of the Pentateuch —Exodus, Leviticus, Numbers, Deuteronomy. There is no Tannaitic midrash on Genesis, since Genesis has no halakah; the Law came through Moses. The names of the Tannaitic *midrashim* known through the Middle Ages to recent times were as follows: The *Mekilta* (of Rabbi Ishmael) on Exodus, *Sifra* on Leviticus and *Sifre* on Numbers and on Deuteronomy. In more recent times other midrashic expositions have been identified as deriving from Tannaitic times, viz., *The Mekilta of Rabbi Simeon ben Yohai* (on Exodus), *Sifre Zuta* on Numbers, *Midrash Tannaim* (Mekilta on Deuteronomy) on Deuteronomy.

Although these works were redacted in post-tannaitic times, they are regarded as belonging to the tannaitic period by reason of their language and the authorities cited in them, which are in the main tannaitic.

The *Mekilta* ascribed to Rabbi Ishmael has been rightly shown to have affinities with the other works known to have been associated with the school of Rabbi Ishmael. D. Hoffmann has shown that the Tannaitic *Midrashim* fall into two types, thus: Type A, *Mekilta* (of R. Ishmael), *Sifre* on Numbers, *Midrash Tannaim* (= Mekilta on Deuteronomy) on the one hand, and on the other Type B, *Mekilta of R. Simeon ben Yohai, Sifre* on Leviticus, *Sifre Zuta* and *Sifre* on Deuteronomy. Type A, D. Hoffmann would attribute to the School of R. Ishmael and Type B to the School of Rabbi Akiba. (On these schools see p. 244 above). H. Albeck, while accepting the division into the two types suggested, expressed reservations about the attribution to the schools in question, although it seems to be agreed by scholars that at least Type A *Midrashim* has a greater amount of material from the School of R. Ishmael than Type B, and Type B has more from the School of R. Akiba than Type A.

i. The Mekilta of R. Ishmael.

This tannaitic exegetical *midrash* interprets the main section of the Book of Exodus chapter by chapter and often verse by verse. It begins with Exodus 12:1 and goes on in continuous fashion to 23:19. Following on this it has an exposition of Exod 31:12-17 and 35:1-3. Its *midrash* is both on the legal and narrative sections of the book, and hence is both halakic and haggadic. The language of both parts is pure rabbinic Hebrew with Greek and Latin loanwords. Many of its *beraitot*, given anonymously in the book itself, are in both the Talmuds and other *Midrashim* given in the name of R. Ishmael or some tanna of his school; hence the attribution of the work to R. Ishmael. The title is already attested in the writings of R. Nissim Gaon (11th century). Although the work itself, like the other tannaitic *midrashim*, was apparently compiled and redacted in the later fourth century, its contents can be accepted as going back to the second. I here reproduce some sections of the work, in the translation of Jacob Lauterbach.

> *And the whole assembly of the congregation shall kill it.* (Exod 12:6) R. Eliezer says: Whence can you prove that if all Israel had only one paschal lamb all of them can fulfill their duty with it? From the passage: And the whole assembly of the Congregation of Israel shall kill it.
> *And the whole assembly of the congregation of Israel shall kill it.* On the basis of this passage the sages said: The rite of slaughtering the paschal lamb is performed by three successive groups, an assembly, a congregation, and Israel.

This can be compared with Mishnah, *Pesachim* 5:5-6:

> The Passover-offering was slaughtered (by the people) in three groups, for it is written, *And the whole assembly of*

> *the congregation of Israel slaughter it* — 'assembly',
> 'congregation,' and 'Israel.' When the first group entered
> in and the Temple Court was filled, the gates of the
> Temple Court were closed..... When the first group
> went out the second group came in. As the rite was
> performed with the first group so was it performed with
> the second and the third.

Mekilta Beshallah. 3 on Exod 14:9-14 knows of the tradition of the division of the Israelites into four groups at the
Red Sea:

> The Israelites at the Red Sea were divided into four
> groups. One group said: Let us throw ourselves into the
> sea. One said: Let us return to Egypt. One said: Let us
> fight them; and one said: Let us cry out against them. The
> one that said "Let us throw ourselves into the sea," was
> told: "Stand still , and see the salvation of the Lord." The
> one that said: "Let us return to Egypt," was told: "For
> whereas ye have seen the Egyptians today," etc. The one
> that said: "Let us fight them" was told: "The Lord will
> fight for you." The one that said: "Let us cry out against
> them," was told: "And ye shall hold your peace."

The same tradition is found in the Palestinian Targums of
Exodus 14:13-14.

ii. The Mekilta of R. Simeon ben Yohai.

Simeon ben Yohai, from about A.D. 150, was a tannaitic
sage of the School of Rabbi Akiba. This work that now
bears his name was known in the Middle ages also under the
titles *Sifre of the House of Rab (Sifre de-be Rab), Mekilta of
R. Akiba* and *Mekilta de-Sanya* (Aramaic for "Mekilta of
the Bush," since it begins with the exposition of Exod 3:1 on
the Burning Bush). It was still known in the sixteenth century but was thought to have been lost. However, portions
of it have been recovered in citations in other works (e.g.
Midrash he-Gadol) and in fragments from the Cairo
Geniza.

The known fragments of the *Mekilta of R. Simeon ben Yohai* contain an expository midrash on Exod 3:2,7-8; 6:2; 12:1-24:10; 30:20-31:15; 34:12,14,18-26; 35:2. We cannot say how extensive the complete work was.

The terminology and names of the Rabbis cited indicate that this work belongs to Type B of the tannaitic *midrashim*. In the halakic exposition, names of scholars of the School of Rabbi Akiba predominate, and there is stress on verbal interpretation. The haggadic passages, however, are similar to those of the Mekilta of R. Ishmael and may have been borrowed from it.

iii. The Sifra on Leviticus.

This is a continuous commentary on the Book of Leviticus, chapter by chapter and verse by verse. At times each word in a verse is interpreted. The language is Mishnaic Hebrew, with some Greek words. Like the other tannaitic *midrashim*, *Sifra* was apparently compiled in its present form in Palestine towards the end of the fourth century —but from earlier, tannaitic, sources. The work belongs to Type B of the tannaitic *midrashim*, which is attributed to the School of Akiba. Since the Book of Leviticus contains mainly legal material, *Sifra* is predominantly halakic, with very little *haggadah*.

iv. Sifre on Numbers.

This work is a running exegetical *midrash* on sections of the Book of Numbers, interpreting it chapter by chapter and verse by verse, and sometimes even going into the interpretation of each word in a verse. The present work, like the other tannaitic *midrashim*, was assembled from earlier sources towards the end of the fourth century, and contains midrashic exposition of the following sections of Numbers: chapters 5-12; 15; 18-19; 25:1-13; 26:52-31:24; 35:9-34. In keeping with the legal narrative material of the book itself, *Sifre on Numbers* contains both *halakah* and *haggadah*.

It was once thought that the *midrashim* bearing the titles *Sifre on Numbers* and *Sifre on Deuteronomy* were really but one work. D. Hoffmann, however, has shown that they are distinct in nature. *Sifre on Numbers* belongs to Type A of tannaitic *midrashim*, resembling the *Mekilta of R. Ishmael*, to whose School it is ascribed.

v. Sifre Zuta.

This work, under this and many other titles, was used extensively by the Jews in the Middle Ages but was later lost. Fragments of it, however, have been identified in the Cairo Geniza and modern scholars have been able to identify other texts from it in extracts copied into other Jewish writings. It was given its name *Zuta* (the Aramaic for "slender," "small") to distinguish it from the better-known *Sifre on Numbers*. It probably covered the same extent as *Sifre*, beginning with 5:1 and ending with chapter 35. It belongs to Type B. ascribed to the School of Akiba. Like the other tannaitic *midrashim*, *Sifre Zuta* was probably compiled towards the end of the fourth century, although some scholars believe it was redacted earlier, and probably in Judea (Lydda) rather than Galilee.

vi. Sifre on Deuteronomy.

This work is a midrashic commentary on certain chapters of the Book of Deuteronomy: Deut 1:1-30; 3:21-4:1; 6:4-9; 11:10-26; 15; 31:14; 32-34. Like the other tannaitic *midrashim*, it treats of the text in consecutive fashion, by chapter and verse, and occasionally the individual words within a verse. It is recognized as belonging to Type B of the tannaitic *midrashim*, and thus ascribed to the School of Rabbi Akiba. Like the text it comments on, which is legal and narrative, *Sifre* contains both *halakah* and *haggadah*.

vii. Midrash Tannaim (Mekilta on Deuteronomy).

Sifre on Deuteronomy, just considered, is of Type B of the tannaitic *midrashim*, and ascribed to the School of Akiba. D. Hoffmann surmised that in ancient times a halakic commentary on Deuteronomy from the School of Ishmael (Type A) must have existed. Several fragments of just such a *midrash* were found in the Cairo Geniza and published by S. Schechter in 1904. Later other portions of it were identified in excerpts in medieval Jewish writings, e.g. in the *Midrash ha-Gadol.* This work is given the title *Midrash Tannaim* or *Mekilta on Deuteronomy.* The extant fragments of the work, however, are too meagre to permit a sure judgement as to the extent or more exact nature of the original, even with regard to its title. It is clear, however, that it belonged to Type A.

6. Exegetical Midrashim
of Early Amoraic Period — 400-500

The period A.D. 400-640 is regarded as the golden age of haggadic *midrashim.* The oldest of these is *Genesis Rabbah,* from about 400, and in this the literary form and constructions are already found in a highly developed form, indicating a lengthy period of development before this. These *midrashim* are characterized by a lengthy proem at the beginning of the complete *midrash* or of a chapter, a proem presumably imitating the beginning of a structured homily.

i. Genesis Rabbah.

This is the oldest of the exegetical *midrashim.* It is a continuous exposition of the Book of Genesis, chapter by chapter and verse by verse. It is written in Mishnaic Hebrew with some Galilean Aramaic, and uses earlier sources which were in part oral and also possibly written. Its composition is to be assigned to about A.D. 420, as it cites rabbis who flourished in the latter part of the fourth century.

ii. Lamentations Rabbah.

This work is an exegetical *midrash* on the book of Lamentations, following chapter and verse. It brings together different interpretations and *haggadoth.* It was composed in Palestine. Its language is a mixture of Mishnaic Hebrew and Palestinian Aramaic. It is later than *Genesis Rabbah,* which it uses, and was compiled from earlier sources by a single author, it would seem, towards the end of the fifth century.

7. Early Homiletical Midrashim of the Amoraic Period
— A.D. 450 to 600

The homiletical *midrashim*, as distinct from the exegetical, explain only the opening verse or verses of the weekly section read in the synagogue. They follow the triennial cycle current in Palestine. As homiletic *midrashim* from the earlier period 450 (or so) to 600 we may instance *Leviticus Rabbah, Pesikta de-Rab Kahana.*

Greater detail on such writings belongs more properly to books on Rabbinic writings rather than to a work such as this one on intertestamental literature. Mention of them, however summary, in this work is considered legitimate because they can be regarded as containing early traditional material from tannaitic and even pre-Christian times.

8. Aramaic Targums.

The word *targum* both in Hebrew and Aramaic means "translation," a translation of any sort, not merely an Aramaic translation of the Hebrew scriptures, much less an actualizing, paraphrastic, one. However, the preponderant use of the word in both these languages is for the Aramaic version of the Hebrew Scriptures. In the present section of our work we shall consider especially these targums that have been transmitted to us by rabbinic Judaism. Since, however, these are but the more recent versions in the long history of the translation of the Hebrew Bible, we shall first of all say a little on the earlier translations.

i. Early Greek Renderings: the Septuagint, Aquila, Symmachus.

In the section dealing with Hellenistic Judaism we have already considered the early Greek translations (above pp. 215-220). Each of these in its own way reflects something of the prevailing interpretative mentality of the age and area in which it was composed. We have already seen how the ideas

of later times have actually been read into the text of the
Scriptures in the process of the final redaction (above pp. 40f).
The longer text of Jeremiah arose very probably in an
attempt to accommodate developments that had taken
place since the composition of the original text, translated
into Greek in the Septuagint. Later sensitivity was also
probably responsible for certain "emendations" in the
Hebrew text to become canonical in the Masoretic Text, as
for instance when in Deut 32:8 we read: "When the Most
High gave to the nations their inheritance. . . . he fixed the
bounds of the peoples *according to the number of the
children of Israel*," instead of "according to the number of
the children of God," that is the angels, as the Septuagint
and an early Hebrew fragment of the passage from Qumran
has. Evidence of the influence of later messianic expectat-
tions is probably present in the Septuagint rendering of Jer
31:8 (38:8 in the Greek text). In the context God is speaking
about the ingathering of the exiles from all parts of the earth
in a new exodus, all very much in language and imagery
similar to that of Second Isaiah (cf. e.g. Isa. 35; 42:16). In
this context God says of the returning exiles: "among them
the blind and the lame" — in Hebrew *bam 'iwwer upisseah*,
or in continuous unvocalized text: *bm'wrwpsh*. The Septuagint rendered: "(Behold . . . I will gather them from the end
of the earth) in the feast of passover" — *en heortē phasek*, as
if it read the Hebrew as *bᵉmo'ed pesah* (*bm'dpsh*), the letters
r (*resh*) and *d* (*daleth*) being easily confused in later Hebrew
script. Prevalence of the belief that the Messiah or messianic
redemption was to occur at Passover would have helped the
misreading of the Hebrew.

We have seen earlier (above pp. 216-220) that from the
mid-second century B.C. onwards the old Greek translation
was to undergo recensional activity designed to bring it
more and more into line with the Hebrew text, considered
canonical and authoritative. The recension was governed by
a certain understanding of what a translation should be. An
extreme example of a translation being governed by a definite exegetical stance can be seen in the rendering of Aquila,
a disciple of Rabbi Akiba (see above p. 220).

ii. *The Targums of Job and of Leviticus 16 from Qumran.*

We have briefly considered both these works in the chapter devoted to the Qumran literature. The former work may have been composed as early as the mid-third century B.C., although some scholars opt for a date about 100 B.C. It is not easy to determine why the translation was made, and why it was used in Qumran, where it probably was brought from outside. As a translation it represents a fairly literal rendering of the original Hebrew, without any sectarian bias. The Aramaic rendering of Leviticus 16 is also a literal rendering of the Hebrew text, although in this does not differ from the other known targums of the passages in question. We have noted above that as a translation it is linguistically nearer Onkelos than the Palestinian Targums, but in some other ways is closer to Codex Neofiti of the Palestinian Targums than to Onkelos (see above p. 117). The translation seems to date from the second century B.C. and probably came to Qumran from outside the community. These two texts, however, tell us very little about what translation principles governed the Aramaic renderings of the Bible that might have existed in the second or first century B.C.

iii. *The Targum of Onkelos.*

This targum is a translation of the entire Pentateuch. It was given its final redaction in the Jewish academies of Babylonia, not in Palestine, and was vocalized and given a masora there. However, it was always Jewish tradition, and now the opinion of scholars in general, that it originated in Palestine. It was unknown, however, in Palestine until taken there after the Arab conquest, and possibly as late as the tenth century. It is written in a literary form of Aramaic, that is now seen to have similarities with that of the Qumran texts. As a translation it tends to be literal rather than paraphrastic, especially when compared with the Palestinian Targums of the same books. It does, however, tend to avoid anthropomorphisms, and has for some time been recognised as opting for a paraphrastic rendering in poetic passages, for example Genesis 49. Closer examination has revealed that it contains much more haggadah than was formerly suspected of having been the case, and furthermore that its haggadah and understanding of the Hebrew text is often that found, and given at greater length, in the Palestinian Targums of the Pentateuch.

iv. *The Palestinian Targums of the Pentateuch.*

Together with Onkelos, which was redacted and unified and became the official targum of Judaism, first in Babylon and later in the West, we also have another rendering of the Pentateuch in a form of Aramaic which is almost identical with that of the Palestinian Talmud and *Midrashim*. This rendering is not preserved in a unified text. Instead of this we have what is basically the same paraphrastic, interpretative, tradition in a variety of forms which are generally now referred to as Palestinian Targums of the Pentateuch, although at an earlier stage of targumic research the rendering was more often referred to in the singular: the Palestinian Targum of the Pentateuch. This Palestinian Aramaic rendering is found in two complete versions, i.e. the Targum in Codex Neofiti 1 of the Vatican Library and in the work known as the Targum of Pseudo-Jonathan. It has also survived in the fragments of complete targum texts found in the Cairo Geniza, in the collected excerpts known as the Fragment Targums and in citations in earlier texts and in medieval Jewish writings.

Codex Neofiti 1 was discovered in 1949 in the Vatican Library by Prof. J. Millas Vallicrosa and Alejandro Díez Macho. They had come there in search of manuscripts of Targum Onkelos and found Neofiti 1 catalogued as an Onkelos text. Its existence was registered in a note by Professor Millas Vallicrosa. In 1955 it was identified by Professor Díez Macho for what it really was: a complete text of a Palestinian Targum of the Pentateuch. The edition of this text, and the interest it generated, helped immensely to promote research in the area of the Palestinian Targums. A colophon to Codex Neofiti tells us that it was written in Rome for Maestro Ayyidio (Giles of Viterbo, O.S.A.) in 1504. Despite the fact that the copy was made so late, the actual text of the targum in Codex Neofiti is considered to be old. Just how old is still a matter of debate: some would say from the second century A.D., others that it is basically pre-Christian.

The Targum of Pseudo-Jonathan is a rather curious composition. It contains a targum of the entire Pentateuch. In some sections it is either identical with, or extremely close to, Onkelos in both content and Aramaic. In other parts it has the Palestinian Targum paraphrase, in Palestinian Aramaic. It has some very old sections; occasionally it appears demonstrably pre-Christian. But there are also some demonstrably late items, such as the mention by name of Adisha and Fatima, the wife and daughter of Mohammed (Gen 21:21), of the Six Orders of the Mishnah (Exod 26:9), and of Constantinople (Num 24:24). It seems to borrow from the Mekilta (as in Exod 14:2) and has some unexplained peculiar similarity with the *Pirke de-Rabbi Eliezer* — a medieval composition which, in fact, may be dependent on Pseudo-Jonathan. It remains for future research to unravel secrets such as these.

From the Cairo Geniza we have fragments of five manuscripts (numbered from A to E) of Palestinian Targums. These have been assigned dates by Prof. Paul Kahle as follows: A, late seventh or early eighth century; E, A.D. 750-800; B, C and D, the latter half of the ninth century. These texts are in Palestinian Aramaic and contain the same peculiarities of the Palestinian Targum with which we are familiar from other texts — the same tradition in a variety of formulations.

We also have a further manuscript with Palestinian Targum material from the Geniza. This is MS F from the eleventh century. However, unlike the others it is not a fragment of a complete targum manuscript. It is a manuscript for liturgical purposes and contains certain targum texts for Jewish festivals: Passover, Shevuoth, Simhat Torah, and —according to the heading, for Hanukkah, although this is now lost. The text known as "The Fragment Targum" was first published by Felix Pratensis in the First Rabbinic Bible of 1517-1518. Since then a number of manuscripts with similar texts have been identified: Paris, Bibl. Nat. Ms Hebr 110 (=P); Vatican, MS Ebr., 440 (=V); Nürnberg, Stadtbibliothek Solger 2.2° (=N); Leipzig, Universität B.H. (=L); New York, Jewish Theological Seminary (=J); London, British Library Or. 10794 (=Br); Moscow, Günzburg 3 (=Mos); Sassoon MS 264 (Sas) and finally, a text recently discovered by Dr. Julia A. Foster in the Cambridge Univesity Library, Taylor-Schechter Geniza Collection T.S. AS 72,75,76,77. Michael Klein has shown that these can be reduced to two major recensions V and P. The *editio princeps* of 1517-18 was based on the Nurnberg MS and its margins. The Moscow MS is copied from the Nürnberg text and the Sassoon MS is copied from the second edition of the *Biblia Rabbinica*, thus again with the Nürnberg text. He has also shown that the Vatican, Leipzig and Nürnberg texts all belong to one and the same family. The Paris MS is the sole representative of a distinct family and so also are the texts in the Jewish Theological Seminary and the British Library. A further point to be noted with regard to the fragments in question is that they cannot be reduced to any common original. There was no original "Fragment Targum" as such; we must speak rather of Fragments Targums, fragments from Palestinian Targum texts copied onto other manuscripts, or into special collections, for what precise reason we cannot say.

With regard to the date to be assigned to the Palestinian Targums — while some scholars maintain that they are early (as already noted with regard to Neofiti) others are adamant that the Galilean dialect in which they are composed requires a date from the third or fourth centuries, at the very earliest.

v. The Targum of the Prophets.

In Jewish tradition this work is ascribed to a certain Jonathan and known as the Targum of Jonathan. Like Onkelos, it received its final form in the Jewish Academies of Babylon and attained official status in Judaism. The Aramaic is of the same nature as that of Targum Onkelos.

The nature of the translation is, however, not altogether

uniform. That of the Former Prophets is literal. The rendering of the Latter Prophets (Isaiah, Jeremiah, Ezekiel) is less uniform and variant traditions show through to a greater degree. The nature of these, however, has not yet been properly investigated.

The date to be assigned to the work is far from certain. Its final redaction may have been in the third or fourth centuries. From a study of the language of the Targum of the Former Prophets and its position within the Aramaic Dialects (Tel-Aviv 1975), Abraham Tal (Rosenthal) concluded that the relationship between the language of the Targum in question and that of the Palmyrene and Nabatean inscriptions and of the Qumran texts seems to indicate that this section of Targum Jonathan is not to be dated later than the crushing of the Bar-Kochba revolt (A.D. 135). If this were so, a similar *terminus ad quem* could be postulated for the Targum of Onkelos and that of the Latter Prophets. Scholars who accept Tal's contention tend to assign a date of the third-fourth century, at the earliest, for the composition of the Palestinian Targums. With regard to this date assigned on linguistic grounds to the Targum of the Former Prophets (and by implication to Onkelos and the Targum of the Latter Prophets), it appears in my view to deduce too definite a historical conclusion from linguistic principles. Future research will probably nuance these conclusions.

vi. The Targums of the Hagiographa.

It does not appear that the Hagiographa (i.e. the books of the third section of the Jewish Canon) had official standing in the Jewish Synagogal liturgy. For this reason no liturgical translation was required. And yet all the books of the Hagiographa, with the exception of Daniel, Ezra and Nehemiah (in part already in Aramaic), have Aramaic translations. These, however, do not appear to have been widely used among the Jews, as they are not much cited by medieval authors. It can be doubted if they were known or used at all in Babylonian Jewry, since we have no Babylonian manuscripts of any of the Targums of the Hagiographa. In general the Yemen got its tradition of Targum from

Babylon, but not with regard to the Hagiographa, which seems to have come to it from Palestine. The targums of the Hagiographa were, apparently, composed in Palestine at different times, but in good part in the post-tannaitic period. Sufficient research has not yet been done on these targums to permit any definite conclusions. Many of them, in fact, have yet to be critically edited. For some of them we have more than one translation, or at least recension. Thus, for instance, in the case of the Book of Esther which has two, or possibly even three, targums. There is a shorter and longer recension in the case of Lamentations and also of Canticles — the former recension used in the Yemen. These Targumim seem to have been the work of individuals, rather than of communities or schools. But, to repeat, no definite conclusions can be reached until the fundamental work of critical editions and source analysis has been carried out.

9. *The Antiquity of Rabbinic Tradition*

In taking the story of rabbinic literature beyond the first, down to the fifth or sixth century, I am mindful of the limits posed by the title of the present volume. The extent of the literature highlights the problem of using rabbinic material as evidence for Judaism of the intertestamental period. It also focuses attention on the nature of rabbinic material itself, and on the relationship of this to an earlier, Pharisaic, tradition roughly contemporary with that of Qumran.

A consideration of the Mishnah, the oldest source, will give an indication of the problem. In this the bulk of the authorities cited are from the second century, and from the post-135 A.D. period at that. Mention is indeed made of Hillel and Shammai (both of whom died about the beginning of our era) and of their respective schools. The tradition records the existence of no important teacher between Hillel and Gamaliel I (presented in one, but uncertain tradition as the grandson of Hillel). Tannaitic tradition (Mishnah, *Soṭa* 9:15; *Nedarim* 9:1, *Aboth* 4:2) recognizes the importance of Gamaliel I (teacher of Paul according to Acts

22:3; see also Acts 5:34-39), but records little of his sayings. His son Simeon was also a renowned Torah scholar in his day and active in public life in the early days of the Jewish War (66-68), but is not given as an authority in rabbinic sources. It is only with the fall of Jerusalem in A.D. 70 that the chain of transmission really starts, and from this point of view the first generation of Tannaim begins with A.D. 70, although the Tannaitic Age itself may be traced back to the deaths of Hillel and Shammai. The teachers most frequently cited in the Mishnah for the period A.D. 70-130 are the following: (a) *for period 70-100*: Rabbi Yohanan ben Zakkai, practically the reorganizer of Judaism after 70 (23 times), a Rabbi Zadok or Zadduk (about 16 times, although two persons may be involved), R. Hanaiah, captain of the priests (12 times), R. Eliezer ben Jacob (40 times, but, again two persons of the same name may be involved); (b) *second generation, period 100-130*: Rabban Gamaliel 11 (84 times), R. Joshua (ben Hananiah) (146 times), R. Eliezer (ben Hyrcanus) (324 times), R. Eleazar ben R. Zadduk (22 times), R. Ishmael (71 times), R. Akiba (278 times), R. Tarfon (51 times) — and eight others. Rabbi Hanina, the "Captain of the Priests," a leading Torah scholar, relates in the Mishnah what his father did in the temple and what he himself saw. In the Mishnah he acts almost exclusively as a witness to details of the priestly cult. R. Eliezer ben Jacob, from the end of the first generation, had an uncle who served as a levite in the temple. He himself is mentioned frequently as having provided information on the description of the temple given in the Mishnah tractate *Middoth*. In fact, later tradition even ascribes the writing of the entire tractate to him.

The question posed by this evidence is whether we can go back beyond the Tannaim and A.D. 70 and trace the tradition, whether halakic or haggadic, back into the earlier first century and even into pre-Christian times. It appears that we can. To begin with, this stress on named teachers for the period 70 onwards seems to derive from the nature of the transmission. It was then that the rabbinic teachers took over the control of Judaism. The older order, with the

Sanhedrin and the rule of the Sadducean High Priests, had vanished from the scene.

It is extremely unlikely that a tradition was created *ab ovo* by this new generation of teachers. Their task would have been much more likely one of consolidation, transmission and formulation or reformulation. The process of developing the *halakah* had begun in its most recent, tannaitic, stage with Hillel, Shammai and their schools. Without denying the creativity that was undeniably part of the post 70 scene we can presume that the bulk of what they transmitted in halakic as in haggadic lore had been inherited by them from their predecessors, which we can accept as having been the Pharisees.

10. Rabbinic Tradition Heir to Pharisaism.

Rabbinic tradition takes it that the oral Law can be traced back to Moses and Mount Sinai, just as the written Law can. In the opening chapter, the tractate *Aboth* of the Mishnah gives us the chain of transmission, from Moses through Joshua, the Prophets, the men of the Great Synagogue (after the exile), the Five groups of Pairs of which Hillel and Shammai are the last. Rabban Johanan ben Zakkai, the father of post-Destruction Judaism is presented as having received the (oral) Law from Hillel and Shammai. In this evidence the technical terms for transmitting tradition are used: "to receive," "to commit" or "hand on."

> Moses received the Law from Sinai and committed it to Joshua, and Joshua to the elders, and the elders to the Prophets; and the Prophets committed it to the men of the Great Synagogue.... Simeon the Just was of the remnants of the Great Synagogue...Antigonus of Soko received (the Law) from Simeon the Just...Jose ben Joezer of Zeredah and Jose ben Johanan of Jerusalem received (the Law) from them..... Hillel and Shammai received (the Law) from them..... Rabban Johanan ben Zakkai received (the Law) from Hillel and Shammai (*Aboth* 1:1-4,12; 2:8).

With Johanan ben Zakkai the chain of transmission ends. The purpose of the piece was to show the continuity of the tradition. What is important for our purpose here is the awareness within rabbinic tradition that the post-70 situation was but a continuation of an earlier tradition, and immediately of that received (and developed) by Hillel and Shammai. It matters little that the final stage of the tradition (of A.D. 70 and later) really knew very little, if anything at all, of the immediate post-exilic situation, designated by the generic expression "the men of the Great Synagogue."

This earlier, pre-70, stage of the tradition was the Pharisaic one. That this was so is confirmed by the fact that pre-70 authorities of the rabbinic chain of tradition are in other sources described as Pharisees. Thus, for instance, Rabban Simeon (ben Gamaliel) of the Mishnah (*Aboth* 1:17,18, *Kerithoth* 1:7) is said by Josephus (*Life* 38 §191) to have been of the sect of the Pharisees. Likewise with Rabban Gamaliel of rabbinic tradition; he is called a Pharisee and teacher of the Law in Acts 5:34.

What rabbinic sources say about the oral law and the traditions conforms to what the New Testament (the Gospels in particular) tells us about the tradition of the Pharisees in Jesus' day and what Josephus has to say concerning the traditions of the Pharisees of his own day and in earlier generations. Thus, for instance, in Mark 7:3,5, we read that the Pharisees, and all the Jews, do not eat unless they wash their hands, *observing the traditions of the elders*, and when they come from the market place, they do not eat unless they purify themselves; and there are many such traditions which they observe, the washing of cups and pots and vessels of bronze. The Pharisees and the scribes are represented as asking Jesus why his disciples do not live *according to the tradition of the elders*, but eat with hands defiled. As part of his reply Jesus calls their traditions the traditions of men (7:8). They make void the word of God through their tradition which they hand on (7:13); cf. parallel passage in Matt 15:2-9. Paul, the erstwhile Pharisee, in Gal 1:14, speaks of the inordinate zeal he once had for the traditions of his fathers.

Josephus writes about the Pharisees in his first work, *The Jewish War* (2,8,14 §§ 162-163), composed soon after A.D. 73, and on more than one occasion in his later work *Jewish Antiquities*, written around A.D. 100 or somewhat later. His summary account in the *War* must be reckoned some-what inexact, in some matters. However, in it he notes the devotion of the Pharisees to the exact interpretation of their laws:

> The Pharisees are those who are esteemed most skilful in the exact explication of their laws.

He writes in a similar vein concerning the Pharisees when discussing the rift that arose between them and John Hyrcanus (*Antiquities* 13,10,6 §§ 293-296):

> For the present I wish merely to explain that the Phari-sees had passed on to the people certain regulations handed down by former generations and not recorded in the Laws of Moses, for which reason they are rejected by the Sadducean group, who hold that only those regula-tions should be considered valid which were written down (in Scripture), and that those which had been handed down by former generations need not be observed....

The context of this same passage indicates that by the time of John Hyrcanus (134-104 B.C.) the Pharisaic tradi-tion was both well developed and well established among the people. Hyrcanus was at first a devotee of theirs but Josephus (*Antiquities* 13,10,6 §§ 293-296) tells us that when they fell from favour, he abrogated the regulations (in Greek *nomina*) which they had established for the people. The Pharisees were out of royal favour until the reign of Queen Alexandra (76-67 B.C.). Josephus tells us (*Antiquities* 13,16,2 § 408) that this ruler "restored those practices which the Pharisees had introduced, according to the traditions of their fathers, and which her father-in-law Hyrcanus had abrogated." From then on the power of the Pharisees over the masses continued unabated. Writing of the events of the census in A.D. 7 Josephus notes that so great was their influence over the people, that whatever the Pharisees did concerning divine worship, prayers or sacrifice the people performed according to their direction (*Antiquities* 18,1,3 § 15). This would have been the situation as Josephus himself knew it about A.D. 50 and later.

Pharisaism was a movement which arose because of a special understanding of what the Jewish religion was, or should be, and of what constituted a proper relationship with God. It is not easy to define what were the essential elements of its view of reality and the relationship of the believer to God, but we can presume that throughout the history of the group these were established well enough to act as a sustaining force and guiding principle. From one point of view Pharisaism was no more than normative, post-exilic, Jewish religion. The point was made by Emil Schürer towards the beginning of the century in his classic *A History of the Jewish People in the Time of Jesus Christ* (English translation 1901), and what he says has not been altered in the revised English version recently edited by Geza Vermes, Fergus Miller and Matthew Black (1979). His words, in the recent revised edition, are as follows:

> No peculiarity emerges from this characterization of Pharisaism which might distinguish it from Judaism in general during the period of the Second Temple. Regarded as a spiritual orientation, it was simply identical with the trend adopted by the main body and the classical representatives of post-exilic Jewry.

The equation, however, is not complete. The very name the Pharisees bore implies or means "separation." They were a distinct body within the Jewish nation. To continue the words of E. Schürer:

> Nevertheless, the Pharisees formed a party within the nation, an *ecclesiola in ecclesia* ... The Pharisees must have obtained their name from a separation in which the main body of the people did not participate, in other words, from having set themselves apart, by virtue of

their stricter understanding of the concept of purity, not only from the uncleanness of the Gentiles and half-Jews but also from that uncleanness which, in their opinion, adhered to a great part of the people itself. It is in this sense that they were called the 'separated' or 'self-separating'. . . . .

Other scholars would say that their pursuit of ritual cleanness derived from their desire to live the "spirituality" of the ministering priests of the temple, from their wish to extend to all Israel the "sanctity" required by the Law of these priests, and from the importance they attributed to the table fellowship in which they and their followers partook of food in a state of ritual cleanness.

It is quite clear, however, that their tradition was a strongly held one, and that they believed that the mass of the people should follow their understanding of Jewish religion, the regulations (*nomima*) mentioned by Josephus (*Antiquities* 13, 10, 6, § 296) which probably correspond to the *taqqanot* of rabbinic sources. These were special enactments made by the scribes as occasion demanded.

In such circumstances it can be presumed that the main body of the earlier scribal, Pharisaic, lore passed over into post-A.D. 70 Judaism. That there should have been change and reformulation is but natural: this was already taking place in the lead up to A.D. 70 in the debates between the rival schools of Hillel and Shammai. But the presumption is that these were limited in nature and that all of them were within the Pharisaic, scribal tradition.

We may also presume that the haggadic tradition is equally old and here there is probably greater reason for so believing since there would have been less cause to change radically in this matter.

To say that this continuity existed between post-70 A.D. rabbinism and the earlier scribal and Pharisaic tradition does not, however, mean that we can presume that any individual item of *halakah* or *haggadah* is early or antedates the destruction of Jerusalem. It is equally clear that there was a change and development. For this reason it would be quite illegitimate to take a rabbinic tradition from either the tannaitic or amoraic period and use it without proper analysis as evidence for Jewish practice or belief in an earlier period. Criteria are needed for discerning the age of rabbinic traditions. Much study has been devoted to this matter for some time past and it is still receiving attention —whether it be in the area of rabbinic tradition in general or of the targums in particular. The nature of the present volume, devoted as it is to the broader area of Jewish literature over three centuries, precludes more detailed examination of the question here.

11. Some Early Writings with Rabbinic Traits

I end this section on Rabbinic literature, and the overall survey itself, by treatment of some works which may help us go back beyond rabbinic writings proper to an earlier stage of the same tradition.

i. 2(4) Esdras and 2 Baruch.

When considering both these works in the chapter on Apocalyptic literature it was noted that they were related, partly in themes, thought and language, to rabbinic writings. They were probably composed some time after the fall of Jerusalem in A.D. 70 by someone who had been trained in the rabbinic schools.

ii. The Biblical Antiquities of Pseudo-Philo.

I finish this survey with consideration of a work which was composed towards the very end of the intertestamental period and in a sense may be regarded as representing the beliefs of the vast body of Palestinian Jews of its day, a kind of synthesis of the development that had been going on for generations. Even if it cannot with any great degree of certainty be taken as representing Pharisaism or rabbinism, it merits inclusion as the final item in this survey.

The Biblical Antiquities of Pseudo-Philo (*Liber Antiquitatum Biblicarum*) is extant in Latin only and in a late

Hebrew translation of the Latin. The original language was most probably Hebrew. In its present form, it gives the narrative of the Hebrew people from Adam to Saul, although it probably was once more extensive. In places it merely gives the biblical text. More often, however, it has introduced additional material on the text, although not always in the expected place. It is a rich source for Jewish tradition as known in Palestine, in certain communities at least, during the first century A.D. Its traditions, emphases and themes are very important for the study of first century Judaism, especially of the Pharisaic or rabbinic type, and also may be of importance for understanding the New Testament. The author's interests, for instance, have been compared with those of St. Luke, particularly in the third Gospel.

Among its legends on biblical persons we may note Milcah announcing the coming of Abraham (4:11); the tower of Babel and Abraham saved from the furnace (6:3-18); Isaac and his sacrifice offered instead of that of a lamb from the flock for an odour of sweetness, i.e. as the *tamid* offering (32:1-6;18:5: "and because he resisted not, his offering was acceptable in my sight and for the blood of him did I choose this people"); Amram and Moses (ch. 9); the birth of Moses announced to Miriam (ch. 10); Moses in glory coming down from the mountain (12:1), etc.

Regarding theological concepts, Pseudo-Philo's lack of interest in the temple is remarkable. He is, however, not anti-priest. He praises the true priests in praising Phinehas (28:3). The author's lack of interest is explained by some through the book's origin in the synagogue context.

The work gives the history of the covenant; it treats of the greatness of Israel and of the Law, the everlasting Law created before the birth of the world. He lays special stress on the Ten Commandments and speaks at length on them (11:6-13;25:7-14;44:6f.). Another favourite theme of his is divine providence; he also has a special interest in the role played by women in sacred history. He reminds his readers that all men have sinned, are sinners (3:9;19:8) and sin results in death (13:8-9; 27:7 . . . .). The sinner is called on to repent; God's mercy is great. "For although our sins do overabound, nevertheless his mercy filleth all the earth" (39:6). With regard to life after death, God will give life to the just (who are dead) at the moment he chooses (51:5); the wicked will be punished. In the intermediate stage between death and the resurrection, there is no room for conversion (33:5); the dead cannot intercede for the living (33:5; cp. 2 Baruch 11:5; 85:2). Only the living can intercede, like Moses (19:3) or Samuel (64:8). During this period awaiting the resurrection the just sleep (3:10;19:12;51:5) and repose (19:12;28:10). They are in "the secret places of souls" (21:9); "in the treasure houses of souls" (32:13); cp. 2(4) Esdras: *promptuaria*. Finally come resurrection and the judgment: ". . . when the years of the world shall be fulfilled, then shall the light cease and the darkness be quenched; and I will quicken the dead and raise up from the earth them that sleep: and Hell shall pay his debt and destruction give back that which was committed unto him, that I may render unto every man according to his works and according to the fruit of their imaginations" (3:10)

The book makes no reference to a Messiah; it is always God himself who acts. The ministry of angels is mentioned; also the activity of the holy spirit, which is associated with prophecy. The spirit of God came upon Maria (Miriam) by night and she saw in a vision the birth of Moses (9:10). The holy spirit abided in Balaam to make him prophesy (18:11). The Judges, as well as prophets, were possessed of the holy spirit. The holy spirit is connected with prayer and praise. Debborah is thus exhorted: "Sing praises, sing praises, O Debborah. . . and let the grace of a holy spirit awake in thee, and begin to praise the works of the Lord" (32:14; cf. Luke 1:67-79). Frequent mention is also made of light and illumination.

With regard to the origin of the *Antiquities*, a natural setting would be the synagogue liturgy, in a Pharisaic setting. A recent editor of the work, C. Perrot thus explains this rereading of biblical history: "This particular rereading of Israel's history, would it not enter into the general picture of biblical rereadings, carried out in particular in the course of the synagogue service before the destruction of the Temple? . . . . Not that we should see in the *Biblical Antiquities* a compilation of synagogue homilies, but rather a corpus of haggadic traditions, for the use of targumists and homilists in particular." Whatever of this opinion, the *Biblical Antiquities* is rich in parallels to rabbinic and targumic midrash.

With regard to the date of composition, opinion differs. Some authors (e.g. C. Perrot, D. Harrington) believe it dates to before A.D. 70. Others (in part because of what it has on the Sacrifice of Isaac) would date it A.D. 70-135. Thus P. R. Davies and B.D. Chilton; see 4 Maccabees, p. 237 above.

8. CONCLUSIONS

Now that we have brought our survey of Jewish literature during the intertestamental period to a close we can reflect on the evidence and consider its significance from various points of view. Before we review the achievement of the intertestamental period proper, however — that is from 200 B.C. onwards — it is better first to consider for a moment the spiritual situation of Judaism at the threshold of this era.

1. The Situation of Jewish Belief 200 B.C.

Recent studies, as we already noted, have shown that the origins of the apocalyptic genre and the existence of certain apocalyptic books go back beyond the Book of Daniel, and at least into the late third century B.C. This means that already by that time the belief existed that "God had created not one world, but two," that there was another world beyond this in which men would be rewarded and punished, in which the souls or spirits of the dead awaited a day of judgment and a future resurrection. This same belief implies that there was an element in man, be it called soul or spirit is indifferent, which could subsist without the body and could also in this state experience either happiness or suffering. This is a noteworthy advance beyond the earlier Hebrew conception of man, and of the Hebrew concepts of *nepesh* and *ruah*. The explanation may well be that the philosophical content of the Greek terms *psyche* and *pneuma* was transferred to the two Hebrew ones.

This awareness that existence beyond this one was a forum for reward and punishment also helped Israelite thought cope with a problem that was becoming more acute since the exile, namely that of retribution. The older view, put forward for the nation as a whole by the Book of Deuteronomy (especially chap. 28) and in the Books of Chronicles for the individual, that good and evil were rewarded and punished in this world was challenged by Job, and practically derided by Ecclesiastes. In two Psalms we seem to have intimations that death could not spell the end of union with God, at least for his pious ones (cf. Pss 49:15 and 73:24): they would, in some way, be taken by God to himself, somewhat as Henoch was (Gen 5: 24). The Hebrew positive view of the material creation would gravitate towards belief in bodily resurrection rather than in immortality, without resurrection.

It may be possible to trace this belief in a bodily resurrection back further still and find reference to it in Isa 26:19, where the following words of consolation are addressed to the persecuted Jews: "Thy dead shall live, their bodies shall rise. O dwellers of the dust, awake and sing for joy! For this dew is a dew of light, and on the land of the shades thou wilt let it fall." This promise is made in the context of a renewal of the nation, and it appears that more is intended than a mere national resurrection, as was the case on Ezekiel 37 (see also Hosea 6:2; 13:1, 14). A little earlier, speaking of the feast to be given by Yahweh on Mount Zion, the promise was made that the Lord would swallow up death for ever (Isa 25:8). The difficulty of assigning a date to this section of the Book of Isaiah (the so-called "Apocalypse of Isaiah") is well known. Some would date it as late as the overthrow of Babylon by Alexander in 331, which need not be much earlier than the date of the Enochic *Book of the Watchers* (1 Enoch 1-36).

Another belief widely accepted in Judaism by 200 B.C.

was the existence of angels and demons and their intermediary role. Their activity is central to apocalyptic thought
moulds.

2. *Political Events in Judea during the Intertestamental Period.*

In the political and religious fields the intertestamental
period was one of deep changes for Palestinian Judaism.
The age began roughly with the transfer of power in Palestine from the Egyptian Ptolemaic to Syrian Seleucid control. Soon afterwards the campaign of Hellenization in
Palestine was to begin, and carry with it a chain of sad
events that ate deeply into the soul of Israel. The reader will
find a catalogue of them at the end of John Collins' work in
volume 15 (pp. 366-368) of this series.

In 175 Antiochus Epiphanes came to the Seleucid throne.
The high priesthood that should have stood for spiritual
values got caught up in the Hellenization movement. In
175-174 Jason of the Hellenizing party succeeded in obtaining the high priesthood by bribery while his brother Onias
III, the legitimate high priest of the Zadokite line, was at
Antioch on a mission to the King of Syria. In 172 Jason was
outbid for the priesthood by Menelaus, a priest not of the
house of Zadok. Onias was a religious man, respected by the
upholders of orthodoxy. He was the son of the High Priest
Simon II, whose praises are sung by Ben Sirach (Sirach 50).
The removal of the priests of the house of Zadok from
power could not have failed to wound deeply the souls of the
faithful. Matters were worsened by the massacre of Onias
III at Antioch in 170. The persecution began in earnest in
167 when "the abomination of desolation" desecrated the
altar and the temple in Jerusalem. The Maccabean revolt
soon got under way, with sufficient success to have the
temple purified and reconsecrated in 164. But the Maccabean revolt that began as a war for God and religion soon
degenerated into a mere power struggle. Less than twelve
years after the purification of the temple from the defile-

ment of the Gentiles, Jonathan Maccabee himself accepted the high priesthood from none other than a Gentile upstart king, Alexander Balas, who posed as the son of the archpersecutor Antiochus IV. "King Alexander to his brother Jonathan, greeting .... And so we have appointed you today to be the high priest of your nation; you are to be called the king's friend...... So Jonathan put on the holy garments (cf. Exod 28:1-39, 39:1-26) in the seventh month of the one hundred and sixtieth year (= 152 B.C.), at the feast of tabernacles, and he recruited troops and equipped them with arms in abundance" (1 Mac 10:18-21). The linking together of priestly power and military might, and this on the occasion of a feast that looked towards a better and renewed future, must have proved hard to bear for those who a short time previously had supported the armed revolt. But worse was to come when this union was solemnized by the people themselves for Simon Maccabee, Jonathan's brother and successor. 1 Macc 14:25-49 tells us that on Mount Zion a record on bronze tablets was set up on pillars. It was to a high priest not of the house of Zadok — to "Simon the son of Mattathias, a priest of the sons of Joarib and his brothers" (1 Macc 11:29). And on that same year, 140 B.C., "the Jews and their priests decided that Simon should be their leader and high priest for ever, until a trustworthy prophet should arise" (1 Mac 11:41).

It came perilously near the prerogatives of "the priest after the order of Melchizedek" of Ps 110:4. Both Jonathan's and Simon's actions seem to have alienated the affections of the religious elements of the population from the Maccabeans and their successors the Hasmoneans. It is widely believed that it was one of these events which occasioned the break of the Qumran community with the official priesthood, and that the Wicked Priest, who was the opponent and persecutor of the Master of Justice (the Founder of the Qumran Community), was either Jonathan or Simon. It was probably the close connection with the wording of the declaration in Simon's favour (1 Macc 11:41) which explains the rather curious absence of any use of Ps 110 from Jewish messianic testimonies during the intertestamental period, although the parallel Ps 2 is interpreted messianically both in Qumran and the Psalms of Solomon.

Disappointment with the Hasmonean house must have increased, if anything, during the post-Maccabean period. Even the military successes of John Hyrcanus would hardly bring the religious element among his people to acquiesce wholeheartedly in the combining of the high priesthood and military leadership in one for whom the priesthood was but an appendage to civil and military power.

The Maccabean high priesthood reached its nadir with the internecine strife between Hyrcanus and Aristobulus II. This gave the Romans a pretext to intervene in Palestinian affairs and have Pompey annex the Hasmonean kingdom to the Empire, making it part of the Roman province of Syria in 63 B.C. From 37 to 4 B.C. it had a certain autonomy once again under Herod the Great. His death takes us to the New Testament period. By the turn of the era dissatisfaction with Roman rule was growing and the scene was being set for the disastrous war against Rome which broke out in A.D. 66, to be crushed by the destruction of Jerusalem in A.D. 70. The Second Jewish Revolt of A.D. 132-135 was mercilessly put down by Roman might. This history is mentioned here only as a backdrop for considering of the literature and thought that went on partly in spite of disasters, partly because of them.

3. Literary Creativity During the Intertestamental Period

One feature of the entire intertestamental period that cannot fail but impress is the spiritual alertness and the literary creativity so much in evidence.

This had begun, of course, already before the year 200 B.C. The apocalyptic movement had produced two major sections of what now is the *Book of Enoch*, namely *The Book of the Watchers* and *The Astronomical Book of*

Enoch. Some extra-canonical Testament writings had also been composed, such as the *Testament of Levi,* and possibly also the *Testament of Amram,* and of *Kohath.*

In Palestine, presumably in Jerusalem, about 180 B.C., the Book of Sirach was composed. Pseudo-Eupolemus' work was probably composed about the same time, in Greek and possibly by a Samaritan. The persecution of Antiochus gave rise to the Book of Daniel. *The Assumption of Moses* and *The Enochic Dream Book* (1 Enoch 83-90) also probably date from the same period.

The mid-second century probably saw the rise of the three well-known groups, the Sadducees, Essenes and Pharisees. Two biblical works, Esther and Judith (the latter not in the Hebrew Canon), unconnected with these divisions, may have been composed about the same time. Also from about the same time, and unconnected with any division in Judaism, comes the *Third Book of the Sibylline Oracles,* this a product of Egyptian Jewry.

The Teacher of Righteousness, the founder of the Qumran Community, was apparently a personality of literary creativity. From him may come some, if not all, of the *Qumran Hymns,* and this about 140 B.C. The *Book of Jubilees* is assigned by some to the period (128-125 B.C.). From roughly the same period comes the *Temple Scroll* of Qumran. The *Epistle of Enoch* (1 Enoch 91-107) cannot be much later. The earliest of the *Qumran Rules* (*The Community Rule*) dates from about 125-100, and *The Damascus Rule* possibly from about 100 B.C. The First Book of Maccabees may have been composed about the same time and 2 Maccabees some twenty years later.

The first century B.C. was also one of literary creativity. From Egyptian Judaism comes the Book of Wisdom and some of the earlier writings of Philo, possibly *3 Maccabees* and the *Testament of Job.* Qumran remained creative, both in the later first century B.C. and the first part of the first Christian century. It was probably during this period that the Qumran *Pesharim, War Rule, Messianic Rule* and the *Genesis Apocryphon* were composed.

To roughly the same time we may assign such works as

The Apocryhon of Ezekiel and *The Life of Adam and Eve*.
The *Ascension of Isaiah* is often dated to the turn of the era.
A new edition of *The Assumption of Moses* seems to have
been composed early in the first Christian century. From the
same first century A.D. come, very probably, *The Biblical
Antiquities* of Pseudo-Philo, *4 Maccabees*, *The Apocalypse
of Jannes and Jambres*, *The Apocalypse of Abraham*, *The
Parables of Enoch* (1 Enoch 37-71) and *The Testaments of
the Twelve Patriarchs*. Shortly after the fall of Jerusalem
Josephus Flavius produced his *History of the Jewish War*.
The theological problems and the soul searching which the
same disaster occasioned gave rise to *2(4) Esdras* between
A.D. 70 and 100. A similar work appeared somewhat later,
and probably in part as a response to 2(4) *Esdras*. It is the
work known as *2 Baruch*. About the same time, and ca.
A.D. 100, Josephus produced his monumental *Jewish
Antiquities*. Finally, about this same time, after the fall of
Jerusalem, rabbinic Judaism as reorganized by Johanan
ben Zakkai was busily developing its own tradition, inherited from its Pharisee predecessors, a tradition that would
be consigned to writing towards the end of the second
century in its law code known as *The Mishnah*.

Together with these works of a more formal nature, we
must also take account of the compositions of a liturgical
and contemplative character which we have considered in a
special chapter above. The mid-second century B.C. was,
apparently, a creative period with regard to these as well,
and the composition and re-editing of such works continued
right down to the end of the first century A.D. and indeed
later.

4. Development of Religious Ideas During the Intertestamental Period.

i. Sadducees, Essenes and Pharisees.

It was most probably the Maccabean Revolt and its
aftermath that forced different groupings within Judaism to
clarify their ideas as to where they stood with regard to the

direction which the course of their people's religious history was taking. With this clarification the three well-known groups Sadducees, Essenes and Pharisees emerged, sometime about 150 B.C. The origins of each group may well have lain much farther back in the past.

Our knowledge of the Sadducees derives in the main from the New Testament and from Josephus, and in both, their beliefs tend to be contrasted with those of the Pharisees. Acts 23:8 says that "the Sadducees say that there is no resurrection, nor angel, nor spirit; but the Pharisees acknowledge them all." Their denial of the resurrection is referred to again in Mat 22:23, Mark 12:18, Luke 20:27, cf. Acts 4:1, 2. In the words of Josephus, the Sadducees "deny the continued existence of the soul and the punishments and rewards in the underworld" (*War* 2, 8, 14 § 165). "According to their teaching, souls perish together with bodies" (*Antiquities* 18, 1, 4 § 16). According to Josephus, there was also a difference between the Sadducees and Pharisees concerning the role of "destiny" (most probably meaning divine providence) in human affairs. The Pharisees "make everything dependent on destiny and on God and teach that the doing and causing of good is mostly the business of men but that destiny co-operates in every action" (*War* 2,8,14 § 163). "They maintain that all is brought about by destiny. Yet they do not thereby deprive the human will of its own activity...." (*Antiquities* 18,1,3 § 13). The Sadducees, on the contrary, "deny destiny wholly and entirely, and place God beyond the possibility of doing and planning evil. They say that good and evil are at man's choice and that the doing of one and the other is according to his discretion" (*War* 2,8,14 § 164). "They deny destiny, maintaining that it is nothing, and that human things do not come about by its means. They ascribe all things to ourselves, inasmuch as we are ourselves the cause of prosperity and that we incur misfortune through our own folly" (*Antiquities* 13,5,9 § 173). The attitude to the oral law, to material not found in the Law of Moses, was a fourth manner in which the Sadducees differed from the Pharisees. "The Pharisees," Josephus writes (*Antiquities* 13,10,6 § 297), "have imposed on the people many laws from the tradition of the elders (*ek pateron diadoches*) not written in the Law of Moses." It was quite otherwise with regard to the Sadducees. In the words of Josephus (in the same passage just noted): "The Sadducean group say that only the written regulations are to be esteemed as lawful, and that those which derive from the tradition of the fathers are not to be observed."

The other differences between Sadducees and Pharisees derive basically from their relationship to later tradition. Their attitude to the resurrection and the afterlife is fundamentally that of earlier Hebrew tradition, that commonly presented in the Hebrew Scriptures before Daniel. They would not have accepted the newer view that came in with apocalyptic as found in the Enochic *Book of the Watchers* and in Daniel. They also seem to have refused to admit that the later development in angelology corresponded to anything in the world of reality. Their attitude to providence is less easy to understand, but it may represent little more than basic teaching of the ancient wisdom literature on human responsibility pushed to extremes.

The Sadducees probably derive their name from the priest Zadok, who gave his name to the priestly house which provided Israel with its high priests until Onias III was ejected from it by the Hellenizing party and Jason was replaced by Menelaus. They would represent the ruling priestly aristocracy, which retained their original name even after the Zadokites no longer controlled the high priesthood. They were by tradition conservative and when the differences arose in the understanding of what Judaism was, they became one of the three rival groups. The basic break probably came with the Hasidim during the persecution of Antiochus in Maccabean times. The Hasidim in time would have branched off in two directions, the one lay and other levitical or priestly. The lay movement would have issued in the Pharisees, the levitical in the Essenes and Qumran Community. With these three groupings there now emerged three ways of understanding Judaism. The bulk of the population seems to have favoured the Pharisaic tradition and to have been more influenced by it than by the others. However, it may well be that the popular religion, the faith of the masses, mainstream Judaism, was relatively independent of Pharisaism, and indeed of any particular group, even though it would have been influenced by various movements and traditions, the apocalyptic as much perhaps as by Pharisaism.

ii. *The Afterlife and the Resurrection.*

Once belief in an afterlife became accepted in Judaism, together with the attendant doctrine on rewards and punishments for the individual beyond the grave, the manner of understanding the nature of this otherworldly existence took at least two forms. One branch of it stressed the existence of the soul or spirit either in happy union with God, or in a state of punishment, without reference to any bodily resurrection. This is the form of belief that would have appealed to the Greek mind. We find it in the *Wisdom of Solomon*, written at Alexandria about 50 B.C. It also seems to be the belief in the afterlife held by the author of *4 Maccabees* (see above pp.235-237). It may also have been a form of belief fairly common in Palestine. In the *Book of Jubilees* we read that the spirits of the righteous dead have much joy (*Jubilees* 23:31). No mention, however, is made of any resurrection. Nor is there any evidence that the Qumran monks believed in a resurrection of the body. It must be confessed, however, that there is also little evidence for a belief in any afterlife on the part of the Qumran community. The emphasis in their writings is on union with God through membership in the community.

Although belief in the resurrection can be traced back to the third century B.C. at the latest, it was to become one of the distinguishing tenets of Pharisaism. It was probably scribes of the Pharisee persuasion who had it become widely accepted among the masses. As a point of doctrine it was part of a larger pattern of eschatology, connected with the general judgement and the new age. And once the central belief of a resurrection body became accepted, speculation arose with regard to the nature of the resurrection body, its identity with the body once borne on earth and such like. Elaborate discussion of matters such as these, however, is beyond the scope of this concluding chapter.

iii. Messianic Belief.

Israel's future hope could take shape either in personal or impersonal messianism. In one sense impersonal messianism — that is, the belief in a new age without reference to a personal messiah as God's agent in its inauguration — is something of a contradiction in terms, but it serves the purpose of expressing one of the forms which Israel's hope for the future took on many occasions. During the Babylonian exile there seems to have been little interest in the advent of any personal messiah. Of the exilic prophets the only clear reference to this belief is found in Ezekiel 34:23 (see also Ezek 37:21-23, 24a). There is no mention of a Son of David in Second Isaiah's grand vision of the future (Isa 40-55), nor in that of Third Isaiah.

The events of 522 B.C. and the actual rebuilding of the Temple appear to have aroused hopes for the restoration of the Davidic Dynasty and the advent of a son of David, and with this the fulfilment of a prophecy of Jeremiah (Jer 22:24). This seems clear from the texts of Hag 2:20-23 and Zech 6:12-13. Some other prophecies on the advent of a personal Messiah embedded in the collected oracles of earlier prophets may also date from about this same period, for instance Jer 33:14-26 (see above pp.35f).With the removal of Zerubbabel, on which this messianic hope centred, the expectation itself apparently vanished. There is no evidence that there was any messianic expectation during the remainder of the Persian period, that is 515-333 B.C. The apparent belief of the restored community that the earlier prophecies were fulfilled already in the restoration would have left little place for any such expectation.

In Zech 9:9-10 we do have a prophecy of the advent of a peaceful messiah. This text probably dates from the beginning of the Greek period (330-300 B.C.)

It could be argued that what messianic expectation there was between 300 and 150 B.C. was also of the impersonal kind. This is the form taken by the future hope in the Book of Daniel. A certain caution, however, is called for in this regard since expectation of the advent of a personal messiah may have been alive in certain circles, although not expressed in new compositions. The sacred tradition, one must remember, contained a number of texts with personal messianism (Isa 9:1-7; 11:1-5; Pss 2:72; 89 — the later tradition seemed to have fought shy of reading Ps 110 as a messianic prophecy). The prayer for the deliverance and the restoration of Israel found in Sirach 36:1-17 reminds us that the hope for the appointed time (Sir 36:8a) could come to expression in the most unexpected places. This prayer, however, contains at most an impersonal messianism.

However, in the litany of praise found after Sirach 51:12 in the Hebrew text of the work (see above p. 177f) — a composition probably going back to before 170 B.C., if not to Sirach's day — mention is made of the Redeemer of Israel, who gathers the dispersed of Israel, who builds his city and his sanctuary, and who makes a horn to sprout forth for the house of David. Such sentiments seem to indicate the resurgence of a form of individual messianic expectation. This would be in keeping with the text of 1 Enoch 90:37-38 (a text that seems to date from before 153 B.C.; see above p. 62) which seems to refer to a personal messiah. The same expectation probably held true for Egyptian Judaism at the same period; in the *Sibylline Oracles* III, 652-795 we have the vision of the future messianic age with mention of the king from the east (literally: "from the sun") whom God will send. Even if the author is thinking here of a Greek king, rather than the Son of David (see above p. 229), the text still is evidence for Jewish expectation of a personal, saviour king.

The belief and hope in the advent of a personal messiah, and Son of David, is clearly expressed in the *Psalms of Solomon* (Pss Sol 17 and 18), composed about 50 B.C. (see above pp. 186-188.)

The vicissitudes of messianic expectations in Qumran are not altogether easy to follow. During the life of the founder, the Teacher of Righteousness, there was probably none. Later, and possibly about 100 B.C., belief in a personal messiah, or messiahs, began to be expressed, and continued to be voiced more clearly and strongly with the passage of time. A feature of Qumran expectations was the belief in the advent of two messiahs: a political and a priestly one, the messiah from Israel and the messiah from Aaron. Together with these two, the community also believed in the advent of a Prophet, obviously the person seen as referred to in Deut 18:18-19. At the turn of the era the expectation of a personal messiah, the Son of David, can be presumed to have been general among the Jews. This expectation survived the destruction of Jerusalem and still finds expression in *2(4) Esdras* and *2 Baruch*.

While there were shades of difference with regard to the office and mission of the messiah, the central belief concerning him was that he would be a human being born as other men, with the chief role of leading his people to war and victory against the Roman invader, freeing his country and restoring the fallen throne of David.

iv. Biblical Interpretation.

We have seen in the first chapter that during the earlier post-exilic period, and until the canonization of individual books, the process of interpretation went on within the community and its results were in part incorporated in works that were to become sacred and canonical. After this canonization, the interpretative process went on but had now, perforce, to be handed on as something distinct from the tradition which it interpreted.

Presumably, all sections of Judaism (not counting the Samaritans), the Sadducees as well as others, accepted this canonical post-exilic scriptural corpus. They inherited a Bible that was in part interpretation. What the Sadducees are presented as objecting to, and rejecting, was the view which regarded traditions not contained in the Scriptures as obligatory and normative. Of course, even the Sadducees must have been the unwitting heirs to an understanding of the Scriptures that was not found in the biblical text itself, somewhat as the conservative theologian Sirach (whom we may regard as a proto-Sadducee) identified Wisdom with the Law of Moses (Sir 24:23) — a non-biblical tradition central to the position of the Pharisees!! The Sadducees probably did not accept the later view which regarded the entire Bible as prophetic, a view that would appear to have been common by the beginning of the intertestamental period. But even this much is not certain, since Sirach seems to have shared this common approach to the written word of God; see above pp. 42f. If we knew more about the Sadducees we might find it necessary to nuance our views of them, views in good part dependent on what we read in Josephus.

The Essenes, Qumran monks and Pharisees may have shared a common origin in the Hasidim of Maccabean times. They would have been heirs to a common approach to the scriptures — the midrashic one. At their foundation they would both have inherited an interpreted Bible. Portions of this older interpretation may have been passed on respectively in the Qumran interpretative texts and in rabbinic tradition. Examples of such common interpretation have been isolated by some scholars.

The same midrashic approach to the scriptures continued to be a major factor behind the interpretation of both the Qumran monks and the rabbinic scholars. Although the techniques of one and the other differed, nevertheless their approach to the sacred text like the circumstances of the times were shaped in common. This made for a continued similarity in the results of their respective interpretative activities.

Another factor to be borne in mind in intertestamental biblical interpretation is the continued existence and creativity of the apocalyptic movement, a movement which influenced both Qumran and the rabbis but remained independent of both. This, too, would make for a certain amount of common interpretation.

One further point to be borne in mind with regard to

intertestamental interpretation of scriptures both in Qumran and in rabbinic tradition is that in both it seems to have been "authorized," of an official nature. It was carried out within a definite community and cannot be regarded as the exercise of individuals acting on their own. Qumran tradition tells us that interpretation was the revealing for the Community of mysteries hidden in the scriptures. The meaning of these was first and foremost revealed to their founder, the Teacher of Righteousness. After him, the meaning would have been disclosed to attested priestly and levitical interpreters. It was not something spontaneous, but was rather carried out within a given community, and by attested leaders acting in accord with a given tradition. It must have been somewhat the same in the Pharisaic and rabbinic tradition, where in good part instruction and development would have taken place within the scribal schools. We are not well informed as to how this biblical interpretation was carried out, but it does appear that it was a controlled operation, one performed by authorized scholars.

We have spoken about the interpretation within schools, and the larger traditions within Judaism. What of the common people? How unified was the understanding of tradition given to them? It would probably be fair to say that there was a fair measure of agreement in their interpretation of the Bible. Much more work, however, needs to be done in this regard before we can speak on the point with any great confidence. Instruction would have come to the masses through the synagogues and the schools connected with them. These can be said to go back to Ezra's reform (see above pp. 24-28). For the latter part of the intertestamental period, these institutions appear to have come heavily under the influence of the Pharisees and their scribes. It is quite probable, nonetheless, that the common people had communicated to them more than the Pharisaic traditions. The many works of non-Pharisaic origin composed during the period must have had a readership. And from this readership the contents and message of these works would have seeped through to sections of the common people.

v. Priestly Tradition and Spirituality.

I end these concluding reflections with some words on the tradition and spirituality of priests and levites. The priestly tradition in Israel seems to have suffered from an identification, however unconscious, of the priesthood with the Sadducees. The Sadducees at most were the ruling priestly aristocracy. They were the powerful and the wealthy element of the priesthood. But the number of the Sadducees must have been insignificant when compared with that of the priests in general, which was so great that it had to be divided into twenty-four courses. Each of these courses served for a week in the temple of Jerusalem. And corresponding with this, the levites and the people were also divided into twenty-four groups. And as the priests and levites functioned according to their course in the temple, the corresponding lay group of Israelites (the *Ma'amadim*) assembled in the local synagogue to read the opening chapter of Genesis, to pray in unison with the course of priests and levites and to manifest the solidarity of synagogue and temple. All this witnessed to the religious unity of Israel, and sacred duties were carried out in a devout manner as detailed in the Bible. The priestly class probably underwent a special training, and possibly in accord with a priestly tradition enshrined in certain writings. J.T. Milik, as we have seen above (pp. 91-94) thinks that we have examples of such works in the *Testaments of Levi, Amram* and *Kohath.* The priesthood probably had its own halakah, and this in part may be found in the halakah presented by Josephus in his writings (see above pp. 239f). The central prayers of Judaism, some of which we have studied above (pp. 165-210), may also have originated in priestly circles. I believe that this priestly tradition and spirituality merit further examination.

It is one of the unexplored areas of the intertestamental period, this period so rich in its creativity and in the heritage which it has bequeathed to both Judaism and Christianity.

CHART OF LITERARY COMPOSITIONS

DATE	EVENTS	LITERARY COMPOSITION
Persian Period (539-333 B.C.)		
538	Edict of Cyrus	
520	Rebuilding of temple	Prophets Haggai and Zechariah
ca. 500		Third Isaiah
445-433	Mission of Nehemiah	
428(or 398)	Mission of Ezra	Beginnings of rabbinic tradition (??)
ca.450		Malachi
ca. 350		Apocalypse of Isaiah (Isa 24-27)
		The Chronicler
		(1,2 Chronicles, Ezra-Nehemiah)
333-332	Destruction of Persian Empire. Greek Rule	
Greek Period (333-63 B.C.)		
323-198	Palestine under Ptolemies of Egypt	
312		Pseudo-Hecataeus of Abdera (Gr)
ca. 300		Pseudo-Eupolemus (Gr)
4th-3rd cent.		Enochic *Book of the Watchers*
		(1 Enoch 1-36)
do.		*Astronomical Book of Enoch*
		(1 Enoch 72-82).
do.		Aramaic *Testament of Levi*

Date	Events	Texts
do.		*Aramaic Testament of Kohath*
do.		Hebrew *Testament of Naphtali*
do		Deutero-Zechariah (Zech 9-14)
ca. 250		Greek Septuagint translation of Pentateuch
ca. 250		
250-100		Later Greek translations Targum of Job (Qumran) Targum of Leviticus 16 (Qumran)
220-205	Palestine passes from Ptolemaic to Seleucid rule; Mention of Gerousia of priests and scribes in ruling position (*Ant* 12,3,3 §142)	Demetrius (Gr)
198		
200-150		Aristobulus (Gr)
2nd cent		Artapanus (Gr)
do.		Theodotus of Shechem (Gr)
180		Sirach
ca. 175		Proto-type of *Shemoneh Esreh* (Hebrew Sirach 51:12)
187-175	Seleucus IV. Beginnings of Hellenization. Resisted by High Priest Onias III.	
175	Onias, on visit to Seleucus, ousted from High Priesthood by his brother Jason	
175-164	Antiochus IV Epiphanes	

Date	Event	Literature
172	Jason ousted from High Priesthood by non-Zadokite Menelaus.	
171	Onias III murdered	Philo the Elder (Gr)
do. 170		Saga of the Tobiads (Gr)
ca. 170		Apocryphal Psalm 154 (11QPs 154)
do.		
167-164	Persecution of Antiochus Rebellion of Maccabees- Mention of Hasidim (1 Mac 2:42-44). Hasidim join with Maccabees.	
ca. 164		The Book of Daniel The Assumption of Moses (original version) Enochic Book of Dream Visions (1 Enoch 83-90)
162	Alcimus, "priest of the line of Aaron" made High Priest Hasidim withdraw support for Maccabees	
160-150	Judas Maccabee	Jason of Cyrene (Gr)
160-142	Three sects, Sadducees, Pharisees, Essenes, first mentioned for his reign	
158-157		Eupolemus (Gr)

Date	Events	Texts
ca. 150		Book of Judith *Acts of Judas Maccabee* *Sibylline Oracles, Book III* (Gr) *Words (Liturgy) of Heavenly Lights* (Qumran)
152	Jonathan appointed High Priest	
ca. 150	Qumran: Man of Lies, Wicked Priest, Teacher of Righteousness	Qumran *Hymns* Qumran *Community Rule* Qumran text on *New Jerusalem*
142	Simon Maccabee declared High Priest	Qumran *Temple Scroll*
142-104	John Hyrcanus	
	Hyrcanus breaks with Pharisees. Sadducees in favour	
125-105		Enochic *Book of Giants*
ca. 124		2 Maccabees
ca. 114		Greek Esther
ca. 100		Ezechielus, Tragic Poet (Gr) *Letter of Aristeas*
ca. 100		Qumran, *Damascus Document, Angelic Liturgy* (Qumran) 1 Maccabees *Prayer of Manasseh* (possibly) *Admonitions of Enoch* (1 Enoch 91-107)
103-76	Alexander Jannaeus: resisted by Pharisees. At death advises wife make peace with Pharisees	

Date	Event	Literature
76-67	Alexandra Salome. Pharisees regain royal favour	
Roman Period (63 B.C.-180 A.D.)		
63	Conquest of Jerusalem by Pompey. Palestine part of Roman Empire, in province of Syria	3 Maccabees
		Wisdom of Solomon (Gr)
50		*Psalms of Solomon*
ca. 48	Qumran monastery destroyed	
37 (or 31)		
25 B.C.-A.D. 50		Philo Judaeus (Gr)
1st cent B.C.		*Testament of Job*
		Qumran *Blessings*
		Qumran *Midrash on Last Days*
		Qumran *Messianic Anthology*
		Qumran *Pesharim*
		Qumran *Genesis Apocryphon*
		Qumran *Pseudo-Daniel* text
		Qumran *Prayer of Nabonidus*
		Qumran *Messianic Rule* (1QSa)
		Qumran *War Rule*

ca. 7 B.C.	Birth of Jesus Christ	
1st cent A.D.		*The Parables of Enoch* (1 Enoch 37-71)
		2 (Slavonic) Enoch
		Life of Adam and Eve
		(The Apocalypse of Abraham)
		Testament of Abraham
		Biblical Antiquities of Pseudo-Philo
		4 Maccabees
		Testament of Twelve Patriarchs
A.D. 38-ca. 100	Flavius Josephus	
ca. 78		Josephus, *The Jewish War*
		Josephus, *Antiquities*
ca. 100		Josephus, *Life*.
80-100		Josephus, *Against Apion*
		2 (4) Esdras
ca. 100		*2 Baruch*
early 2nd cent.		*3 Baruch* (Greek *Apocalypse of Baruch*.)
132-135	Second Jewish Revolt	Bar Cochba Letters
ca. 180		Completion of the *Mishnah*
		The *Tosefta*

Acknowledgements for Passages Cited

RSV for 2(4) Esdras, 1 Esdras, 3 Maccabees, 4 Maccabees, and the Prayer of Manasseh.

R.H. Charles, general ed., *The Apocrypha and Pseudepigrapha of the Old Testament in English*, vol. I,II, Oxford: At the Clarendon Press, 1913, reprint 1963 for The Book of Jubilees, The Testament of the Twelve Patriarchs (Test Judah), Aramaic Geniza Fragment of Testament of Levi, 2 Baruch, and the Psalms of Solomon.

Translation of Qumran texts (unless otherwise noted) taken from G. Vermes, *The Dead Sea Scrolls in English*, second edition, Penguin Books, Ltd. (Harmondsworth, Middlesex, England, 1975).

Citations from 1 (Ethiopic) Enoch taken from *The Ethiopic Book of Enoch*. A new edition in the light of the Aramaic Dead Sea Fragments by Michael A. Knibb in consultation with Edward Ullendorf, vol. 2, Oxford: At the Clarendon Press, 1978.

Citations from texts of 11Q Psalms Scroll taken from editio Princeps by J.A. Sanders, *The Psalms Scroll of Qumran Cave 11 (11QPs^a)*, (Discoveries in the Judeana Desert, vol. 4), Oxford: At the Clarendon Press, 1965.

Citations from the *Jewish Prayer Book* from: *Daily Prayer Book. Ha-Siddur Ha-Shalem*. Translated and Annotated with an Introduction by Philip Birnbaum, Hebrew Publishing Company, New York, 1949.

Citations from the *Mishnah* from: *The Mishnah*. Translated from the Hebrew with Introduction and Brief Notes by

Herbert Danby, Oxford University Press, London: Geoffrey Cumberlege, 1933.

Palestinian text of *Eighteen Benedictions*, according to a Geniza fragment, in the translation of Solomon Schechter, from *Jewish Quarterly Review*, Old Series 10(1898), pp. 656-657.

Bibliography

CHAPTER ONE: *Formation of the Tradition*

Emil Schürer, *The History of the Jewish People in the Age of Jesus Christ (175 B.C. — A.D. 135)*. A new English version revised and edited by Geza Vermes, (Edinburgh: T. & T. Clark, vol. I, 1973; vol. 2, 1979). Volume 3 to appear later.

Since the first edition of the original German in 1874 this has been recognized as the authoritative work on the period. An English translation of the second and revised edition of the German was published soon after the German edition of 1886. The new English revised edition is made in the light of the many developments that have taken place since and will long remain the basic up-to-date compendium for all students of the period.

Peter R. Ackroyd, *Israel under Babylon and Persia*, New Clarendon Bible IV (Oxford University Press, 1970). A useful book on the exilic situation and the thought of the exilic age, on the Restoration and on the life and thought of post-exilic Judaism.

D.S. Russell, *The Jews from Alexander to Herod*, New Clarendon Bible V (Oxford University Press, 1967). This work, by a recognized authority in the field, treats of the history of the period, of the religion (the foundation of Judaism, religious ideas, parties within Judaism) and the literature (the canonical and apocryphal i.e. deutero-canonical), in some detail and more briefly with 1 Enoch, Jubilees and the Qumran Hymns.

D.S. Russell, *Between the Testaments* (London: SCM Press, 1960).
This earlier work by the same author treats of the cultural and literary background in part I and devotes II to the Apocalypticists, their message and method.

Martin McNamara, M.S.C., *Targum and Testament* (Shannon, Ireland: Irish University Press, Grand Rapids: Eerdmans, 1972).

Martin McNamara, M.S.C., *Palestinian Judaism and the New Testament*, Good News Studies 4 (Wilmington, Delaware: Michael Glazier, Inc. 1983).

George W. E. Nicklesburg, *Jewish Literature between the Bible and the Mishnah. A Historical and Literary Introduction* (Philadelphia: Fortress Press; London: SCM Press, 1981).
In nine chapters this work, by a recognized authority in the field, discusses the books of the Apocrypha and Pseudepigrapha and the Dead Sea Scrolls against the relevant historical background and in chronological order. The discussion of each work is accompanied by learned notes and a rich bibliography.

Leonhard Rost, *Judaism outside the Hebrew Canon. An Introduction to the Documents* (Nashville: Abingdon, 1976).
The German original of this work was published in 1971. It has an introduction on the Hebrew and Greek Canons, a brief summary of the history of the period and the intellectual milieu. It then treats of the individual works of the Apocrypha and Pseudepigrapha and has a final section on the major Qumran writings. There is a supplement on Ahikar and Pseudo-Philo.

Brevard S. Childs, *Introduction to the Old Testament as Scripture* (Philadelphia: Fortress Press, 1979).
Pays special attention to the final, canonical shape of the books in question.

James H. Charlesworth, *The Pseudepigrapha and Modern Research with a Supplement*, Society of Biblical Literature, Septuagint and Cognate Studies (Chico: Scholars Press, 1981).
A reprint with a supplement of the 1976 work, *The Pseudepigrapha and Modern Research*. An invaluable work for the Pseudepigrapha of the Old Testament, by reason of its special introductions and exhaustive bibliography on the doctrinal content of the works.

CHAPTERS TWO AND THREE:
Apocalyptic Literature and Testament Literature

R.H. Charles, ed., *The Apocrypha and Pseudepigrapha of the Old Testament in English* with introductions and critical and explanatory notes on the several books, 2 vols. (Oxford: Clarendon Press, 1913, reprint 1963).
Volume 1 contains the Apocrypha (i.e. the deuterocanonical books together with 1 Esdras, 3 Maccabees, Prayer of Manasses), volume 2 the Pseudepigrapha, together with the *Letter of Aristeas*, the Mishnah treatise *Pirke Aboth*, and also the *Story of Ahikar* and the fragments of a Zadokite Work (texts of which were also later found in Qumran). The work is still indispensable by reason of its English translations, introductions and notes.

Addison Wright, *The Literary Genre Midrash* (Staten Island: Alba House 1967).
A detailed study of the subject. Important even though the author's understanding of midrash has been queried.

Roger Le Déaut, "A propos A Definition of Midrash" (in French), in *Biblica* 60 (1959), 395-413; an English translation by Mary Howard in *Interpretation* 26 (1971), 259-282.
Actually a review article of A. Wright's work on midrash, this is an important study in its own right.

Renée Bloch, "Midrash," *Supplément au Dictionnaire de la Bible*, vol. 5, (Paris: Lethellieux, 1957). English translation by Mary Howard Callaway in *Approaches to Ancient Judaism: Theory and Practice*, edited by William Scott Green, Brown University Judaic Studies 1 (Missoula: Scholars Press for Brown University, 1978), pp. 29-50.
A seminal, and still important, work in the modern study of midrash.

John J. Collins, *The Apocalyptic Vision of the Book of Daniel* (Missoula: Scholars Press for the Harvard Semitic Museum, 1977).
A major work by a leading scholar in the field. Among other matters, it treats of the origins of apocalyptic and of the availability of older Babylonian, Canaanite and Egyptian material to the later Jewish scribes.

John J. Collins, editor, *Apocalypse: The Morphology of a Genre* (*Semeia* 14, 1979).
Of the seven studies in this issue of *Semeia* two by the editor are of interest for this present work, namely, the introduction, "Towards the Morphology of a Genre" and "The Jewish Apocalypses."

Paul D. Hanson, *The Dawn of Apocalyptic. The Historical and Sociological Roots of Jewish Apocalyptic Eschatology* (Philadelphia: Fortress Press, revised edition 1979.
This work treats of the Phenomenon of Apocalyptic in Israel, its background and setting, on apocalyptic eschatology in the later apocalyptic writings. The body of the book deals with Third Isaiah and its presumed setting in Israelite society. There is a somewhat similar treatment of the post-exilic writings and situation: Haggai, Zechariah and Chronicles, with a special treatment of Second Zechariah (Zech 9-14).

Paul D. Hanson, "Apocalyptic, genre" and "Apocalypticism" in *The Interpreter's Dictionary of the Bible*. Supplementary Volume (Nashville: Abingdon, 1976), pp. 27-28, 28-34.

A later elaboration of the same author's views on these subjects.

D.S. Russell, *Between the Testaments* (London: SCM Press, 1963).

D.S. Russell, *The Method and Message of Jewish Apocalyptic 200 B.C. - A.D. 100* (London: SCM Press, 1964). The first part of this book treats of the nature and identity of Jewish apocalyptic. Part two is on the method of Jewish Apocalyptic (the decline of prophecy and the rise of apocalyptic), characteristics of the apocalyptic writings, the apocalyptic consciousness, apocalyptic inspiration, apocalyptic and the interpretation of prophecy. Part three treats of the message of Jewish apocalyptic: on its teaching concerning human history, divine control, angels and demons, the time of the end, the messianic kingdom, the traditional messiah, the Son of Man, life after death. The author's earlier work, noted in the preceding number, treats of these themes in a less detailed manner.

Walter Schmithals, *The Apocalyptic Movement. Introduction & Interpretation* (Nashville, New York: Abingdon Press, 1975). This is the translation of a work first published in German in 1973. It treats of the thought-world of Apocalyptic, of its origins, of its history in Judaism and Christianity, with special emphasis on the Books of Daniel and Revelation. At the end of the work we have a sketch of the development of the movement down to the present day.

H.H. Rowley, *The Relevance of Apocalyptic. A Study of Jewish and Christian Apocalypses from Daniel to the Revelation* (London: Lutterworth Press, second edition 1947). This work which has been very influential in its day can still be profitably consulted.

Robert W. Funk, editor, *Apocalypticism (Journal for Theology and Church 6, 1969)* (New York: Herder and Herder).

Although the chief interest in this issue is on the bearing of apocalypticism on the New Testament and Christian theology, there are some essays in it on the larger question of apocalypticism as such.

Leon Morris, *Apocalyptic* (London: Inter-Varsity Press, 1972).

James H. Charlesworth, *The Pseudepigrapha and Modern Research* (Missoula: Scholars Press for the Society of Biblical Literature, 1976; reprint with a supplement, 1981). Apart from the treatment of the individual books, there is an extremely rich bibliography on apocalyptic in pp. 46-52, 253-259.

J.T. Milik, *The Books of Enoch. Aramaic Fragments of Qumran Cave 4* (Oxford: Clarendon Press, 1976).

Michael A. Knibb, in consultation with Edward Ullendorf, *The Ethiopic Book of Enoch. A New Edition in the Light of the Aramaic Dead Sea Fragments.* Vol. 1: Text and Apparatus. Vol. 2: Introduction, Translation and Commentary (Oxford: Clarendon Press, 1978).

CHAPTER FOUR: *Literature of the Qumran Community*

Joseph A. Fitzmyer, S.J., *The Dead Sea Scroll. Major Publications and Tools for Study.* (Missoula: Scholars Press for the Society of Biblical Literature, 1975; reprint with an Addendum, 1977).

J.T. Milik, *Ten Years of Discovery in the Wilderness of Judaea* (London: SCM Press, 1959).
Although one of the earlier works on the subject, it still remains one of the standard books in the field. It is by the leading scholar in the decipherment of the Scrolls.

Frank Moore Cross, Jr., *The Ancient Library of Qumran and Modern Biblical Studies* (New York: Doubleday Anchor Books, Revised ed. 1961).
Another of the great works on the subject, and again by a recognized specialist in this branch of learning.

Geza Vermes, *The Dead Sea Scrolls. Qumran in Perspective* (London: SCM Press; second ed., 1982).
A further book by a scholar of renown who has been active in the study of the Scrolls for many years. Together with the usual treatment of the history and identification of the people who wrote the scrolls, this work has a chapter in which a brief, but authoritative, analysis is given of each of the works from the Qumran library.

Geza Vermes, *The Dead Sea Scrolls in English* (Harmondsworth: Penguin Books, second ed., 1975).
An English translation of the more important works from Qumran, together with a general introduction on the community, and special introductions to each of the works. This small work is indispensable for any serious student of the Dead Sea Scrolls.

Helmer Ringgren, *The Faith of Qumran. Theology of the Dead Sea Scrolls.* (Philadelphia: Fortress Press, 1963).
An excellent summary of the beliefs of the Qumran monks, as expessed in the Scrolls, together with a chapter on the organization and cult of the Community and its place within the history of religion.

Frank Moore Cross and Shemaryahu Talmon, editors, *Qumran and the History of the Biblical Text* (Cambridge, Mass., London, England: Harvard University Press, 1975).

F.F. Bruce, *Biblical Exegesis in the Qumran Texts* (London: Tyndale Press, 1960; Grand Rapids: Eerdmans, 1959).

Maurya P. Horgan, *Pesharim: Qumran Interpretations of Biblical Books* (Washington: Catholic Biblical Association of America, 1979).

Jacob Milgrom, "The Temple Scroll", *The Biblical Archaeologist* 41 (1978), pp. 105-120.
A detailed analysis of the Temple Scroll, without translation.

Johann Maier, *Die Tempelrolle vom Toten Meer.* Übersetz
und erläutert von Johann Maier.
A German translation of the Temple Scroll, with introduction and notes.

CHAPTER FIVE: *Prayer and Prayers of the Intertestamental Period.*

Philip Birnbaum, *Daily Prayer Book. Ha-Siddur ha-Shalem*,
Translated and annotated by Philip Birnbaum (New
York: Hebrew Publishing Company, 1949).

S. Singer, *The Authorised Daily Prayer Book of the United
Hebrew Congregations of the British Commonwealth of
Nations*, with a new translation by the late Rev. S. Singer
(London: Eyre and Spottiswoode, 1962).

James H. Charlesworth, "A Prolegomenon to a New Study
to the Jewish Background of the Hymns and Prayers in
the New Testament," in *Essays and Studies in Honour of
Yigael Yadin.* Edited by Geza Vermes and Jack Neusner
(*The Journal of Jewish Studies* vol. 33, 1982), pp. 265-
285.

Joseph Heinemann, *Prayer in the Talmud. Forms and
Patterns* (Berlin, New York, 1977).
A study of fundamental importance in the subject. It goes
beyond the Talmud into the origins of the prayers.

L. Zunz, *Die gottesdienstlichen Vortrage der Juden histor-
isch entwickelt*, (second edition, Frankfurt on Main, 1892;
reprint Hildesheim 1966).

I. Elbogen, *Der jüdische Gottesdienst in seiner geschichtli-
chen Entwicklung* (third edition, Frankfurt on Main,
1931; reprint, Hildesheim 1962).
Both these works, of which no English translation is
available, are of fundamental importance for a serious
study of Jewish liturgy.

G. Scholem, *Major Trends in Jewish Mysticism* (third edition, London: Thames and Hudson, 1955: New York, 1961).

G. Scholem, *Jewish Gnosticism, Merkabah Mysticism and Talmudic Tradition* (New York: Ktav Publishing House, 1965).

G. Scholem, "Merkabah Mysticism or Ma'aseh Merkavah," in *Encyclopaedia Judaica*, vol. 11 (Jerusalem: Keter Publishing House, 1972, cols. 1386-1390.
These are three major studies on Jewish mysticism by the leding authority in the field.

Louis Jacobs, *Jewish Mystical Testimonies* (New York: Schoken Books, 1977).

J.J. Petuchowski, *Contributions to the Scientific Study of Jewish Liturgy* (New York: 1970).

Solomon Schechter, "Geniza Specimens," *Jewish Quarterly Review* Old Series, 10(1898), pp. 656-657.
With English translation of the Geniza text with the Palestinian recension of the Eighteen Benedictions.

J.J. Petuchowski and M. Brocke, eds., *The Lord's Prayer and Jewish Liturgy* (London: Burns and Oates, 1978).
An English edition of a work originally published in German: *Das Vaterunser. Gemeinsames im Beten von Juden und Christen* (Freiburg i. Breisgau: Herder, 1974), with M. Brocke, J.J. Petuchowski and W. Strolz as editors.

David de Sola Pool, *The Old Jewish-Aramaic Prayer, the Kaddish* (Leipzig: Rudolf Haupt, 1909: third edition, New York: 1964)

J. Strugnell, "The Angelic Liturgy at Qumran — *4Q serek shirot 'olat hashshabbat*", in *Supplements to Vetus Testamentum* vol. 7 (1960), pp. 318-345.

J.A. Sanders, *The Psalms Scrolls of Qumran Cave 11 (11 QPs^a)*, Discoveries in the Judaean Desert IV (Oxford: Clarendon Press, 1965).

CHAPTER SIX: *The Literature of Hellenistic Judaism*

Emil Schürer, "The Graeco-Jewish Literature," in *A History of the Jewish People in the Time of Jesus Christ*, second division, vol. 3 (Edinburgh: T. Clark, 1885-1891, pp. 156-381); new revised edition in preparation, edited by Geza Vermes, Fergus Millar and Matthew Black.

Martin Hengel, *Judaism and Hellenism. Studies in their Encounter in Palestine during the Early Hellenistic Period*, 2 vols (Philadelphia: Fortress Press; London: SCM Press, 1974).
The classical work on Hellenistic influences in Palestine from an early period: military, social, economic and cultural, and on the religious effects of these.

Victor Tcherikover, *Hellenistic Civilization and the Jews* (New York: Atheneum, 1970; Philadelphia: Jewish Publications Society, 1959).

John Collins, *Between Athens and Jerusalem: Jewish Identity in the Hellenistic Diaspora* (New York: Crossroad, 1983).

John Collins, *The Sibylline Oracles of Egyptian Judaism*, SBL Dissertation Series 13 (Society of Biblical Literature and Scholars Press, 1974)
A detailed study of the Third, Fourth and Fifth Books of the Sibylline oracles.

Ben Zion Wacholder, *Eupolemus: A Study of Judaeo-Greek Literature*, (New York, Los Angeles, Jerusalem: Hebrew Union College, Jewish Institute of Religion, 1974).
A detailed and authortative study of the entire field.
The same author has treated most of the writers in the *Encylopaedia Judaica* (1972).

Samuel Sandmel, *Philo of Alexandria. An Introduction*, (New York, Oxford: Oxford University Press, 1979).

R.J.H. Shutt, *Studies in Josephus* (London: S.P.C.K., 1961).

CHAPTER SEVEN: *The Literature of Rabbinic Judaism and Pharisaism*

E. Schürer, *The History of the Jewish People in the Age of Jesus Christ (175 B.C. — A.D. 135).* A new English version revised and edited by Geza Vermes, Fergus Millar, Matthew Black (Edinburgh: T. & T. Clark, vol. 1 and 2, 1973, 1979).

George Foot Moore, *Judaism in the Early Centuries of the Christian Era. The Age of the Tannaim,* 3 vols. (Cambridge, Mass: Harvard University Press, 1927, 1927, 1930).

Ephraim E. Urbach, *The Sages: Their Concepts and Beliefs* (Jerusalem: Magnes Press, 1975).

Max Kadushin, *The Rabbinic Mind* (New York: Bloch Publishing Company, 3rd edition, 1972).
These three works concentrate on the contents of the rabbinic writings. Moore's work first treats of the development of rabbinic Judaism and of the sources at hand for a knowledge of the subject, and of the critical principles governing the use of these. Then in seven major sections he gives a synthesis of rabbinic doctrine on revealed religion, the idea of God, man, sin and atonement, observances, morals, piety and the hereafter. While this still remains a standard work on the subject, it has been criticized for its neglect of the central place of law in Jewish life.

Hermann L. Strack, *Introduction to the Talmud and Midrash* (New York: Meridian Books, Philadelphia: Jewish Publication Society of America, 1959; first English publication in 1931).

H.L. Strack/ G. Stemberger, *Einleitung in Talmud und Midrasch,* Siebente, völlig neu bearbeitete Auflag, Munich: Verlag C.H. Beck, 1982)
Strack's *Einleitung in Talmud und Midrasch* was first

published in 1887; the fifth edition from which the first
English translation was made appeared in 1920. The first
part contains an introduction to the Talmud (including
the Mishnah and Tosefta), the second part an introduction to the Midrashim. The many reprints show that the
work continue to fill a need, and had not been replaced. It
was, however, hopelessly outdated both in information
and bibliography. G. Stemberger has made a complete
revision of the work, somewhat in the line of what has
been done for Schürer by Vermes, Millar and Black.

Herbert Danby, *The Mishnah*. Translated from the Hebrew
with Introduction and brief Explanatory Notes (Oxford
University Press, 1933).

Jacob Neusner, *The Tosefta*. Translated from the Hebrew;
six vols. (New York: Ktav Publishing House, 1977-1981)

I. Epstein, editor, *The Babylonian Talmud*. Translated into
English with notes, glossary and indices under the editor-
ship of Rabbi Dr. I. Epstein; thirty-five vols. (London:
The Soncino Press, 1935-1952).

Jacob Z. Lauterbach, *Mekilta de-Rabbi Ishmael*, three
vols. (Philadelphia: The Jewish Publication Society of
America, 1933).

H. Freedman and Maurice Simon, editors, *The Midrash
Rabbah*, Translated into English with notes, glossary and
indices (London, Jerusalem, New York: The Soncino
Press, 1939; 3rd ed. 1961).
Ten vols, with index. It has an English translation of the
Midrash Rabbah on the Pentateuch and on the Five
Scrolls.

M.R. James, *The Biblical Antiquities of Pseudo-Philo*
(London: S.P.C.K., 1917; reprinted with prolegomenon
by Louis H. Feldman, New York: Ktav Publishing
House, 1971).

Charles Perrot and Pierre-Maurice Bogaert, with collaboration of D.J. Harrington, *Pseudo-Philon. Les Antiquités Bibliques,* 2 vols. Sources Chretiennes (Paris: Editions du Cerf, 1976).

John Bowker, *The Targums and Rabbinic Literature. An Introduction to Jewish Interpretations of Scripture,* (Cambridge: University Press, 1969).

M. McNamara, *Targum and Testament. Aramaic Paraphrases of the Hebrew Bible: A Light on the New Testament* (Shannon, Ireland: Irish University Press; Grand Rapids: Eerdmans Publishing Company, 1972).

Roger Le Déaut, *Introduction à la littérature targumique* (Rome: Biblical Institute Press, 1966).

Jacob Neusner, *The Palestinian Talmud. A Preliminary Translation and Explanation* (Chicago: University of Chicago Press 1981-   ; in progress.)